THE SAN JUAN WATER BOUNDARY QUESTION

CANADIAN STUDIES IN HISTORY AND GOVERNMENT

A series of studies edited by Kenneth McNaught, sponsored by the Social Science Research Council of Canada, and published with financial assistance from the Canada Council.

The San Juan
Water Boundary
Question

BY JAMES O. McCABE

~~~~~~

UNIVERSITY OF TORONTO PRESS

TO MY WIFE

CONTENTS

CONTENTS

THE SAN JUAN WATER BOUNDARY QUESTION

CHAPTER ONE

ORIGIN AND EARLIEST STAGES OF A DISPUTE

THE AUTHORS of the Oregon Treaty of 1846 could never have suspected that the obscure phraseology of their work would produce a new boundary quarrel which would more than once during the following generation threaten to precipitate a war between Great Britain and the United States. The complacence with which the prime minister, Sir Robert Peel, and the foreign secretary, Lord Aberdeen, accepted their removal from office in 1846 would not have been so easy had they foreseen that the treaty, one of their few crumbs of comfort in surrendering power, was to produce a quarrel almost as acrimonious as that over Oregon.

The first article of the treaty had decided that the boundary line along the forty-ninth parallel should run "to the middle of the channel which separates the continent from Vancouver's Island; and thence southerly through the middle of the said channel, and of Fuca's Straits to the Pacific Ocean." The negotiators had apparently neglected the fact that there was more than one channel west of the mainland at the forty-ninth parallel. The British had used Captain Vancouver's chart of 1798 which shows only one body of water, the Gulf of Georgia, between the mainland and Vancouver Island at this point. The British Foreign Office had drawn up the terms of the treaty of 1846 which was accepted without the alteration or addition of a single word by the government of the United States. At the forty-ninth parallel there was no difficulty about the exact line, for the Gulf of Georgia was indubitably the "channel which separates the continent from Vancouver's Island." The vagueness of the language subsequently used by Lord Aberdeen, who framed the treaty, concerning the geography of the area between the mainland and Vancouver Island, and the failure to attach a map to the treaty of that year are sufficient to make it abundantly clear that the British government, or at least Aberdeen, had not carefully consulted cartographical authorities in drawing up the draft of the treaty.

Sir John H. Pelly, governor of the Hudson's Bay Company, had been consulted by Lord Aberdeen on May 16 before the foreign secretary drew up his draft of the Oregon treaty which the Americans accepted without alteration. Pelly put the substance of the discussion into writing a few days later, saying that on reflection he felt that "the Water demarkation [sic] line should be from the center of the water on the Gulf of Georgia on the 49° along the line coloured Red as Navigable on that Chart made by Vancouver (a tracing of which I enclose) till it reaches a line drawn through the center of the Straits of Fuca, the only objection to this is giving to the United States the valuable Island of Whitby [Whidbey] but I do not see how this can be avoided in an Amicable adjustment."[1]

The ink on the treaty was barely dry when the Hudson's Bay Company hastened to advise the government of the fact that there was more than one channel west of 49° N and to warn them of a possible conflict over claims. Accordingly, Pelly interviewed Lord Palmerston, Aberdeen's successor at the Foreign Office, on July 29, 1846, and gave him his opinion of the questions likely to arise from the treaty of the previous month. He explained that the space between 49° N and 48° 20′ N (where the Strait of Juan de Fuca opens) contains numerous islands with passages between them, but he opined that there could be no doubt that the "largest" passage, "that used by Vancouver," was meant as the boundary. At Palmerston's behest, Pelly put his views in writing and forwarded them to the Foreign Office.[2]

It was thus early apparent that a new controversy would arise, or indeed had arisen, as to which channel—Rosario Strait nearer the mainland or Haro nearer Vancouver Island—was that meant by the Oregon treaty. The Americans, as we shall see later, contended for Haro, and the British for Rosario. Lying between the disputed straits are a number of islands extending over about 170 square miles, the most important of which is San Juan, covering nearly a third of the island area in the disputed region.[3]

The views of both sides were coloured, as they had been from the earliest days of the Oregon controversy, by a desire to secure the harbours of Puget Sound which both saw as the really valuable part of the territory. It was deemed essential to secure easy access to the entrance to Puget Sound and all the valuable harbours within it.

The United States was to base its claim mainly upon contemporaneous evidence, that is, upon the argument that the negotiators of 1846, Lord Aberdeen and Richard Pakenham on the British side and Louis McLane, James Buchanan, and President Polk on the American, had clearly demonstrated their intention to adopt the line following Haro Strait. But the Americans had neglected to insist that Haro Strait should be specified in the Oregon treaty, and the British based their claim on incomplete information. The knowledge of the geography and topography of the chief negotiators on both sides in 1846 was flagrantly incomplete. Both thought that only one channel existed west of the mainland; the Americans thought it was Haro and the British thought the only channel was that taken by Captain George Vancouver in 1792, namely, Rosario Strait. The possibility of the existence of more than one channel seems never to have been understood in Buchanan's discussions with Pakenham, or in McLane's with Aberdeen. The British later gave as their reason for this the excuse that, though trouble over the actual boundary line had been foreseen by them in 1846, "this consideration being of less importance than the conclusion of the Treaty, the Treaty was concluded and signed."[4]

The British government took no immediate action on Pelly's letter mentioned above, but a despatch from Sir Richard Pakenham, British minister at Washington, dated March 17, 1847, served to remind them that the line of demarcation ought to be more accurately defined. Palmerston replied at once urging Pakenham to hasten adjustment in order "to obviate future disputes." Continuing the co-operative policy pursued throughout the Oregon negotiations, the Foreign Office at once got in touch with Sir George Simpson of the Hudson's Bay Company and desired him to prepare a memorandum on the treaty of 1846. The result was a document that did little more than advise that, since more than one channel exists west of the mainland at the forty-ninth parallel, a commission should be appointed to determine which one was meant by the treaty.

The cumbersome and slow Foreign Office machinery had been set in motion with the result that the permanent under-secretary, H. U. Addington, who had been at the Foreign Office since 1842, that is, throughout the most contentious years of the Oregon question, prepared for Lord Palmerston a memorandum on the subject of the Pacific water boundary.[5] He foresaw trouble over possession of the islands west of British Columbia unless the two countries agreed that "channel" meant navigable channel, in which case two naval officers, one British and one American, could effect an agreement. If, however, the "channel" were taken to mean the whole water area between the continent and Vancouver Island, Addington subscribed to Simpson's view that a commission would be necessary to trace a line down the middle of the channel on the same principle "as the islands in the St. Lawrence." Palmerston's note attached to the memorandum is concise enough: "Suspend negotiations till Admiralty reports received," and Pakenham was told a fortnight later that the Admiralty survey of the disputed area being still unfinished, and the greater part of the territory still unexplored, he was to do nothing meantime.[6]

The calm nature of all this was rather the reverse of what many had expected from warriors like Palmerston and Polk. The ratification of the Oregon treaty in 1846 had disposed of the most pressing and acrimonious dispute between the United States and Great Britain, but the auspices for continued good relations were not good. The characters of the two statesmen had played a great part in bringing agreement at the time it did. Thus settlement might have come a year earlier but for the tenacity and obstinacy of President Polk who refused to accept a line below 54° 40' N unless the Senate first agreed to accept less. One of the factors hastening settlement, on the other hand, had been the imminence of the advent to the Foreign Office of Lord Palmerston. Sir Robert Peel, the prime minister until June, 1846, had known after the previous December that his government would have a short life and a coalition of his opponents was sure to bring Palmerston in as foreign secretary. Both the Americans and Peel's followers, not to mention the queen and the French, had felt trepidation at the prospect of Palmerston's return to office, for Palmerston's foreign policy, summarized in his own words, asserted that "influence abroad is to be maintained by the operation of one or other of two principles—hope and fear. We ought to teach the weaker powers to hope that they will receive the support of this country in their time of danger. Powerful countries should be taught to fear that they will be resisted by England in any unjust acts, either towards ourselves or towards those who are bound in ties of amity with us."[7] The policy to be followed towards the United States was more specific. We may certainly preserve peace, Palmerston argued in the *Morning Chronicle*, and express our admiration of American institutions, but we must maintain our honour and our rights. To let the Americans have this so-called barren tract of Oregon is not going to prevent war; rather will it invite hostilities, for, if we yield in this, the United States will soon pick a quarrel. Acquiescence would only be interpreted in America as a surrender to transatlantic menaces.[8]

Fear of Palmerston had been a potent factor in impelling the two governments to seek a peaceful solution of the Oregon controversy. The American minister in London, Louis McLane, had written home that Peel's government would not be in office after July 1, 1846, and this rather than any embarrassment caused by the Mexican War induced the Americans to seek a peaceful solution. The foreign secretary, Lord Aberdeen, had been fully aware of this: "The conduct of my predecessor and expected successor ... had filled Mr. McLane with the greatest alarm, which, I presume, was shared by the Government of the United States."[9] McLane was writing in similar vein to Secretary of State Buchanan.

With the belligerent Palmerston at the Foreign Office, therefore, after June, 1846, and a confident, exultant president who was convinced that the best way to "treat John Bull was to look him straight in the eye," it might have been expected that Anglo-American relations would be strained, and that even the relatively minor water boundary dispute would be used to precipitate trouble. Fortunately, this did not prove to be the case. Palmerston seemed determined that the Oregon sequel should not intrude itself to complicate relations, while Polk found the remaining months of his tenure of office occupied with the Mexican War.

Thus it was that, in December, 1847, John F. Crampton, who succeeded Pakenham as British minister at Washington, was instructed to obviate future disputes by securing a speedy arrangement of the Pacific Coast boundary dispute. It was believed that only one channel had been hitherto surveyed and used, namely, that laid down by Captain Vancouver on his chart, and it seemed reasonable to assume that in employing the word "channel" the negotiators of the Oregon treaty had had in view this particular channel. Palmerston expressed the hope, therefore, that this channel would be mutually agreed upon, though he disingenuously instructed Crampton to remind the American secretary of state that its adoption would mean more islands falling to Great Britain than to the United States. Enclosed with his despatch was a copy of instructions to commissioners which advised the use of Vancouver's chart as the basis of any deliberations.[10] It is obvious that Palmerston was unable to foresee any insuperable difficulty in the way of a swift and satisfactory adjustment, and there is nothing new in his approach. He is retaining the fallacious British devotion to Vancouver's chart, and he is continuing quite correctly to base his line upon the advice of the Hudson's Bay Company.

Crampton duly carried out his instructions and Secretary of State James Buchanan in reply, intimating that there was little likelihood of inconvenience arising on the American side, asked for an offer in writing to put before the president. He affirmed that he had never seen Vancouver's chart (yet he was a principal negotiator in 1846) and hesitated therefore to adopt its line as the geographical channel; while negotiating in 1846, however, he had taken the channel mentioned in the treaty to mean "navigable channel."[11]

If Great Britain was slow to act, the United States was not less so. During 1848, however, there was some correspondence between George Bancroft, United States minister in London, and Lord Palmerston, Bancroft using every occasion to assert that the boundary line passed through "the middle of the channel of Arro." The Foreign Office deliberately refrained from commenting on or correcting Bancroft's assertion. The permanent under-secretary at the Foreign Office spotted the alleged error, however, and sought the advice of Palmerston. The great man replied in character: "Thank him and say that the information contained in these charts [survey reports sent by the Americans] as to soundings will no doubt be of great service to the Commissioners to be appointed by assisting them in determining where the Line of Boundary described by the Treaty ought to run."[12] In the later stages of the dispute the United States made much of "this repeated reminding" of Lord Palmerston that Haro was "the channel through the middle of which the boundary is to be continued."[13]

Crampton's note to Buchanan suggesting the appointment of commissioners was dated January 13, 1848, but no mention of the matter was made by the Americans until the autumn of the following year when Crampton sought an answer to his earlier note. Secretary of State Clayton, in reply, informed him that Congress was to be asked to make the necessary appropriation if it acceded to the choice of commissioners.[14] Unfortunately, nothing was done yet.

The governments having failed to act, their respective subjects who were directly concerned in the allocation of the disputed islands proceeded to play their part in the controversy. A British subject named Pattle had gone from Vancouver Island to establish two log huts on Lopez Island in 1852 with a view to trading with the natives. The whole plan proved abortive, however. The Hudson's Bay Company agents had taken formal possession of San Juan island in July, 1845, a note to that effect having been erected on a wooden tablet. In 1850 the company established a fishing station there and three years later this was supplemented by a sheep farm.

On the American side there was activity also. An Act of August 14, 1848, organized Oregon Territory, comprehending all United States territory north of 42° west of the Rocky Mountains.[15] In January, 1853, Island County was established, covering part of the mainland and all the San Juan Archipelago. At that time Island County had about two hundred inhabitants; later it was divided up so that Whatcom County was erected with the archipelago within its limits.[16] In the winter of 1852-3 United States settlers on the islands in the archipelago asserted claims on behalf of their country to possession of the islands in question. This presented a problem for Governor James Douglas of Vancouver Island and, thoroughly alarmed, the governor hastened to seek instructions from his superiors at the Colonial Office in London.[17] Douglas (knighted in 1863) had been a Hudson's Bay Company employee from boyhood and was a government servant from 1851 to 1858 when he became governor of both Vancouver Island and British Columbia.[18]

The Colonial Office seems to have been unfamiliar with the subject and so assistance was sought from the Foreign Office. The latter simply instructed Crampton in Washington not to mention the affair to the American Secretary of State unless it was deemed important enough to demand urgent settlement; otherwise, he was to allow it to remain in the background at a time when several more pressing and likely to be protracted questions, notably the fisheries dispute, British maritime claims, and the rival positions in Central America, were pending between Great Britain and the United States.

The dispute over the Canadian fisheries, one of the most clamant matters of controversy between the two countries, was no new one. Its origin went back to the treaty of 1783 whose Article III gave Americans fishing privileges on the Grand Banks of Newfoundland, in the Gulf of St. Lawrence, "and also on the coasts, bays and creeks of all other of His Britannic Majesty's dominions in America," plus rights of drying and curing fish on the unsettled bays and harbours of Nova Scotia and Labrador.

The American fishing industry had flourished in the last decade of the eighteenth century, and the fishermen of the colonies were soon unable to compete with it. The War of 1812 had been received with delight by the colonial fishermen because it finished the liberty granted in 1783. The fishing rights were discussed at Ghent, but no agreement was reached. Soon after Ghent a series of incidents had occurred to bring the fisheries to the notice of both governments. A conflict of opinion about "rights" and "liberties" ensued until in 1818 a new arrangement was arrived at which worked without an excess of friction for nearly twenty years. Inevitably problems arose from the interpretation of the agreement of October, 1818.

Till 1854 the fisheries were an almost constant source of dispute and irritation which might have flared into serious trouble. Forcible exclusion of American fishermen and the refusal to allow time to buy bait and supplies in colonial ports produced an atmosphere of bickering and nervous reaction. The inevitable explosion came in 1852 when, at the request of the government of Nova Scotia, the British government sent a naval force "to assure the observance of the Convention." The United States reaction was sharp and productive of an outburst of anti-English feeling. A frigate was sent to protect American claims. The President's message of December, 1852, fortunately went some way towards mollifying the colonists when it was intimated that the United States government were prepared to negotiate on the fisheries and on Canadian reciprocity. Negotiations did come, and the first article of the Reciprocity Treaty of 1854, in addition to securing to the Americans the liberty obtained in 1818, conceded the liberty to take fish in Canadian waters. The Americans also gained free navigation of the St. Lawrence River, Canadian canals, and Lake Michigan. At least for the next dozen years the fisheries problem was out of the way, though we shall see that it became a subject of great friction during the later stages of the water boundary controversy.

The trouble between the two countries over Central America which the Foreign Office mentioned was the most important one in the 1850's, and the irritation it caused much resembled that produced by developments in the water boundary area in the same years. Great Britain had controlled Belize, the modern British Honduras, for 180 years and since 1841 she had had a protectorate over the Indians of the Mosquito Shore, governed from Jamaica, and claimed sovereignty over the Bay Islands, an area near British Honduras inhabited by people of British stock. Nicaragua protested at the British occupation of the Mosquito Protectorate, but its appeals to the United States then occupied with the Mexican War went unheeded. Palmerston, however, was well aware that the Americans, gorged by recent huge territorial gains and fortified by President Polk's restatement of the Monroe Doctrine, would soon challenge British claims in Central America.[19] It was just the kind of situation that Palmerston loved to exploit, and it must be remembered that, with the exception of most of the year 1852, he was a member of the government until his death in 1865.

Though President Polk hesitated to give assurances to Nicaragua, he was not inactive in Central America. In December, 1846, his representative negotiated with New Granada (now Colombia) a treaty which gave the United States and its citizens exclusive right of way across the Isthmus of Panama. By 1848 a whole concatenation of circumstances had developed to direct American attention to the Panama isthmus. Mexico had been overwhelmingly defeated and forced to cede huge tracts of territory. Almost synchronizing with the conclusion of the Mexican War came news of the first gold strike in California followed by the amazing helter-skelter from all over the Union towards the new El Dorado. A transcontinental railway was envisaged, while American capitalists, led by Cornelius Vanderbilt, also planned access to California via the isthmus. The idea of a canal, often mooted before, approached realization. Once again, as in Texas, Oregon, Canada, the old enemy stood in the way of the Americans. As a great commercial state Great Britain was interested in the future of any canal that might control one of the great highways of the world, and her possession of Jamaica and the West Indies also gave her a stake in the whole Caribbean area.

The Whig, Zachary Taylor, who succeeded Polk in March, 1849, and his secretary of state, John M. Clayton, were both pacifically minded, and Clayton honestly believed that a ship canal connecting the two great oceans would do much to perpetuate peace between Great Britain and the United States. The upshot was the Clayton-Bulwer Treaty of April 19, 1850, which aimed at putting the two nations on an exactly equal footing so far as the projected canal was concerned. But the first article of the treaty, the main one, was interpreted differently by both sides. The Americans thought the article comprehended a British withdrawal from the Mosquito Shore; the British, on their part, maintained that the treaty in no way affected the Mosquito Protectorate. Instead of settling the controversy, the treaty merely created a distinctly uneasy situation.

Not only was the Central American isthmus a source of dispute between the United States and Britain in the 1850's, but Cuba and slave-trade developments also exacerbated relations. The smuggling of slaves became rampant, and the United States filibustering expeditions aimed at assisting Cuban rebels against the Spanish colonial government were another problem. Southerners thought that Cuba might fall to Great Britain or become a republic. Palmerston feared an attempt at annexation of Cuba by the United States, and he sought to strengthen the Spanish hold on the island and also to stop the slave trade. British cruisers were instructed to intercept American filibustering expeditions. The impact of this policy soon showed its effect on the Southern states, which saw the British action not only as a reassertion of the old Right of Search but also as a device to hasten the accession of Cuba to the British Empire. It seemed to many Americans in the early 1850's that Great Britain was seeking to establish a considerable empire in the West Indies and Central America, and in 1852 Secretary of State Edward Everett, notoriously a friend of England, felt compelled by events to declare American policy. He asserted an exclusive United States interest in Cuba, and he reiterated the "manifest destiny" of all European possessions in the Western Hemisphere to fall under the United States. These views were denounced by the British Foreign Office in February, 1853, when the foreign secretary asserted that Britain had possessions in the Western Hemisphere which gave her "an interest in this question which she cannot forego."

In March, 1852, the British government had taken the extreme step of awarding the Bay Islands the status of a Crown colony. This was an astounding intimidatory move in view of the apathy of all British parties to colonial affairs, and the step was interpreted as a move towards making the Bay Islands a base to menace the transisthmian canal project which might restrict British commerce. Coming as it did during the presidential campaign of 1852, it proved to be excellent fodder for the anti-British politicians. But President Fillmore, in his December message, offered to negotiate on the fisheries and Central America, and there followed in 1854 the happy interlude of the Reciprocity Treaty which opened the fisheries to the Americans and United States markets to the Canadians. Despite the destruction of Greytown by American warships about the same time and the inane Ostend Manifesto of October, 1854, a document which supported slavery and contained a ridiculous declaration that Spain ought to sell Cuba to the United States to make her land (Spain) "a centre of attraction for the travelling world," there was no rupture.

In the middle of 1854, therefore, the international situation was not exactly serene, and added to Central American complications Britain was meeting the heavy burden of the Crimean War which broke out in March. It is no wonder, therefore, that, as we have noted, Crampton was advised to keep quiet about the Pacific water boundary. This, however, did nothing to lighten the burden of Governor Douglas whose position was becoming increasingly difficult as Americans persisted in their attempts to settle on the disputed islands. He continued to resist all these endeavours because he realized that the three main islands in the San Juan Archipelago, Lopez, Orcas, and San Juan, were all very valuable, not only on account of their strategic situation with respect to Vancouver Island, but also because of their productive salmon fisheries, forests of timber, and great extent of arable land. Further, in accordance with his instructions from the Colonial Office, Douglas determined to keep possession of these valuable territories and maintain them as *de facto* dependencies of Vancouver Island, a herculean task for which only a small number of hired labourers were available.

While the government hesitated to move, the situation in the disputed area continued to assume a graver aspect. Douglas's despatches became more and more alarming, and the sequel was the despatch of instructions to him by the Hudson's Bay Company to secure possession of the islands of San Juan and Lopez, both of which were to be occupied and turned to some use by the company's servants. The plan obviously aimed at anticipating official American action. Douglas at once (December 15) sent Captain Stuart to take possession of Lopez Island with authority to give grants of land. Douglas was able to tell the Colonial Office on November 21, 1853, that so far he had been able to keep the Americans off the disputed islands of the archipelago. "I accordingly proceeded to warn the parties, who had commenced building huts on Lopez Island that they were committing a trespass . . . I moreover informed them that the spot which they proposed to occupy would be reserved for the use of Her Majesty's Government . . ."[20] As we have seen, the Hudson's Bay Company's agents had taken formal possession of San Juan in July, 1845, and had a fishing station and a sheep run there.

Douglas's report apparently caused concern in the Colonial Office, for a copy was sent immediately to the Foreign Office with a request for instructions and the query: "Is there any information in the Foreign Office with regard to the Islands in the Canal de Arro?" To this the foreign secretary, Lord Clarendon, attached his comments: "Is it a matter of importance that this affair shd. be settled; if so, Mr. Crampton must again call attention of U.S. Govt. to it; if not, it might be well not to add another question to the many now pending & not likely soon to be arranged."[21] On September 21, 1854, the colonial secretary, Sir George Grey, told Douglas: "I have to authorise you to continue to treat those Islands as part of the British Dominions," an important instruction in the light of what followed in the next few years.

This instruction to Douglas arose from the submission of data on the island dispute to the Queen's advocate and to the Foreign Office. The advocate gave his views on the legal position, and Addington, the under-secretary at the Foreign Office, presented a new memorandum, much more pointed than the last. Starting off with the astounding statement that in the negotiations of 1846 the present trouble had been foreseen, "but this consideration being of less importance than the conclusion of the treaty, the Treaty was concluded and signed," the memorandum goes on to reiterate the statement that Rosario Strait is the navigable channel meant by the treaty. Douglas had acted quite correctly in dispossessing the American squatters, and it would be politic for him to continue to do so without ostentation or force.[22]

The Americans were also set upon establishing themselves on the disputed islands. A land speculator, William Webster, told Douglas that he had traded in the waters around Vancouver Island "free from any Custom House restrictions," and he protested against paying any customs duties. Douglas rejected the protest because by the treaty of 1846 it was "the navigation of the Ship Channel leading into the Gulf of Georgia and the Straits of Juan de Fuca, the outlet of that Channel which remains free and open to both parties, and not the Ports of Vancouvers Island nor of the Coast of American Oregon."[23]

It was to defeat American attempts at settlement that a beginning was made with British settlements under the authority of the Hudson's Bay Company. The latter advised Douglas to make free grants of land of up to 500 acres to any British subject prepared to occupy and improve the land. This plan was a complete failure, and not a single person seemed to have the means and capital. This impelled the Company to take their own steps and accordingly another servant, Charles J. Griffin, was established on San Juan at the end of 1853. In the following January Griffin was made a J.P. and magistrate "to enable him to treat the U.S. Collector of Taxes on San Juan as a common offender."[24] In reply to a question, Douglas told the colonial secretary that "the Executive authorities in Oregon have not by any overt act contested the sovereignty of Great Britain over these Islands, neither do I suppose they will attempt any open act of aggression."[25] But the position was changing and the extension of American influence was leading to a more positive policy on the part of the Americans.

Not all the early development of the dispute was diplomatic, and synchronizing with the agitation in the Colonial and Foreign Offices there was developing in the disputed area the first of a series of "incidents." An American collector of customs, I. N. Ebey, was appointed in the spring of 1853 by the executive of Washington Territory to the charge of Puget Sound District. He insisted that the sheep landed on San Juan by Griffin were liable to seizure because they had entered without paying duty. On May 3, 1854, he landed on San Juan to be followed next day by Governor Douglas, on the call of Griffin. Douglas landed James Sangster, British collector of customs on Vancouver Island, with instructions from Douglas to superintend the islands in the San Juan Archipelago west of Rosario Strait. Sangster lost no time in telling Ebey that he was on British property.

After two days Ebey left the island, but he appointed Henry Webber as inspector of customs on San Juan. Griffin issued a warrant for the arrest of Webber, which Sangster unsuccessfully attempted to implement. Griffin was at this point instructed by Douglas to treat Webber as a private individual "amenable to the Laws of the Country which afford him protection" and he was not to arrest him unless he broke the law. Ebey asked Griffin questions about his status, and Sangster did the same with Webber. The latter encamped behind the Hudson's Bay Company establishment and refused to leave. When the British attempted to arrest him he produced a revolver; fortunately for the cause of peace, Griffin refused to arm the five men in his company.[26]

Both sides appear to have been satisfied with the outcome of the incident, for Douglas felt that the Americans had been made familiar with the fact that he would assert the British claim with determination, and Ebey was able to assert that "the Authority of the U.S. has been established & successfully maintained over the Islands in dispute" though he thought the Territory would doubtless now become a "matter of Negotiation."[27]

Douglas lost no time in advising his government of these developments, and they were raised with the American secretary of state with a reiteration of Douglas's threat that the moment Webber "commits any infringement of the Law or interferes with the Rights or Property of British Subjects by attempting to exercise an Authority which cannot be recognised . . . a warrant is to be issued for his arrest and is to be served at all hazards." But it is also urged that the settlement of the question of the boundary between British and United States possessions in the area is of "urgent importance."[28]

The United States govenment acted no less quickly. The British representative in Washington was told that the Americans shared the British desire for settlement of the boundary dispute. Application had been made to the last session of Congress for an appropriation to defray the expenses of marking the boundary, but the House of Representatives had done nothing, "not it is presumed from any indisposition to provide the means for the purpose indicated but from a want of time to become properly acquainted with the subject. It shall again be brought to the notice of Congress early in the next session . . ."[29] In his reply to Ebey, Secretary of the Treasury Guthrie, was explicit: "the question of jurisdiction will be settled by a boundary commission between the two Governments but in the meantime you will continue to hold possession."[30]

Douglas's reports to the Colonial Office continued grave and almost hysterical. The appearance off San Juan of a United States revenue cutter with six guns convinced him that they were "resolved to gain forcible possession of the disputed Territory, and I hardly know how to prevent them."[31] However, when the colonial secretary got his despatch and enclosures of May 17, 1854, giving details of the Ebey-Griffin incident, his reply, which was first submitted to the Foreign Office, was specific and approving: Douglas was to continue to treat the islands of the San Juan Archipelago as British. Triumphantly, Douglas announced to the Colonial Office that "there is not a single American citizen on any of the Arro Islands." He had survived a visit to San Juan by the acting governor of Washington Territory and three attempts by an American sheriff to levy certain taxes, for he "always managed to have a superior force." On February 27, 1855, he was able to boast to the company that the trial of strength with the Americans at the end of the previous year had gone to him, and "I hope it is now virtually decided that the place belongs of right to our Government." He welcomed a visit paid to him by Governor Stevens of Washington Territory who suggested that they should both leave the settlement of boundaries to their governments.[32]

A rather more serious attempt by American officials to interfere with the Hudson's Bay Company's position on San Juan came on March 30, 1855, when Sheriff Ellis Barnes landed on the island with a party of eight compatriots and two Indians, each with a brace of revolvers. Douglas reported that the British were outgunned and outnumbered, but he regretted that they did not display a "more resolute bearing." Sheriff Barnes demanded payment from Griffin of eighty dollars in taxes, and when Griffin repudiated liability the American forcibly seized forty-five sheep of which eleven escaped and the remainder were taken away.[33]

Douglas at once complained to Governor Stevens, asking him if Barnes's actions had been authorized by him or by Washington. A claim for damages estimated at nearly £3,000 was presented. He reminded Stevens that San Juan had been in the possession of British subjects for many years, "and it is, with the other islands in the Archipelago de Arro, declared to be under the jurisdiction of this Colony, and under the protection of British laws. I have also the orders of Her Majesty's Ministers to treat these Islands as part of the British dominions."[34]

Stevens in a temperate reply explained the American position. An Act of the Legislative Assembly of Oregon prior to the separation from Washington Territory had declared the boundary to be through the Haro channel so that San Juan was included in Washington Territory. The sheriff was therefore acting under the law, and the Governor must sustain him. The ownership of San Juan remained as settled in 1846 and can in no way be affected by the possessions of British subjects. In any case, the "contemporaneous exposition of the Treaty, as evinced in the debate in the United States Senate, shows the Canal de Arro to be the boundary line as understood by the United States at that time."[35]

It was therefore the explosive actions of their citizens in the disputed area that prompted the two governments, after an almost inactive lapse of four years, to give consideration to the water boundary. The British government could not be blamed for apathy and inactivity, because they had tried more than once to have commissioners appointed to settle the boundary line. At this time the chief obstacle was the tardiness of the United States' "appropriation" machinery, and the British government could not be charged with negligence or lack of diligence in introducing the subject to the Americans. Written appeals like that of Crampton to James Buchanan on January 13, 1848, based on Palmerston's instructions of the preceding December 18, had proved abortive, for Buchanan did not even vouchsafe an answer.

The four years' diplomatic hiatus which followed was broken by the reaction arising from events in the disputed area itself. President Pierce's secretary of state, William Marcy, proved sincere in his efforts to end the controversy and his first step, taken on June 2, 1853, was to initiate measures for a survey of the western boundary of Washington Territory. Accordingly, Haro and Rosario channels were surveyed and a chart published in the following year. This was accompanied, in December, 1853, by a statement in the President's annual message stressing the desirability of adjusting the northwest boundary.[36] His message of the following December went a step further by recommending the appointment of a joint commission to run the boundary. The recommendation was repeated again in December, 1855, for "by reason of the extent and importance of the country in dispute, there has been imminent danger of collision between the subjects of Great Britain and the citizens of the United States, including their respective authorities in that quarter." He coupled this with the suggestion that the possessory rights of the Hudson's Bay Company, protected by the treaty of 1846, should be bought out.

The third article of the treaty of 1846 had provided that the possessory rights of the company and of all British subjects "who may be already in the occupation of land or other property lawfully acquired within the said territory, shall be respected." It was a right to be held by mere occupancy but was to expire the moment occupancy was abandoned. Already in 1852-3 negotiations were proceeding in London for the sale of these possessory rights. It was therefore in the interests of the company to have their pre-1846 holdings as extensive as possible. This may or may not have induced Governor Douglas to neglect to mention in his depatches to the Colonial Office the fact that the company had established itself on San Juan at the end of 1853. Douglas had informed the colonial secretary that he was treating the Haro islands as a *de facto* dependency of Vancouver Island. The islands, he said, were "unoccupied by any Settlement of whites."[37] Charles Griffin, however, a clerk in the company's service, had been established on San Juan after, he said, "being given explicitly to understand by [Douglas] that this was British Territory and that he should be protected by his Country from all Foreign Aggressors."[38] Griffin was deemed by the Colonial Office to be "an independent British subject who would be more likely to be respected by the Authority of the United States than those of the Hudson's Bay Company."[39]

This evasive and reprehensible step drew from the secretary for the colonies, Henry Labouchere, a sharp reprimand to Douglas for failing to make it clear that Griffin was a company servant and not a private individual so that the company "were applying to the Secretary of State for the Foreign Department for compensation for damages done to their property on the Island of San Juan by the Americans, at a time when the Colonial Office were without information except of certain alleged injuries inflicted on a Mr. Charles Griffin."[40]

This helps to explain why the British government were determined not to allow the possessory rights of the Hudson's Bay Company to be entangled with the water boundary dispute, and their policy on this was admirably summarized in a typically Palmerstonian memorandum which said: "Tell Sir John Pelly that as to the sale of the Property possessed by Hudson's Bay Company South of Boundary Line, it is a matter of entire indifference to H.M. Govt. whether that Sale takes place or not except insofar as it may be for the Mutual and equal advantage both of the U.S. Government & of Gr. Br. . . ."[41]

It was apparent that the chain of events was being forged too rapidly for effective control. It was realized by the governments concerned that they must direct their agents to operate with discretion and forbearance, or the consequences might be grave. Representations from Washington Territory accompanying copies of correspondence in April and May, 1855, between Douglas and Governor Stevens of Washington Territory prompted Secretary of State William Marcy to write: "The President does not conceive that he can take any steps

towards that object [fixing the boundary] without the authority of Congress ...
He has instructed me to say to you that the officers of the Territory should
abstain from all acts, on the disputed grounds, which are calculated to provoke
any conflict, so far as it can be done without implying the concession to the
authorities of Great Britain of an exclusive right over the premises. The title
ought to be settled before either party should attempt to exclude the other by
force or exercise complete and exclusive sovereign rights within the fairly
disputed limits." [42]

A copy of this instruction was sent to Crampton by Marcy with the suggestion:
"I presume that the Government of Her Majesty will be willing to recommend
to her subjects along the boundary in question a similar course until the line can
be established. In this way I sincerely hope all collision may be avoided."
Crampton replied at once, concurring completely in Marcy's sensible views and
intimating that he was sending a copy of the letter to the Canadian government
so that the same forbearance "would be inculcated in British subjects." [43]

The potential danger of the situation had therefore been made obvious to both
governments, and both seem at last to have become infected with some of Douglas's anxiety. The Ebey incident, while of little moment intrinsically, had proved
to be the spur necessary to rouse the two governments. The incident also served
to hasten an appropriation bill through the House of Representatives; unfortunately, however, the Senate rejected it. This was a keen source of disappointment
for Britain at a time when, engaged in the Crimean War, she was particularly
anxious to maintain peaceful relations with the United States. She feared that
the recurrence of trouble on the Pacific Coast might precipitate war, but after
the failure of the United States to appoint a commissioner to define the boundary line she had to be content with taking steps towards obviating another clash
of interests in those parts. It was very fortunate, therefore, that she found Marcy
sympathetic and understanding.

So far, that is, until 1855, when the Marcy-Crampton understanding formulated
a standard of discipline which was to endure for several years, the water boundary or, as it was later called, the San Juan controversy, had been treated more or
less casually by both interested governments. This is explained by the remoteness
of the area in dispute, the procrastinating policy of the United States, Great
Britain's extreme apathy in matters colonial, and both countries' preoccupation
with much more pressing problems. The water boundary could not be expected
to have the same significance in the eyes of the Colonial Office that it had in
those of James Douglas. It was thus early apparent that only when, if ever, a
local clash of interests threatened to expand and involve greater issues would
either government seek a final and conclusive settlement. What greater issues
might be at stake? Throughout the whole of the water boundary dispute, as also
during the later stages of its parent, the Oregon controversy, two concurrent,
mainly philosophical movements—that of anti-imperialism in England and that
of "manifest destiny" in the United States—were most prominent, and each contributed its part towards inspiring and defining the official attitude to the
problem. Their combined effect was considerable, and appreciation of the weight
of their joint influence makes it a matter of much wonder that Canada managed
to remain a member of the British Empire.

In Anglo-American relations Canada was Britain's weak spot. On the one hand, British Liberals strongly resented the claims of Canada upon the mother country, and they looked forward to the time when Canada should be free of British control; on the other, the protagonists of the "manifest destiny" idea strongly resented Britain's control of the vast area to the north of the United States. Liberal governments were, to say the least, apathetic in their attitude to Canadian affairs and many Americans mistakenly accepted this as evidence of general weakness in British foreign policy. Only very strong provocation would justify a British government, Liberal or Conservative, fighting a war which could jeopardize Lancashire's great cotton trade to retain defenceless Canada. The Americans early perceived this, and they were accordingly inclined to be exacting in their attitude to Britain, particularly as far as Canada was concerned. They believed, and many Englishmen shared their view, that it had become a maxim of policy with Britain that all controversies with the United States must be in some way amicably settled. "The idea that, happen what may, England will never really declare war with this country has become so deeply rooted that I am afraid nothing short of actual hostilities would eradicate it," said Lord Lyons, British minister at Washington, to Lord John Russell.[44]

The anti-colonial agitation in England was a powerful factor affecting the foreign policy of successive governments. Early in the century the Philosophical Radicals had applied their principles to the theory of colonial government and had found that to protect the colonies, keep them in dependence, and prevent them from smuggling, fleets and armies were necessary and, because the colonies yielded no revenue, the mother country had to pay for them.[45] The *Westminster Review* in 1830 called colonies "impediments to commerce, drawbacks on prosperity, pumps for extracting the property of the many for the benefit of the few, the strongholds and asylums of despotism and misrule." It was the fond belief of Liberal free-traders that application of their ideals would lead to the loss of the colonies. Moreover, they argued, it was inevitable that the larger colonies at least should become independent in the course of time; Spanish, Portuguese, and American example all pointed that way. As the colonies grew, they would naturally seek independence to develop their ideals and enhance their power.

The general public was of course little exercised over the question and knew next to nothing of the geography and importance of England's colonial possessions. When colonial affairs were due for discussion Parliament was often "counted out," and colonial policy before the late sixties was in the hands of professional politicians and permanent officials. The little public interest that was aroused over colonial matters among the British people was confined to humanitarian societies.

Statesmen in the middle of the century, if they did not actually favour the grant of independence to the colonies, were almost unanimously convinced that ultimate separation was inevitable and that diplomacy should aim at making the parting as amicable as possible. Thus Sir Robert Peel, beyond affirming a desire to remedy specific grievances, was quite unprepared to make any radical change of imperial policy. He regarded the empire "primarily as a liability, an addition to the burdens, heavy enough without it, of government and of defence."[46] Even the minority who ignored the financial burden imposed by the possession of colonies argued that as independent states they could be quite as profitable to the mother country.

The budgets of the Peel government of 1841-6 and the repeal of the Corn Laws represented the triumph of the Adam Smith school of economic thought which was based on the principle that the regulation of trade by government was ineffectual and merely retarded the free development of all trade. But most conclusive evidence of the consistent attitude of successive governments to colonial development is to be found in the views of the permanent under-secretaries at the Colonial Office. During the period 1836 to 1871 there were but three such officials there: Sir James Stephen, 1836-47, Herman Merivale, 1847-59, and F. C. Rogers (later Lord Blachford), 1859-71.

In Stephen's eyes, for instance, the colonies were useful for absorbing the mother country's surplus population, but he considered them to be a "wretched burden" and favoured the development of colonial self-government as a step towards independence.[47] The object of the Colonial Office was to encourage the colonies to prepare for independence for their own sake and at the same time to relieve the mother country of her large share, usually 90 per cent, of the cost of colonial administration and defence. But connection should last just as long as the connection was profitable to both countries; separation, which was inevitable, should come amicably.[48]

The colonies, according to this commonly held view, were a *damnosa hereditas* which constituted a grave danger to the equanimity of the mother country because their contiguity to foreign countries introduced persistent and unnecessary causes of war. Canada in particular, as the neighbour of the United States, was a constant source of diplomatic trouble and the frequent incidents which arose between Great Britain and the United States produced a feeling of exasperation and annoyance in the mother country. According to this view, nothing could be more provoking than the threat of war with the Americans in the place and manner most disadvantageous to Great Britain, on behalf of a colony which was of little intrinsic value and many of whose people at one time or another spoke glibly of annexation to the United States.

It is easy, therefore, to understand the irritation of the British government when incidents on San Juan arose to disturb their composure. The island was something of a powder barrel which caused great anxiety and, especially after its occupation by American troops in the years after 1859, there was acute danger of an explosion. The continuous and oft-expressed concern, therefore, of diplomatists like Lord Lyons, British minister in Washington during the extremely thorny period after 1858, about the situation on the island is hardly surprising.[49]

The effect of the introduction of free trade in Great Britain had had a disastrous influence on Canadian commerce and induced Canadian businessmen to look southward for redress. The repeal of the Corn Laws in 1846 had driven Canadian produce down the New York channels of communication, destroying the revenue which Canada expected to derive from canal dues and ruining at once mill-owners, forwarders, and merchants. The consequence was that private property became unsaleable in Canada, while the United States tariff wall meant that Canadian produce could find no market to the south.[50] To aggravate matters, British money and labour went to the United States to make railways and develop industries at a time when Canada was ignored. Inevitably, therefore, there was annexationist sentiment in Canada which reached its zenith in 1849 though not its extinction until the seventies.

With the return of prosperity in the fifties after the failure of the diverse expansionist groups to unite on a common policy, the movement suffered temporary extinction and was never again revived, at least in Upper or Lower Canada, with so much hope of success. Still it could be used, and was indeed used, to unsettle Canadians and make them dissatisfied with the imperial connection. Annexation became chiefly the cause of a minority of malcontents whose influence waned with the winning in 1854 of reciprocity, which "gave to Canada most of the advantages of annexation without its defects."

In view of the general British conviction that colonies were "millstones round the imperial neck," it is natural to ask whence sprang the incentive to retain them or, more specifically, why were such strenuous efforts made to hold on to Oregon and later to the San Juan Archipelago. The British thought of Oregon as a barren tract, but a point of honour was involved. It was a twofold one, the abstract principle of which was threatened by surrendering to American threats a region to which Great Britain felt she had a just claim; the dread of loss of prestige among foreign powers was present—the danger of what one British journal called "the world's sneer." The concrete aspect of the point of honour involved the abandonment of the interests of the Hudson's Bay Company in North America, and the embarrassment of the company's presence in Oregon had been a major factor in inspiring the stubborn British attitude on Oregon. The company, which had done so much to guard Oregon jealously against American encroachment, had been "let down" over Oregon and any repetition of what some called the "Oregon surrender" would be political dynamite. The pontifical *Times* had said: "The Hudson's Bay Company has a very strong case with our government and its interests must not be sacrificed to American ambition and aggression." [51] And "we cannot compromise our countrymen's interests." [52]

On the American side there was the expansionist movement inspired by the term "manifest destiny," a picturesque phrase which became the battle-cry of a very considerable movement. After the Revolution the United States had been too occupied with domestic problems till early in the nineteenth century to devote much attention to territorial expansion. Their mild success in the War of 1812 was the first step in a series which in the middle forties engendered the idea of manifest destiny. The promulgation of the Monroe Doctrine, the beginning of overland emigration to the Oregon Territory, the manoeuvres to secure Texas and California, were all steps in the movement which, with the election as president of the political "dark horse," James Polk, protégé of the arch-expansionist, ex-president Andrew Jackson, achieved the stage of articulation with the famous cry of "Fifty-four forty or fight." In 1845 there appeared, in the *Democratic Review*, whence it was transferred to the House of Representatives debate on Oregon, the phrase "manifest destiny." It was asserted that the best and strongest title to Oregon was by the right of the United States' "manifest destiny" to "overspread and to possess the whole of the continent which Providence had given them for the development of the great experiment of liberty and federated self-government entrusted to them." [53] The phrase took an important place in the national vocabulary, and it became the rallying-cry of expansionists from Polk to Seward and Sumner.

The expansionist movement was the expression of the American feeling that democracy had approached perfection in the United States, and Americans wanted to prove that democratic institutions could go hand in hand with territorial greatness and power. Accordingly, it was inevitable that Texas, Mexico, California, and even Canada, should all eventually come under the Stars and Stripes; indeed, it was the duty of Americans to extend their institutions to these territories. Thus, Lyman Beecher claimed the United States to be ". . . still the richest inheritance which the mercy of God continues to the troubled earth. Nowhere beside, if you search the world over, will you find so much real liberty, so much equality, so much personal safety, and temporal prosperity; so general an extension of useful knowledge, so much religious instruction, so much moral restraint . . ." [54]

Standing in the way of the full achievement of manifest destiny was one country—Great Britain. By her influence in Mexican affairs she had delayed the acquisition of California; her place in the counsels of Texas retarded the annexation of that territory; there had been much evidence that by her claims in Oregon she had stood in the way of United States expansion on the northwest coast; her presence in Central America was retarding a solution of the isthmian problem; her possession of Canada complicated all Anglo-American relations and presented a perpetual problem to the expansionists of the United States. British control of the West Indies menaced American domination of the Gulf of Mexico. The presence of the British in Central America, where they might be empire-building, retarded the neutralization of what was to become the canal area.

It is obvious that the two movements—anti-colonialism in Britain and manifest destiny in the United States—would have their effect upon the solution of the San Juan water boundary question. Manifest destiny made possession of the island an essential of a vigorous policy which exalted territorial expansion, and only a decline in the fervour with which the movement or idea was viewed would make possible an American attitude suitable for settlement. On the other hand, the comparative equanimity with which territorial cession on the American continent would have been viewed by many in Great Britain in the middle of the nineteenth century concurred with the spasmodic evidence of annexationist activity in Canada to encourage a situation, so far as Great Britain was concerned, of official inaction and apathy. A change could be expected only if the "Little Englanders" of the British Isles or the enthusiasts for manifest destiny of the United States were to move into oblivion.

CHAPTER TWO

THE WATER BOUNDARY COMMISSION

In August, 1856, the United States made a move to settle the water boundary dispute. On August 11, Congress passed an Act empowering the president to appoint commissioners to act in conjunction with British government commissioners and to take other necessary steps for the demarcation of the boundary west of the mainland at the forty-ninth parallel. Intimation of this action was conveyed to the foreign secretary, the Earl of Clarendon, on August 28 by Mr. G. M. Dallas, American minister in London, and Clarendon replied at once that Her Majesty's government received the news "with great satisfaction." [1]

Captain James C. Prevost and Captain George H. Richards were to be the British commissioners, the latter as chief surveyor and astronomer acting under the instructions of Prevost to whom he was second in command. [2] The instructions to the commissioners were drawn up by Lord Clarendon in consultation with Herman Merivale, permanent under-secretary at the Colonial Office, and E. H. Hammond, foreign under-secretary. The instructions began with a brief review of the attempts to settle the controversy, and this was followed by directions to the commissioners on the manner of procedure, this part of the instructions being identical with those prepared by Viscount Palmerston in 1847. First of all, the commission was to determine where the forty-ninth parallel strikes the sea; then to trace the line of boundary westward to the middle of the channel between the mainland and Vancouver Island, seeking to obtain Point Roberts for Great Britain; the line thus reaches the Gulf of Georgia, through the middle of which it runs, until it ceases to be the only channel.

"So long as there is only one Channel separating the Continent and Vancouver's Island, no doubt can be entertained; and therefore the centre of the Gulf of Georgia, as far as the latitude where it ceases to be the only Channel, and the centre of the Strait of Fuca till it ceases also to be the only Channel between the Continent and Vancouver's Island, appear to Her Majesty's Government to be fixed points in the line of boundary—and it is only as regards the space between these two points that any difference of opinion as to the proper Channel can exist."

"There can be little doubt that the Channel through Rosario Strait was the Channel which the negotiators of the Treaty had in view when they proceeded to define verbally the boundary between Her Majesty's possessions and those of the United States. It was at the time . . . the only known navigable Channel, and was laid down as such on the Charts." There is a "far less safe and convenient passage known as the Canal de Arro" which the American commissioner would probably claim as the boundary, and Prevost was to point out that this channel did fit the treaty definition of the boundary. The treaty provided for the boundary taking a southern direction; if it was to follow the "Canal de Arro" it would have to proceed for some distance in a direction nearly due west, and the treaty made no provision for such westerly direction.

The instructions mentioned with approval the views on the boundary of Governor James Douglas of Vancouver Island, who strongly held an opinion in favour of Rosario Strait as the boundary line, and a copy of his despatch to the Colonial Office of February 27, 1854, giving his views was enclosed with Clarendon's instructions to Prevost. Douglas's chief arguments, accompanied as they were by a map of the whole area, a facsimile of Vancouver's chart, and a copy of Preuss's map of 1848, were briefly as follows: (1) The Haro Channel was not properly a part of the Gulf of Georgia nor of the channel leading from it into the Strait of Juan de Fuca. (2) The term "said channel" required that the line should follow the Gulf of Georgia, and no other channel, for the treaty of 1846 stipulated that the line should be drawn "southerly," "through the middle of the *said channel.*" (3) The Gulf of Georgia certainly extended as far south as McLoughlin's Island, from which the boundary would naturally follow the line of Rosario Strait. (4) The spirit of the treaty was to allow free egress from and ingress to and from the Gulf of Georgia, and only Rosario Strait satisfied that.[3]

If the commission considered that Rosario Strait was not indicated by the treaty they would be "at liberty to adopt any other intermediate Channel which they may discover . . ." At the same time Captain Richards was to initiate an accurate survey of the area to discover if there was another navigable channel among the group of islands lying between the mainland and Vancouver Island.

Clarendon had now arrived at the point of importance for Great Britain. Prevost was reminded that there are important islands lying between Haro and Rosario straits, and these had always been considered by Great Britain as "appendages" of Vancouver Island, and their possession was essential to the "quiet possession" of Vancouver Island. Prevost, therefore, must use his "utmost efforts" to convince the American commissioner to accept this view and he was furnished with a variety of American maps, including that of Charles Preuss, on which "you will find a line drawn through Rosario Strait as the line between the British and American Possessions."

If he was unable to convince his colleague that Rosario was the channel of the treaty, he was to attempt to discover if there was a third channel intersecting the islands "more accurately" answering the description of the treaty; if there was one, he was to get the American commissioner to agree to adopt it. It was impressed on him that Great Britain wanted the dispute settled; he was exhorted to establish as clear a line as possible in order to obviate trouble in the future.

"But if you are satified that the British claim is unquestionably sound, and you are unable to come to an understanding on the subject with your American Colleague, you will then propose that you should lay before your respective Governments, either jointly or severally, a statement of the points on which you disagree, and the reasons by which each of you supports his opinion."[4]

Prevost sailed from England on December 23, 1856, and arrived at Esquimalt, Vancouver Island, on June 13, 1857. The American commissioner, Mr. Archibald Campbell, who had been appointed on February 14, left New York on April 20 and arrived on June 22. Before beginning their discussions five days later the two commissioners exchanged copies of their instructions.[5] It is significant that, although Campbell presented a full copy of his instructions, Prevost withheld part of his. Thus in the copy handed over to Campbell, there was no mention of some of Clarendon's statements and arguments, notably that Rosario Strait was the only known navigable one, that Haro Strait did not accord with the definition of the treaty; the arguments and contentions of Governor Douglas; the British need to have the islands in order to secure "quiet possession" of Vancouver Island; the possibility of finding a third channel and the British government's great anxiety to have the question settled. This stood out in sharp relief against the simplicity of the instructions of Secretary of State Marcy to Campbell who was told merely to "determine and mark the boundary line between the United States and the British Possessions as described in the first article of the treaty . . . of 1846." [6]

This duplicity did not augur well for the success of the Water Boundary Commission. It is obvious that Prevost was not being allowed to have a free hand in determining the line of demarcation, and that was a definite obstacle to free discussion and decision. His instructions make it clear that he might contend for Rosario Strait as boundary but never Haro, and the American commissioner's allegation that he did not have a free hand was justifiable. The quest for a middle channel which might be said to satisfy the terms of the treaty was now initiated, and we shall see that most subsequent British negotiators were hypnotized by this pursuit of a middle-channel alternative to either Rosario or Haro straits. It is true that the United States minister, G. M. Dallas, subsequently asked for and received a copy of Prevost's instructions, but by that time (February, 1859), the two commissioners had reached a deadlock. [7]

Several formal talks followed the first meeting of the commissioners and it was "mutually admitted that through the Gulf of Georgia and through the Straits of Fuca there would be no difficulty in tracing the boundary line, but as to the direction in which it should proceed through the space situated between these waters, we found that our opinions differed widely." In short, Campbell stood out for the Haro channel; Prevost demanded Rosario Strait. [8] Prevost rested his opinion upon the wording of the treaty of 1846, while Campbell tended rather to argue upon contemporaneous evidence which sought to explain the intentions and views of the negotiators and others directly concerned in the signing and ratification of the Oregon treaty.

Campbell produced copies of despatches from Louis McLane, United States minister in London in 1846, along with reports of speeches by Senator Benton, to prove that the United States had in mind the Haro Strait when concluding the treaty. Thus, McLane, in his despatch of May 18, 1846, had recounted the substance of an interview with Lord Aberdeen, in the course of which the foreign secretary had explained the probable terms of his proposition for the conclusion of the controversy over Oregon. In his despatch, McLane definitely mentioned the Haro channel as that to be offered as boundary; moreover, a copy of his letter accompanied President Polk's request to the Senate for their advice on signing the treaty.

Senator Benton in a speech in the Senate on June 6, 1846, said that the line established by the treaty's first article

follows the parallel of 49 degrees to the sea, with a slight deflection through the Straits of Fuca, to avoid cutting the south end of Vancouver's Island . . . When the line reaches the channel which separates Vancouver's Island from the continent (which it does within sight of the mouth of Fraser's River) it proceeds to the middle of the channel and thence, turning south, through the Channel de Haro (wrongly written Arro on the maps) to the Straits of Fuca; and thence west through the middle of that Strait to the sea. This is a fair partition of these waters, and gives us everything we want, namely, all the waters of Puget Sound, Hood's Canal, Admiralty Inlet, Bellingham Bay, Birch Bay and with them the cluster of islands, probably of no value, between de Haro's channel and the continent.[9]

Campbell argued that the boundary line defined by Lord Aberdeen in his despatch of May 18, 1846, could not possibly be "tortured" into a line running through the middle of Rosario Strait. It follows that, since Aberdeen's line was not clearly marked, we must fall back upon the motive which induced deflection from the forty-ninth parallel. This motive was simply to give Vancouver Island to Great Britain; Aberdeen's actual words are: "thus giving to Great Britain the whole of Vancouver's Island and its harbours." Finally, if there was any possibility of doubt concerning the interpretation of the treaty of 1846, the British government which framed it ought to have taken all possible steps to preclude a state of doubt and uncertainty. Not only American but even English contemporaneous evidence was clearly on the side of the United States, continued the American commissioner, and the letters of Palmerston, Aberdeen, and Pakenham did not sustain the British argument.

It had been British policy, argued Campbell, studiously to depreciate the value of the small islands in the Haro archipelago as of little or no use and, by way of apology for proposing to take them on the British side of the boundary, the United States was gravely informed that the only large and valuable island in the group, Whidbey, would "of course" belong to them.[10] The Haro Strait, continued Campbell, is the main channel of navigation, being wider, clearer of islands, and shorter than that called Rosario. The "said channel" of the treaty is the main channel, that most conspicuous and open, most adapted to the general purposes of navigation, the shortest channel, that best known to geographical science in 1846; in other words, Haro Strait. It was named on Spanish Admiralty maps of the last century, and it had been accurately surveyed by Captain Wilkes of the United States Navy, whose report of his survey was published in 1845. On Wilkes's map Haro Channel is so designated; Rosario is laid down but given no name.

Commissioner Prevost rested his argument almost entirely upon the words of the treaty of 1846 and concluded that Rosario Strait was the only line which could be justified after a study of the wording. His reasons were: (1) Rosario is the navigable channel of direct communication from the Gulf of Georgia to the Straits of Fuca situated most adjacent to the continent and is consequently the channel "which separates the continent from Vancouver Island." Rosario Channel is a *direct* continuation of the channel of the Gulf of Georgia and answers the phrase, "thence southerly through the middle of the said channel." (2) It admits of the channel being carried through it with less departure from "southerly" than any other channel. (3) Rosario is a more navigable channel than Haro, the free navigation being agreed upon by both parties. Haro has irregular and uncertain currents. (4) Haro does not satisfy because it is not the channel "separating the continent from Vancouver's Island," the continent having already been separated by another channel, Rosario, it runs west as well as southerly for which there is no provision in the treaty.

Prevost answered Campbell's claim that the islands between the continent and Haro Strait are natural appendages of the continent thus: "I reply that in the Treaty I find two fixed points named, the Continent on one hand, and Vancouver's Island on the other, and that I conceive the Continent must be de facto the Continent, as much as Vancouver's Island is de facto Vancouver's Island."

Campbell refused to admit that Rosario Strait was peculiarly a direct continuation of the channel of the Gulf of Georgia but maintained it to be a continuation only in common with other channels. Local experience, argued the English commissioner, was on the British side, "for the uninterrupted body of water flowing from the Gulf of Georgia through the Rosario Strait causes a regularity of current that is not experienced in the other channels." A glance at any map will show that "the waters passing southerly through the Rosario Strait are derived from the Gulf of Georgia alone and uninterruptedly while the Canal de Haro is, in like direction, supplied only partly and indirectly by the waters from the southern termination of the Gulf of Georgia, and partly and more directly from the waters flowing through the passages between Saturna Island and Vancouver's Island." In other words, Rosario channel is more direct.

If "southerly" were taken in the strict sense, the treaty would become a nullity, the American commissioner had claimed, for the term related equally to the Strait of Juan de Fuca, where it was impossible for the boundary line to be carried in a southerly direction and he argued that, therefore, the term must only be used generally and in contra-distinction to "northerly." Prevost answered that where the wording of a treaty can be strictly adhered to, this must be done; where it cannot, the evident intention of the treaty should be sought. He quotes from Vattel to illustrate: "It is not allowable to interpret what has no need of interpretation."

In the fourth point of his rebuttal, Prevost admitted that the testimony of Benton and McLane was entitled to some weight, but their evidence was merely secondary. The terms of the treaty had been drafted by Britain, but no mention was made of the Haro channel to explain the nature of Benton's and McLane's testimony. Prevost educed two possibilities: Benton used Wilkes's map of 1845 and was therefore misled, "for in carrying the eye along from the termination of the boundary line on the eastern side of the Rocky Mountains, it rests naturally upon Birch's Bay and the 'Canal de Arro' is so conspicuously marked that it *appears* to be the only direct channel" between the mainland and Vancouver Island that bends into the Strait of Juan de Fuca; alternatively, Benton may have relied on the terms of McLane's despatch of May 18, 1846.

The absence of the name Haro in the treaty and in the earliest draft of June 6, made it impossible to accept the testimony of Mr. McLane. It was impossible to believe that Britain would accept Haro channel and thus give up Rosario Strait which was the best known in 1846, whereas the channel claimed by the Americans was not known to be navigable then. In 1846 Rosario was the channel known in England as navigable, it was that used by Vancouver, and it was the Hudson's Bay Company's route to the northern posts. Prevost did not dispute that the United States might have contemplated Haro as the channel of the treaty, but the Americans, he pointed out, had not insisted upon its name being inserted in the treaty.[11]

In his rebuttal, Campbell made much of the argument that the basis of settlement in 1846 had been the forty-ninth parallel and any departure from that line had been effected merely to give up Vancouver Island to Great Britain. Campbell argued that, if the whole of Vancouver Island had been to the north of the forty-ninth parallel none of the islands south of the island would ever have been claimed by Britain. If five-sixths of the islands had been to the south of the forty-ninth parallel, the deflection from that parallel would perhaps have been northerly and the whole island might have gone to the United States. In other words, the sole reason for abandoning the forty-ninth parallel was the interposition of Vancouver Island. As for the navigability of the "said channel," it was a matter of dispute whether Rosario or Haro was the better. The American commissioner dismissed Prevost's argument based on the assertion that Haro was not the channel "separating the continent from Vancouver's Island" as laboured and inconsequential, and he attached no significance to the argument based on the use of " southerly."

The respective arguments proved irreconcilable and, recognizing this fact, Prevost proposed that the channel situated nearly midway between Rosario and Haro straits should be taken as the channel through which the boundary should be run. Prevost had privately come to the conclusion that the rapid increase of settlement of Washington Territory was a menace to the potentially important Vancouver Island, and to assure the "quiet possession" of that island it was imperative that the Island of San Juan, lying between the mainland and Vancouver Island, should be secured to Britain. Already, therefore, we see the shape of things to come: the water boundary question is about to become the San Juan question.

Prevost's suggestion, made on the instructions of Lord Clarendon, that the middle channel situated between Rosario and Haro straits might be accepted as the boundary line was, from the British point of view, ill conceived and unfortunate. To argue vehemently that Rosario was meant in 1846 and then to suggest a compromise was to weaken irrevocably the British case for Rosario. An excellent case could be made out for demanding the line along the middle of the whole area between the mainland and Vancouver Island, but only one channel was meant by the treaty, and to plump for one of the three was to reject the other two. The British commissioner was saying, in effect, that either Rosario or the Middle Channel, both of which gave the strategically important Island of San Juan to Great Britain, fulfilled the terms of the treaty, but never Haro. Campbell had therefore no option but to reject absolutely the offer to compromise along the line of the Middle Channel.[12] Prevost now had to postpone discussions pending the receipt of fresh instructions from the Foreign Office. But the British government were in no hurry to issue fresh instructions, and beyond formal approval of his efforts and promise of further correspondence, Prevost heard nothing more until 1859.[13]

Prevost had been deeply impressed by the strategic value of the islands lying between the two disputed channels, particularly that of San Juan and he allowed this predilection to colour his attitude to the boundary question. He told the Foreign Office:

considering the fast increasing interests of the United States in this part of the world, it appears to me, judging from being on the spot, of the utmost importance that Vancouver's Island should be carefully preserved to Great Britain and the greater the distance of the line of boundary, so much the more must the peaceful possession of the Island be secured . . . but, if the proposition I made for the whole space between the continent and Vancouver's Island, from the southern termination of the Gulf of Georgia to the eastern termination of the Straits of Fuca, to be considered as one Channel, and for the Boundary Line to be traced through the middle of it, so far as islands would permit, could be carried out, it would give the Island of San Juan to the British Government, and would be almost all that is required to ensure the quiet possession of Vancouver's Island.[14]

Again he writes: "as the value of Vancouver's Island to us as a Naval Station and perhaps a terminus of a great railroad scheme becomes generally known, the possession of San Juan as a wall of defence to its peaceful occupation will be equally appreciated."[15]

Prevost omitted to mention, however, that San Juan had considerable importance in American eyes as possession of it meant control of the harbours of Puget Sound, harbours which had fascinated the United States government from the earliest stages of the Oregon dispute. These were the harbours which Benton had mentioned and, although an Englishman might be pardoned for thinking that places with names like Admiralty Inlet had an exclusively English connotation, it was nevertheless a fact that they were in American hands. Commissioner Campbell was just as alive to the importance of San Juan as his British counterpart and his report to Secretary of State Cass of September 25, 1858, explains his views. The islands, he said, "are so situated that they form an admirable landlocked harbour of ample size, accessible by six narrow entrances, in any wind and weather."

With the two commissioners thus bemused in contemplation of the strategic value of San Juan, it is no wonder that they could not come to an agreement over the line of boundary. Each felt that he could not accept the other's view and each also seemed to derive great satisfaction from reminding his government of the importance of the island. Nothing could have been more inflexible than their testimonies to their respective governments. Said Campbell: "I am still of the opinion that if the boundary line had been drawn upon the maps of the day immediately after the conclusion of the treaty, that it would have been drawn through the Gulf of Georgia and Canal de Haro."[16] Prevost was equally emphatic: "I can state my conviction of the Rosario Strait being the Channel of the Treaty in their strict and literal interpretation becomes stronger the more I study and reflect upon the evidence brought forward on both sides . . ."[17]

CHAPTER THREE

A BRITISH PROPOSITION

THE FAILURE of the commissioners to effect a settlement was most disappointing, particularly since a new factor had made itself known while the water boundary question lay in abeyance between the governments and their representatives. This was the Fraser River gold rush of 1857-8 which gave British Columbia and the adjoining islands an importance they had never before enjoyed. The discovery of gold along the banks of the Fraser River attracted throngs of gold-miners from the corners of the earth to British Columbia. The great majority of the newcomers, however, were Americans and the population of American towns on the Pacific Coast was severely depleted. Since all prospective gold-miners had to procure a license at Victoria on Vancouver Island, that settlement increased almost overnight to the status of a city. It became obvious that British Columbia, Vancouver Island, and the adjacent islands would thenceforward assume a prominent place in North America and, what was more important, many squatters, the great majority of them Americans, settled, "staked their claims," on the islands of the Haro archipelago, openly declared the territory to belong to the United States, and refused to budge. The colony of British Columbia had been established in 1858, with James Douglas as governor, and a body of Engineers was stationed at New Westminster. The stage was therefore set for another act in the disturbing drama enacted by the two governments.

Fortunately the British government perceived the danger and took immediate and comprehensive steps to achieve a solution. The whole problem was such a perplexing one for them that strict unanimity of departmental opinion could not be secured. Copies of Captain Prevost's despatches were sent to the Admiralty and to the Colonial Office in an attempt to amass all available evidence and opinions in order to arrive at the best possible course to be pursued. During 1858, therefore, there was considerable inter-departmental activity and correspondence.

The Colonial Office advised arbitration as the best means of settling the controversy, which was tantamount at that stage of development to shirking or at least shelving the issue.[1] When in May, 1858, Lord Stanley was succeeded at the Colonial Office by Sir Edward Bulwer-Lytton, a more positive policy was embarked upon, and the new secretary concurred in the increasingly prominent view that San Juan was indispensable to the safety of Vancouver Island; in other words, the risk of a possible adverse decision by an arbiter could not be taken.

Of all the government departments at this stage of the affair, the Colonial Office was undoubtedly the most active and aggressive. Stanley had been at best a lukewarm minister, because he was not very much interested in the colonies. Bulwer-Lytton, on the other hand, was by nature dynamic and positive. He accepted the pale policy of the government after protest and, as he said, "with great reluctance." He stressed the "very serious and critical additions to the difficulties connected with the question which is created by the discovery of gold in British Columbia, and the probability that the Americans will on that account increase their demands in proportion to the delay which allows the popular feeling in America to be fed and swollen by accounts that must stimulate cupidity." Delay of any kind will mean "certain loss and probable danger and that the more immediate the settlement of a water Boundary upon waters that will be swarming with American Vessels the better the chance of fair terms and averted quarrels."[2]

While the lords of the Admiralty reminded the foreign secretary in the Derby government of 1858-9, the Earl of Malmesbury, that no purely naval question was at stake, they were of opinion that the line meant by the framers of the Oregon treaty was to follow the middle of the whole area between the mainland and Vancouver Island. It seemed obvious to them, therefore, that the object of the commissioners should be to trace the most convenient line by which the whole strait could be divided between the two countries, and could be continued as nearly as possible along the middle of the whole water area dividing the continent from Vancouver Island.

Haro channel did not satisfy the treaty proviso that the "navigation of the whole of the said channel and straits south of the forty-ninth parallel of north latitude remain free and open to both Parties." Clearly, argued the Admiralty, the channel meant was the whole area between the mainland and Vancouver Island. This channel begins above, and is greater than, Haro Strait. If the latter had been meant, words of restriction would have been inserted excluding the free navigation of that part of the channel given to the United States. For similar reasons Rosario channel did not completely satisfy. Therefore the lords of the Admiralty said that it would be an advantageous settlement of the question if the boundary line were drawn so as to give to Great Britain the Island of San Juan and they felt that this line might be fairly accepted as a compromise line by the United States. Should that not be conceded, they would advise that the question be settled even by accepting Haro channel as the line. The important consideration in their view was that the United States gained by the question's being left open, every day adding to the number of American settlers in the disputed territory. The precise line of boundary was of minor importance, but the Admiralty insisted that free navigation of the whole water area must be guaranteed to Great Britain.[3] The equanimity with which they viewed a possible adverse award can be explained by the fact that their preponderant naval influence in the Pacific made them ready to ridicule any fears for the safety of Vancouver Island and made them satisfied with mere freedom of navigation in the disputed area.

The Admiralty were well aware of the government's recollection of the effect of agricultural settlement on the development of American claims to Oregon in the years 1843-6, for the incidence of American settlement in Oregon after 1843 had been a vital factor in influencing the United States government's policy. The agitation on behalf of the American pioneer settlers had begun in the twenties and continued annually for over two decades; it had done much to keep the subject before both American and British eyes. The fear that minor local conflicts might spread into a vast national conflagration had weighed considerably with Lord Aberdeen and Sir Robert Peel in 1846; repeatedly they had made mention of the danger of local clashes growing into international ones. This fear explains the Admiralty's view in 1858, and the British government shared this view that the United States gained by delay in adjustment, for every day would add to the number of American settlers in the archipelago. Once established there, their government could neither ignore them nor desert their interest.

The Foreign Office also canvassed the views of Sir Richard Pakenham, who had been British minister at Washington throughout the decisive Oregon negotiations of 1843-6, and of Lord Aberdeen, who had been foreign secretary in the Peel government of 1841-6 and who had drawn up the terms of the Oregon treaty (accepted by the United States without a single alteration or amendment). Copies of the instructions to Prevost, the latter's report on them, the despatches of Lord Napier, British minister at Washington, the Colonial Office opinion, the Admiralty opinion, all were sent to these two diplomatists for their observations.

Lord Aberdeen declared that he was certain that it was the intention of the treaty to adopt as line of demarcation the mid-channel of the straits without any reference to islands, the position and indeed the very existence of which had hardly at that time been accurately ascertained. He had "no recollection of any mention having been made during the discussion of the Canal de Haro or indeed any other channel than those described in the Treaty itself."[4]

Pakenham's conclusion, a very valuable and important one, was that neither Haro nor Rosario would exactly fulfil the conditions of the treaty, which according to their literal tenor would require the line to be traced along the middle of the channel, "meaning, I presume, the whole intervening space...." He was certain that no mention had ever been made of Haro Strait in the course of the negotiations. Sir Richard went on to assert his belief that neither Lord Aberdeen nor Secretary of State Buchanan nor Mr. McLane, the minister in London in 1846, possessed at that time a sufficiently accurate knowledge of the geography or hydrography of the region in question to enable them to define more accurately what was intended to be the line of boundary than is expressed in the words of the treaty. Besides, went on Pakenham, it is certain that Mr. Buchanan signed the treaty with McLane's despatch of May 18, 1846, before him and that he made no mention whatever of Haro Strait as that through which the line of boundary should run in the understanding of his government. Pakenham advised that, since a direct line, as obviously envisaged by the Oregon treaty, could not be conveniently adopted because it would run partly over land, the next best course to pursue would be to trace the line in the direction coming nearest to that required by the treaty.[5]

Preparations were made to go over the whole controversy at the Foreign Office, arrangements being made for Viscount Palmerston, though he was not at this time a member of the government, and Lord Stanley, colonial secretary (after May at the Board of Control) and son of the prime minister, to discuss the whole position with Lord Malmesbury and permanent officials representing the Foreign Office, Colonial Office, and Admiralty. Copies of the correspondence sent to Aberdeen and Pakenham, their replies thereto, and in particular a memorandum by Mr. E. H. Hammond, permanent under-secretary at the Foreign Office, were all placed before the statesmen.

Hammond's memorandum is important because it carried weight with the government as the work of an experienced and knowledgeable servant. Hammond had been in the diplomatic service since 1824 and had been chief clerk at the Foreign Office before he succeeded Henry Unwin Addington as permanent under-secretary in 1854. The dominant note of the memorandum stressed the necessity of securing undisputed possession of the Island of San Juan, and this insistence upon acquiring the island became the basis and chief objective of the British government's policy in the dispute. Hammond saw San Juan as the really desirable island and Great Britain ought to stand out for it. He advised that the Middle Channel, as coming most nearly within the strict definition of the treaty of 1846, might first be suggested and, if refused, Hammond would press for arbitration. If both these proposals were refused, the under-secretary would go the length of intimating that England would act upon her interpretation of what was right, and she would continue to hold San Juan as a purely British possession.[6]

After discussion, it was finally decided to make no proposal until Captain Richards' survey was concluded, since whatever was done would be better accomplished with full knowledge, particularly since it could be safely assumed that the Americans would not voluntarily forego any portion of their pretensions. Further, if resort were to be had to arbitration, it would be wise to have a clear knowledge of the chances resulting from a survey before deciding upon the course to be taken.

Both the Colonial Office and the Foreign Office, therefore, awaited the report of Captain Richards with considerable interest. The Colonial Office saw the danger to British Columbia and Vancouver Island if there was an adverse report upon the usefulness of Rosario Strait, while the Foreign Office perceived the danger of having to recede from their strong position or, alternatively, of having to submit to an arbiter a question which they feared might be decided against them.

The chart and report of the survey party under Richards were finally despatched on November 30, 1858, and reached the government at the end of January of the following year. Its effect was instantaneous and arresting, for in the foreign secretary's own words they went to "establish the American claim that the Canal de Haro was the best navigable channel."[7]

This important report commences with a comparison of the three main channels, Haro, Rosario, and the Middle, the latter sometimes called Douglas Strait.[8] Rosario Strait, the report points out, varies in width from one and a third to six miles, with an average width of two miles. It has strong tides; it contains two great dangers to navigation in the shape of two giant rocks. Its depth varies from twenty-five to thirty-five fathoms. Haro Strait, on the other hand, is two and a half miles at its northern entrance, and it is on the whole wider and deeper than the other two. The Middle Channel is much inferior in capacity, yet it is safe enough for steamships. Its tides are strong at the southern entrance, and yet there is a narrow inlet. All three channels present considerable difficulties to sailing vessels, involving chiefly danger and great delay. So far as steamships are concerned, however, the passages are quite safe during the day and could be lighted at night.

The Richards report emphasizes three points in particular: (1) Vessels passing through the Strait of Juan de Fuca and bound for the Fraser River or Nanaimo on Vancouver Island would unquestionably take the Haro channel since by doing so they would save a distance of twelve to fifteen miles; (2) Haro Strait from its position with reference to British ports must be almost entirely used by British vessels; (3) "To the commerce of British Columbia, to the rising port of Nanaimo, which probably for many years will be the great coal depôt to the coasting trade, which will rapidly rise into importance so soon as Vancouver's Island is open to the enterprise of the Agriculturist and the Settler, this Strait is of equal interest." [9]

It will be seen, therefore, that Richards's report is of the greatest importance in the controversy because, by proving the Middle Channel to be navigable, it gave the British government a valuable, if dangerous, alternative to Rosario Strait in the negotiations. At the same time, by demonstrating the essential superiority of Haro Strait, it weakened the confidence of the British government in the British position and made possible, if indeed it did not actually encourage, the ultimate mismanagement of the British case.

The disappointing nature of the survey report compelled the British government to reconsider their attitude. They could not publicly admit, without serious loss of prestige, that from the point of view of navigability and accessibility their claim to the Rosario channel as the line of boundary was difficult to substantiate. The utilitarian aspect of the problem became paramount with them, therefore, and they arrived at the conclusion that if they could secure rightful possession of San Juan island, they might save face and at the same time strike a blow for the safety of Vancouver Island about which the Colonial Office in particular was so much exercised. It was not going to be easy to acquire full legal title to the coveted island, but after receipt of the report of Captain Richards in January, 1859, the water boundary question became for Great Britain the San Juan question.

The truth is that mere considerations of the phraseology of treaties and the weighing of the pronouncements of statesmen became of minor significance when the naval and military importance of the Island of San Juan fell into the balance. Both governments were aware of the strategic position of the island and both attached to it an almost exaggerated military value. As Canning, first English statesman to appreciate to the full the value of his country's retaining a hold on the Pacific coast, had said, it was becoming increasingly evident that "the trade of the East was that most susceptible of advancement," and the worth of Vancouver Island and the potentialities of the mainland of British Columbia were enormous. For one thing, this area in the region of the modern city of Vancouver, which even then promised to be the commercial centre of the North Pacific, was several hundred miles nearer the East than San Francisco.

The value of Vancouver Island had become well known. It had on all sides safe and commodious harbours; it was well supplied with fresh water; it had four lakes with rivulets to produce good water power; it was covered with excellent timber; its splendid equable climate, with a warm, dry summer, short winter, and heavy dews to take the place of rain, made it an enviable possession for its intrinsic worth as much as for its strategic excellence. There was an abundance of first-class coal, while salmon, cod, and herring flourish in its waters. It had extensive deposits of limestone of superior quality and it was the only point in the Puget Sound area where limestone was found. Gold had been discovered and after the "strike" in the adjacent Fraser River region, the island could conceivably be rich in this respect too.

The key to the possession of this Eldorado was an island which a writer of the time had called the "Cronstadt of the Pacific"—San Juan. It is at once patent that every effort must be made to gain or retain legal possession of this key. It is not too much to say that it was this high evaluation on the part of officials and states-men of both countries that gave the whole question of the boundary west of the mainland the importance and prominence it ultimately achieved and delayed settlement of a controversy that might otherwise have been quite unobtrusively adjusted. Both sides had their quota of experts who could become lyrical in contemplation of the strategic value of San Juan.

The joint commission of Prevost and Campbell had been foredoomed to failure because the principals on both sides had allowed their views to become coloured by their conception of the Island of San Juan as a military and naval stronghold of prime importance. Campbell in his researches had come upon the report of General Persifer F. Smith who had visited the region in 1849-50 and on his return had represented to the president the immense importance of the islands in the San Juan Achipelago. In his report he affirms that

these islands [San Juan, Orcas, and Lopez] form a naval harbour that may be defended against any force if they are fortified as they may be, and the nation that disposes of them thus will absolutely command not only Queen Charlotte's Sound but all those splendid harbours in our territory on the waters of Admiralty Inlet and Puget's Sound, as well as those on the straits of Juan de Fuca and the navigation of that inlet. These harbours are the best on the Pacific coast, for, with the timber that covers the hills bordering on them, and the coal in the adjacent terri-tory as far south as Gray's Harbour, they possess the great advantage of a rise and fall of tide of twenty-one feet, rendering the construction of docks easy and cheap.[10]

Confirmation of this expert view was afforded five years later when Captain George Stoneman of the Dragoons and Lieutenant W. E. C. Whiting of the Engineers reported in very similar terms to the United States government.[11]

In 1860 General Totten, Chief Engineer of the United States Army, was sent to the Haro archipelago to report upon suitable naval and military sites there. In his report to the War Department he confirmed the views of the earlier experts and expressed the opinion that possession of San Juan was absolutely essential to the United States to compensate for the loss of Vancouver Island in 1846. "The presence ... of fast, armed steamers, would exercise an important influence upon the communications between the Straits of Fuca and the Gulf of Georgia, Fraser river, etc., [and] would at all times threaten and harass this communication and completely command it, whenever it should happen to be without the actual presence of a strong convoy ... without the possession of [San Juan] there can be no escape from the paralysis that adverse naval predominance will impose on all our coasts and waters inside Cape Flattery."[12] These views were subsequent-ly adopted *in toto* by the United States Board of Engineers who concluded that

our sole and exclusive possession of Rosario Straits will be of no appreciable military value to us if Great Britain be allowed to possess the island of San Juan ... The possessor of the south extremity of the island of San Juan can easily close the entrance to the President's Passage at will. By establishing a military and naval station at Griffin Bay, on the southeastern shore of San Juan Island, we shall be able to overlook those inner waters equally with Great Britain from Esquimalt harbour, and thus counterbalance the preponderance she is seeking to establish. Ex-cluded from this harbour we shall find no substitute for it, for no harbour of sufficient capacity for vessels of war is to be found east of this point short of Rosario Straits. A harbour in Rosario Strait will not enable us to overlook these inner waters equally with Great Britain.[13]

The official American opinion was based on all these views of their experts, and it was neatly summed up by A. A. Humphreys, Chief Engineer, thus: "Our military interests require us to possess the island of San Juan and an equal joint share of the use of the waters of the Canal de Haro."[14] "Puget Sound" was a magic phrase to the Americans, for their determined stand for their line of boundary during the Oregon negotiations before 1846 had been largely prompted by the high value the United States government placed upon the harbours of Puget Sound. The earliest United States interest in the northwest coast had originated from its coastal and internal trade activities, and John Quincy Adams had early in the century perceived the potentialities of the Puget Sound area. From his time it had been a canon of American policy to get ports in Puget Sound. George Canning, who well understood the need for maritime nations to have harbours available for their commerce, was sympathetic to this part of the American demand, and that is why in 1826 he made the celebrated offer of the Olympic Peninsula. Only deep appreciation of the justice of the American demand could have justified this compromise of the future British position in the Oregon controversy.

The vehemence with which these views were expressed and the universality with which they were held by American experts justify the importance attached by the American government to the possession of San Juan. Indeed, if there was to emerge unanimity about anything connected with the water boundary dispute, it was that about the military value of San Juan. Faith in the justice of the abstract claim to the island might waver, but recognition and realization of its strategic value made the two protagonists unwilling to hear of compromise.

Captain Prevost, on his part, had been deeply impressed by the island's strategic position. He saw a menace to the safety of the whole region in the rapidity with which Washington Territory was being settled and in the fast-increasing interests of the United States in the Pacific Ocean. England must control Vancouver Island as a counterpoise, and Prevost, as a naval expert, considered that possession of San Juan as a wall of defence lying in the line of direct communication between Vancouver Island and British Columbia was essential to the peaceful occupation of the naval base on Vancouver Island.[15] The British government at once adopted Prevost's view. It is to be remembered that, in the middle of the nineteenth century at least, Vancouver Island was potentially more valuable than the mainland of British Columbia. To lose the islands lying between Vancouver Island and the mainland meant for Great Britain the loss of the only navigable channel for sailing vessels, in as much as the navigation of this channel was commanded by San Juan. Prevost believed that Vancouver Island was of greater potential value than the Washington territory, and his conclusion was that, as he told the Foreign Secretary, to lose San Juan "might some day prove fatal to Her Majesty's Possessions in this quarter of the globe."[16] And while Prevost was urging the Foreign Office to recognize the value of San Juan, the Colonial Office was driving home their opinion that the island is "of the utmost importance in a military, maritime and commercial point of view and on account of its close proximity to Vancouver Island."[17]

It was impressed upon the British government on all sides, therefore, that they would be able to realize the aims of the various government departments if they gained the Middle Channel as boundary because such a line would secure the

absolute possession of the Island of San Juan. They could justify their tacit surrender of the claim to Rosario Strait as boundary by officially endorsing the
views of Lord Aberdeen and Sir Richard Pakenham and insisting, accordingly,
that the negotiators of 1846 had meant the line of demarcation to divide equally
between the two countries the whole area lying between the mainland and Vancouver Island. Richards's report had proved the existence of a navigable middle
channel which, if it was not ideal from the mariner's point of view, was nevertheless a fair compromise line which by dividing the whole area into two ap-
proximately equal parts would surely be acceptable to the United States. What
the government neglected to notice, however, was that the United States was
also aware of San Juan's importance and that the Americans were not prepared
to accept the islands east of the Middle Channel as adequate compensation for
surrendering their claim to San Juan.

Once the decision to negotiate for a line which would give them San Juan
had been arrived at, steps were taken to hasten the work of the diplomatists.
Lord Malmesbury was succeeded at the Foreign Office in June, 1859, by Lord
John Russell, and the new secretary soon got to grips with the water boundary
problem. Declaring "honourable compromise" to be his inspiration, he adumbrated the British arguments for Rosario in his instructions to Lord Lyons, British
minister in Washington since the preceding April. But, forgetting the tactical
blunder inherent in the offer of a proposition which surrendered, perhaps not
positively, the line of the Rosario channel, he instructed Lyons to offer the
Middle Channel as boundary line. At the same time Russell took the risk of
completely alienating the United States by a stroke of "diplomacy by ultimatum"
with the assertion that, no matter what the circumstances, Great Britain was
determined to maintain her right to the Island of San Juan; whatever adjustment
of the line of boundary might be effected as the result of negotiation, the United
States must relinquish its claim to that island. Britain was prepared to give up
Orcas and Lopez islands, but she insisted that all three channels in the region
between Vancouver Island and the mainland should remain free and open to
both countries. Apparently quite unaware that the United States also placed a
high value upon San Juan and ignoring the fact that, even if the Americans did
not covet the island, the attempt thus peremptorily to exclude it from the negotiations would reveal its importance, Lord John expressed himself as unable to
believe that the United States could refuse this attractive compromise offer.
Before formulating it he was at pains to have his proposition reviewed by Lord
Palmerston, the prime minister, and by the Duke of Newcastle, the colonial secretary. All were in agreement that, if the proposition was rejected, the only
possible solution was arbitration, in which case Britain would fall back upon her
claim to the line of Rosario Strait.[18]

The British government had thus adopted the compromise plan presented by
Captain Prevost nearly two years previously. That plan had been suggested before the Richards survey report was received because it was then officially
believed, or at least hoped, that a middle channel would be found. Commissioner
Campbell, while at Washington in January, 1858, for the purpose of impressing
upon his government the strategic value of San Juan, had several discussions upon
the water boundary with Lord Napier, then the British minister. The latter had
suggested that provided a middle channel were found, it might be accepted as

an "amicable compromise," though the suggestion was made by Napier "without committing either my Government or myself, or any other person, to a renewal of it at any subsequent period should it not now be accepted."[19]

Unfortunately, the offer was still unacceptable to the United States, and more unfortunately for Britain, the British government could be sure that in future negotiations with that country the reserved British claim to the line of the Rosario would quite properly be ignored and the line of the Middle Channel would be adopted by the Americans as a proposition to be whittled down. The compromise offer was deemed a confession of lack of faith in their claims on the part of the British government, and the confidence with which the United States government asserted and held their views increased in direct proportion to the extent of the British concessions.

On the day that Russell sent off his despatch to Lyons another "confidential" one was forwarded to Captain Prevost, advising him of the new proposition, and declaring his position as commissioner to be in abeyance pending the development of negotiations in Washington.[20]

CHAPTER FOUR

THE HARNEY EPISODE: 1859-60

WE HAVE seen how Great Britain was once more embarked upon a diplomatic method of settling the San Juan dispute, but before discovering the fate of Lord John Russell's offer it is necessary to notice developments on the island itself. Shortly before the despatch of the offer, a crisis had been precipitated on San Juan and word of this was on its way to England while the new British proposition was being transmitted to the United States. Thus it was that the attention of the world was for the first time attracted to the Haro Archipelago by an incident which almost brought war between the United States and Great Britain. The incident, which revolved round the intervention in the area of the American General W. S. Harney, has never been explained satisfactorily and has been shown to be susceptible of various interpretations.

The developing interest in the area had manifested itself in a number of ways, and the gold rush of 1857-8 sharply drew international attention directly to it. Thus the United States government sent a special agent, John Nugent, in August, 1858, to the Fraser River region. Their purpose was to "ensure to our citizens in that quarter the most fair and liberal treatment," and Nugent was wisely instructed to remind Americans "that they have duties as well as rights."[1] Nugent reported that between 30,000 and 33,000 Americans had emigrated to the Fraser River region since May, 1858; but very soon less than a tenth of that number were left because the gold yield proved to be unprofitably low.[2]

The Island of San Juan had been first settled in 1845 by the Hudson's Bay Company, which established a fishing station there in 1850 and, as we have noted, an agricultural establishment in December, 1853. Some Americans, mainly miners returning from the gold rush, had also found their way there, and in 1854, along with other adjacent islands in the archipelago, it was organized as Whatcom County and treated by the Americans as American territory. Taxes were assessed regularly though no serious attempt was made to collect them, and it was estimated in May, 1859, that the company owed 935 dollars as arrears of taxation.[3] H. R. Crosbie, magistrate of Whatcom Country, reported that "there were 4,500 sheep, 40 head of cattle, five yoke of oxen, 35 horses and 40 hogs on the island, the property of the company. . . . There were attached to the Hudson's Bay Company stations, besides Mr. Griffin, eighteen servants, three only of whom were white, and those three were naturalized American citizens and exercized their rights as such at the territorial election last July at which time there were twenty-nine actual settlers on the island." The company of course refused to recognize any right of American authorities, whether federal or territorial, to tax their establishment.

In February, 1859, a group of Americans living on Vancouver Island sent a surveyor to San Juan, and he proceeded to survey land actually occupied by the

Company. This impelled Governor Douglas to ask powers from the Colonial Office to "eject squatters" until the boundary was settled.[4] In consequence, he was instructed to warn off the squatters and maintain British "rights" on the island, at the same time avoiding "giving occasion to acts of violence and merely upholding British possessions by the ordinary exercise of the Civil Power."[5] These instructions had serious implications, for they meant that Douglas could evict American squatters after due process of law in the local courts and they did not exclude the use of force to implement the decisions of the court. If the Americans acted similarly, as they had every right to do as long as the archipelago boundary remained undecided, there would be an inevitable conflict of jurisdiction, with each side evicting the other's squatters until armed hostilities would be certain. Here was a situation demanding the exercise of great discretion.

In April, 1859, an American citizen named Lyman Cutler landed on San Juan and proceeded to establish there what he euphemistically called a farm.[6] On June 15 Cutler was unwise enough to shoot a pig belonging to the Hudson's Bay Company because, he alleged, it was destroying his crops. He called on Charles J. Griffin, the company's representative on the island and offered to pay reparation or replace the pig. That same day Mr. A. G. Dallas, director and president of the council of the Hudson's Bay Company in America, landed from the company's ship, *Beaver*, accompanied by two other officials named Donald Fraser and Dr. W. F. Tolmie. On the following day, the trio accompanied by Griffin called upon Cutler. The latter was under the impression that the three colleagues of Griffin had come from Vancouver Island specifically to demand retribution from him; actually, according to Dallas, he and his friends, who were visiting the Island of San Juan solely for reasons of trade, were there on that particular day entirely by coincidence.[7]

Griffin gave his account of the incident to his superior, Governor Douglas. "I distinctly gave him to understand he had not a shadow of a right to squat on the Island and much less in the centre of the most valuable sheep run I have on the Island. He replied that he had received assurance from American authorities in Washington Territory, that he had a right, that it was American soil, & that he and all other Americans squatting or taking up claims would be protected & their claims recognised as being established on American Soil." Now, went on Griffin, there are sixteen squatters established on the island.[8]

Cutler, who gave his version by affidavit on September 7, explained that he had told Griffin he had acted "in a moment of irritation." His account of the meeting with Dallas, Tolmie, and Fraser makes it clear that tempers were on edge, Dallas's manner annoying Cutler and Cutler's upsetting Dallas. According to Cutler, Dallas threatened that if he did not pay a hundred dollars he would be taken to Victoria on Vancouver Island by Hudson's Bay Company vessel for trial. All four British insisted that it was British soil, Cutler that it was American.[9] Dallas, however, in his later account to General Harney played the whole thing down and after a series of denials affecting his alleged government and company status he categorically denied that he had demanded one hundred dollars "or any sum of money ... nor did I threaten to apprehend him or take him to Victoria. On the contrary I stated that I was a private individual and could not interfere with him." He had suggested to Governor Douglas that an appeal be made to the officials of Washington Territory "requesting them to restrain their citizens on San Juan Island from committing further trespasses. He declined to adopt my suggestion and the matter dropped." "Cutler did not use any threat to me, and I gave him no cause to do so."[10]

It seems remarkable that Dallas neglected to get written corroboration from Fraser, member of the Vancouver Island council, neutral and unconnected with the company, and from Tolmie, particularly as his account of the incident was in dispute: their statements could have clinched matters. Dallas strenuously denied any threat to transport Cutler to Victoria and asserted that he had "fortunately three unimpeachable witnesses to prove this."[11] With his vast experience he must have appreciated that verbally asserting British sovereignty on San Juan was one thing; arresting Americans to prove it was another. Dallas possibly may have hinted at arrest but it is significant that, in spite of his superiority of force, no attempt was ever made to arrest Cutler.

If Dallas's account is true and no threat to Cutler of seizure and transference to Victoria for trial was uttered, the subsequent action by General Harney was totally unwarranted and reprehensible. Cutler's action in shooting the pig was indefensible, but his ready admission of error and his speedy offer of restitution, both confirmed by Griffin and Dallas, tend to cancel out the gravity of his action. On the other hand, even if we accept Cutler's statement that he was threatened with arrest, the fact remains that no attempt at seizure of his person was ever actually made, even though the odds were overwhelmingly in favour of the company's men. There is the additional fact that all through the Oregon dispute, particularly in the trying years immediately preceding the settlement of 1846, the Hudson's Bay Company had invariably been most careful never to take forcible action against any American. Yet they had had to deal with thousands of them, many of them of the worst character and often offering extreme provocation. There had been wordy battles, but nothing more, and it is unlikely that Dallas, son-in-law of Governor Douglas, high in the company's hierarchy, and a servant of the company all his adult days, would take any step calculated to reverse this time-honoured policy. Forcible seizure of Cutler would have been so conspicuously opposed to the Marcy-Crampton agreement of July, 1855, that his government must have instantly repudiated his action. It should also be noted that neither Griffin nor Dallas accepted Cutler's offer of reparation, made both on June 15 and 16—an inexplicable fact.

Cutler communicated his account of the "pig battle" to American officials of Washington Territory, and this synchronized with the presentation of a petition by American citizens on San Juan to Brigadier-General W. S. Harney, commander of the Department of Oregon, seeking military protection against marauding Indians. Harney had received an account of the Cutler-Dallas incident from Paul K. Hubbs, Sr., successor to I. N. Ebey on San Juan, who in turn had had a first-hand version from Cutler. By the time the report reached Harney the significance of the incident had assumed alarming proportions. Dallas and his colleagues, it was now alleged, had been conveyed to San Juan in one of Her Majesty's sloops-of-war and Dallas was designated "Chief Factor" of the Hudson's Bay Company who had been on his way to seize and hold an American citizen.[12] Thus the fundamentals in a situation designed to justify military action were, in Harney's opinion, actively present. Seizure by a foreign official, conveyance in a foreign warship, incarceration in a foreign prison, trial by a foreign court by foreign laws, were all imminent, felt Harney, not only for Cutler but for any American citizen foolhardy enough to settle on the Island of San Juan.

On July 18, General Harney, from his headquarters at Fort Vancouver in Washington Territory, took the extreme step of ordering Captain G. E. Pickett to proceed to San Juan from Fort Bellingham with a force of soldiers for the purpose of protecting the American citizens from Indians and to stop "British interference by intimidation or force" and "to protect our interests in all parts of the sound." If Dallas returned to prosecute his plans for punishing Cutler, he was to be told that he could not interfere with an American citizen. In his report of July 19 to his superior, General Scott, however, Harney hinted at the real reason for his action: the strategic value of San Juan, "offering the best location for a naval station on the Pacific coast" and commanding Vancouver Island whose position on the Pacific was as important to the United States as Cuba's on the Atlantic.[13] Pickett's small initial force, which landed on San Juan on July 27, was to be increased, in accordance with Harney's plans, until it eventually numbered from four to five companies. Harney's move seemed to have the blessing of Governor Isaac I. Stevens of Washington Territory with whom he had consulted; indeed, Stevens' biographer gives the impression that Harney was actually operating upon the advice of the governor.[14]

Harney was using the Cutler incident to justify his intervention. Thus Cutler's affidavit was written on September 7, that is, nearly three months after the "pig battle," and some time after the landing of United States troops on San Juan, and it might reasonably be argued that it was composed with a view to furnishing a reason for Harney's action; at any rate, it is fair to assume that any circumstance deemed prejudicial to Harney's argument was suppressed. Cutler declared himself "convinced that if troops had not been on the island he would have been taken by force and carried before an English magistrate." His extraordinary reason for this belief, goes on the affidavit, "is based on the fact that the English force on board the steam frigates Satellite and Tribune had orders to obey any requisition that Mr. De Courcey [sic] [British stipendiary magistrate on San Juan after July 27] should make on them."[15]

Cutler claimed to think that a writ was to be served on him, but the significant fact is that none was ever issued. Further, fully six weeks had elapsed between the date of the "pig battle" and the landing of the American force on San Juan. Cutler had been thrust into the limelight and possibly he did not relish the idea of retreating to the shadows. That could best be avoided if he could assert that every possible effort had been made to arrest him; so he announced that Magistrate de Courcy had been sent to the island specifically to apprehend him. But the instructions to de Courcy did not even mention him, which must adequately dispose of Cutler's allegation. He alleged that an English constable with a posse had called at his house during his absence on July 29 or 30 to arrest him. But H. R. Crosbie, resident United States magistrate on San Juan after July 29, 1859, does not go so far as Cutler when he states: "The only inference that can be drawn is, had there been no probability of at once an active resistance to the execution of process, the original intention would have been carried out."[16] The astonishing thing is that Cutler was brought before Magistrate Crosbie on July 31 and heavily fined for shooting the pig; what is more astonishing is that Cutler makes no mention of this fact in his affidavit of September 7; and what is more astonishing still is the fact that the fining operation was performed on July 31—a Sunday!

The most that can be assumed in justification of Harney's action, therefore, is that process *might* have been served against Cutler if Harney had not intervened to send in American troops. For his case to be credible Harney had to make it appear that process was at least contemplated and that only his timely intervention had prevented a grave injustice's being perpetrated. His whole case fell to the ground if his intervention did not save Cutler from arrest, and it was not improved by Cutler's palpably false statement that Magistrate de Courcy could dictate orders to the senior naval officers in the area; actually, de Courcy was employed and paid by the civil authorities, and the naval officers were, perhaps only theoretically, subordinate to Governor Douglas, who held the rank of vice-admiral and was therefore senior to Rear-Admiral Baynes, the senior naval officer in the area.

In accordance with instructions from Governor Douglas through the colonial secretary of Vancouver Island, and after the governor had told the British naval authorities in the region that the Americans would land on San Juan, but without knowledge of Harney's instructions to Pickett, Major John de Courcy was taken to the Island of San Juan on July 27, four days after his appointment as British stipendiary magistrate and installed there; on the following day he read his commission to the British settlers, all seven of them. De Courcy was to "warn off" all interlopers, and to "maintain the peace." [17] Obviously, there had arisen a situation fraught with danger and liable to develop rapidly.

De Courcy confronted Pickett and demanded to know by what right he had presumed to land on the island. The captain, while denying that de Courcy had any right to pose such a question, had no objection to informing him that he was acting in accordance with government instructions. The Englishman replied that he was trespassing on British property and warned him off. Pickett's retort was to introduce H. R. Crosbie, American stipendiary magistrate, who in his turn warned de Courcy against acting upon his orders. Fortunately for the cause of peace, however, Crosbie and de Courcy established good relations with each other based on mutal respect for the other's good sense. Crosbie was wise enough to realize the "disastrous consequences" that would follow a collision, and he resolved to do everything possible to avoid one. Thus he was able to write the secretary of state that "Major de Courcy realized the responsibility of his position, and acted throughout the whole difficulty with a discretion and good feeling which tended very much to preserve quiet and peace." [18]

But Pickett's published order was not so reassuring: "All the inhabitants of the Island are required to report at once to the Commanding Officer in case of any incursion of Northern Indians, so that he may take such steps as he may deem necessary to prevent any further occurrence of the same. This being United States territory no Laws other than those of the United States, nor Courts except such as are held by virtue of said Laws will be recognised or allowed on this Island." [19]

Governor Douglas was placed in a quandary, particularly since this military occupation by Captain Pickett on the advice of an important senior officer like the United States commander-in-chief of Oregon seemed to have federal government sanction. He considered the San Juan group of islands to be British property, as he was told to do, but he had no instructions from the Colonial Office, his superiors, that comprehended the contingency which had now arisen. "Trusting that the exhibition of an overwhelming force might prevent resistance and probable effusion of blood," he asked Captain Michael de Courcy, cousin of the magistrate appointed to San Juan and senior naval officer in the region during the absence temporarily in other waters of Rear-Admiral R. L. Baynes, for a powerful vessel to stop the American landing. Captain Geoffrey P. Hornby with his ship, the *Tribune,* was sent at once. He was instructed by Governor Douglas to sail for San Juan with a body of marines to prevent the further landing of American troops, to erect military works, and to assist the civil power. He was also to call upon Captain Pickett and outline to him his instructions, but when he duly called at the United States camp he was unable to find the captain. He decided, therefore, to take no steps to hinder the American landing before he had an opportunity to interview him.[20]

On July 30 Douglas held a conference with Captain Richards of the Boundary Commission and Captain Michael de Courcy, and he found that the two naval officers were strongly opposed to the employment of force against the American troops. Milder measures, in their opinion, would meet the situation. "I considered it highly essential to do everything possible to prevent a collision with the U.S. Forces, and not disturb the amicable relations existing between the two countries...."[21] The governor, while still of the opinion that a display of force by the British was called for, realized that it would be difficult for him to take any positive action without the cordial support of his naval allies. Accordingly, Douglas agreed to modify his instructions to Hornby, revoking that part which told him to prevent the American forces from landing and their erecting military works on San Juan. The British magistrate on the island was also advised not to issue any process against the troops on San Juan.[22] It was further agreed that Captain Prevost, British member of the Boundary Commission, should be asked to get in touch with Commissioner Archibald Campbell, his American vis-à-vis, to induce him to use his influence with Harney to do nothing to produce a collision, and it was also decided that a ship should be sent to overtake the homeward mail at San Francisco so that the British government might have earliest possible notice of the situation and developments. An order to Magistrate de Courcy to summons Captain Pickett before him was countermanded on the very day it was issued, all in the cause of easing the position, on the advice of the senior naval officers.

Governor Douglas got in touch with Captain Prevost immediately and that officer called upon Pickett, who received him at once and was completely frank and open in defining his position. He was merely a subordinate, he told Prevost, carrying out the orders of a superior, sent to the Island of San Juan to protect American citizens and to enable the civil power to carry out the law. The territory belonged to the United States, he went on, and therefore they were justified in all they did to maintain peace and order, but "the strictest orders had been given to protect and respect the property of settlers on the Island, British or otherwise." Prevost hinted that Great Britain might have to send occupation forces also and Pickett, taking this in his stride, assured him that there was room on the island for both.[23]

The local Legislative Council, deliberating in conjunction with the chief officers of Vancouver Island and British Columbia at Victoria, was asked to approve the newly made decision and, with a single dissentient, G. H. Cary, the attorney-general, did so on August 1. The council was prompted by quite different motives from those of the British naval officers. To the council the evidence that the American occupation was a federal action appeared overwhelming, but there were no available forces at hand to repel a federal action, for a large number of the inhabitants of British Columbia and Vancouver Island were Americans, and in the event of an outbreak there would doubtless be what they described as "insurrectionary and filibustering movements." The local militia could not be depended upon, and the British authorities could not hope to maintain sovereignty for more than a short time.[24]

On the same day Governor Douglas issued a proclamation to the effect that "the sovereignty of the Island of San Juan, and of the whole of the Haro Archipelago, has always been undeviatingly claimed to be in the crown of Great Britain...."

The governor, on August 2, ignoring the advice of the council, and professing himself unable "to abandon the Island to a miltary occupation and to a squatter population of American Citizens," instructed Captain Hornby, for the moment senior naval officer in the area in the absence of both Admiral Baynes and Captain Michael de Courcy, to land troops on San Juan in order to sustain the British claim to the island, for the purpose of maintaining the national honour, exerting control over the Indians, and protecting British subjects. At the same time Hornby was told to enter into "full and frank communication" with Captain Pickett.[25] Magistrate de Courcy was told of all this also, and he was also instructed "to be cautious and not to push matters in his department."

The delicacy of Hornby's position is obvious, but fortunately he was fully aware of the fact and prepared to take decisions in keeping with his senior office. The following day, accompanied by commissioners Prevost and Richards, he called upon Captain Pickett. The deputation demanded to know if General Harney was acting upon authority from Washington when he commanded Pickett to occupy San Juan; they protested at the American assertion of a claim; they suggested joint military occupation of the island and withdrawal of both sides' civil magistrates, for they were convinced that injudicious use of civil powers was more likely even than military occupation to initiate hostilities. Hornby, in his account, says that "he pointed out that his proposition was strictly in accordance with the principles laid down in Mr. Marcy's despatch [of July 14, 1855] and that [Pickett's] on the other hand, offered no security against the occurrence of some immediate evil." Pickett's answer was clear and to the point: so far as he knew, General Harney had acted upon orders from his superiors in Washington, and he must refuse to consent to joint occupation because his instructions did not provide for one. He suggested, however, that the dispute ought to be referred to their immediate superiors—Governor Douglas and General Harney.[26]

Each side now knew the other's point of view, and the issue trembled in the balance with everything dependent upon Captain Hornby. The whole episode had, starting with the Cutler-Dallas incident and continuing with the warlike fulminations of Harney and Douglas, now reached a crisis and whether a settlement was to be effected by peaceful means or by force rested with Hornby.

Fortunately, the interview between the two groups of officers had been carried through in a most friendly atmosphere and Hornby had no hesitation in deciding to disobey Douglas's orders of the day before. If he landed, he felt sure that the British case would be weakened, for the British had protested at the American landing and to imitate that action would be "undignified." He rightly believed that the honour of the flag was not at stake and that to have precipitated a war by landing marines would have given a distinct moral advantage to the United States in view of the overwhelming superiority of the British naval forces in that region. Above all, he did not land marines because to do so would have been a breach of the Marcy-Crampton agreement of 1855. "Moreover, if we land, we must land in force superior to his; if once we do that it seems to me that we give up our right of protest against his increasing his forces on the Island. If we once proclaim a right to land at Pleasure by ourselves exercising such a right, we have nothing but force to prevent his landing any amount of men hereafter that he may have at command."[27]

There were four men-of-war of the British Navy in the vicinity of San Juan and Vancouver Island, and Admiral Baynes arrived on August 5 on the *Ganges* to make the total five. They carried 167 guns and had a personnel of 1940 men; in addition, there were over 200 sappers and miners. If they had landed a force, the British would have appeared as aggressors ready to take advantage of temporary weakness, and would therefore have been successful only in uniting American public opinion against their cause. The situation was clearly one for the use of what Lord John Russell called "the utmost temper, moderation and firmness," particularly since Harney was acting without government sanction. In view of the foreign secretary's statement of the same month that Great Britain was not prepared to negotiate unless San Juan was guaranteed to her, there could be no complaint if this arrogant proviso, though conjured up without knowledge of the Harney interlude but following so soon a naval or military attack upon the island itself, were misconstrued.

It would be unfair to say that Governor Douglas was actuated by other than patriotic motives, but it is right to note that he was exasperated at the Americans. The Hudson's Bay Company had engaged in stern economic battle with the Americans on the northwest coast since the beginning of the century and had not, in Douglas's opinion, been adequately compensated for losses sustained by virtue of the Oregon Treaty of 1846. The type of American with whom he normally came in contact was not of the most respectable and he could be excused for looking upon the American squatters with something like contempt. He understood how quickly that type would seize upon any concession or lack of vigour as evidence of weakness to be further exploited. It was undoubtedly humiliating for the British inhabitants of the area to see American troops landed on San Juan without any attempt being made to oppose them in any way. Pioneers respect force and vigorous action more than ordinary men, and there was much to be said for a policy of positive decision. It was not easy for Douglas to consider the situation calmly and with the detachment displayed by the naval officers, though as responsible senior official answerable to the British government he ought to have seen the problem in its widest aspects and ought to have appreciated the wisdom of Hornby's deliberate failure to implement his instructions. Had these been acted upon, it is difficult to see how hostilities could have been avoided. The governor was surrounded by a population bent on forceful retaliatory measures. The local journal, the *British Colonist*, demanded to know "Why were Troops not Landed on San Juan?" for the protection of British subjects. Had bloodshed followed, "we could have appealed to the world." An address of the Legislative Assembly of Vancouver Island asked the same question, for they maintained that troops ought to have been landed "to uphold the honour of our country and our Queen."[28] This was a pioneer population ever ready to demonstrate in favour of what they thought was right, holding their opinions passionately, quick to resent opposition of any kind.

The position changed radically for Douglas in 1858, in more ways than one, when he was appointed governor of Vancouver Island and British Columbia on condition that he cut his official connection with the Hudson's Bay Company. His promotion meant that no longer was he able to use company servants unostentatiously to keep squatters off the disputed islands, and thus the number of American settlers on San Juan grew, to the chagrin of Griffin, who counted "upwards of sixteen," and to the delight of Baynes, who derided Douglas's failure to warn off squatters on the island. His change of post ushered in a series of quarrels between the governor and the company because Douglas became extremely jealous of government rights and interests vis-à-vis the company.[29]

It would be easy to condemn Douglas out of hand for his apparently chauvinistic reaction to the Harney attack, but the British government rather than Douglas stands condemned. They had instructed the governor to "assert rights of occupancy" on San Juan and to maintain "the rights of the British Crown to the Island." The Colonial Office despatch of as recent date as April 30, 1859, which instructed Douglas to "pursue the course indicated by the Earl of Malmesbury," the foreign secretary, was his authority for his action in the Harney matter and, as Douglas reminded the Colonial Office in his report, he had appointed Magistrate de Courcy in direct conformity with the terms of that despatch.[30] The implications of the instructions were clear: he was to exclude American squatters from the island "by the ordinary exercise of the Civil Power," that is, he was to prosecute squatters in the J.P. court presided over by de Courcy, he was to take steps to see that decisions of the court were implemented, and he could apprehend any person who "broke the peace," a phrase of menacing elasticity. All this had arisen from Douglas's efforts at clarification of the San Juan Archipelago situation. He had been impelled to this by reports that, early in February, parties of Americans were visiting San Juan to pre-empt land under United States law and, he told the Colonial Office, "there is no doubt that the whole Island will soon be occupied by a squatter population of American citizens if they do not receive an immediate check."

Douglas in his despatch of February 19, 1859, to the Colonial Office had bluntly reminded the government that "the question of sovereignty was avowedly in dispute," a pointed reminder which had become highly necessary; he had also suggested a solution of the problem. "I would recommend in this juncture an arrangement being entered into having for its object the preservation of peace, and embodying as a condition of primary importance that Great Britain and the United States will unite in preventing the settlement of the Islands in question by ejecting squatters until the line of boundary is definitively traced, and it is decided to which Power they of right belong."[31] There was of course little original in this, for it was the solution proposed by Secretary of State Marcy in his letter to Governor Stevens of Washington Territory in July, 1855, a proposal subsequently accepted by the British minister in Washington, J. F. Crampton.[32] The government's answer to Douglas's proposed solution conceded no possibility of doubt about the legality of the British claim to sovereignty, yet their representative had agreed in 1855 that "the title ought to be settled before either party should attempt to exclude the other by force or exercise of complete and exclusive sovereign rights within the fairly disputed limits."[33] The British government refused to see that if the Americans were squatters on San Juan, the Hudson's Bay Company servants there were in exactly the same category. If the British set up courts, the Americans were entitled to do the same. If the British appointed magistrates to administer British law, the Americans had every right to establish jurisdiction in accordance with American laws. The astonishing thing is that the British government, while admitting that "the question of the boundary in that quarter remains unsettled," were so determined to act unilaterally. Yet they had found Douglas's solution "prudent and moderate," as the Colonial Secretary put it; although the only development in their policy over several years was an instruction marked "immediate" to Lyons in Washington to call the "immediate attention" of the United States Government "to the circumstances."[34] There was in fact practically no difference of tone or content between the instructions to Douglas of Sir George Grey of September 21, 1854, and those of Sir Edward Bulwer-Lytton of April 30, 1859.

To Douglas the Harney-Pickett occupation of San Juan was a flagrant assertion of exclusive sovereignty, and to do nothing, as the naval officers advised, besides being foreign to his character, was to him sheer dereliction of duty. Up to then both sides had had settlers, court, and magistrates on the island, but this was something more and the governor could not allow himself to sit idly by. Douglas did not desire war, though had hostilities been necessary to overawe the Americans on San Juan he would not have hesitated to begin them. He believed a collision was inevitable "in the event of both Governments asserting extreme rights of possession. . . ." His instructions were to assert full British rights to San Juan and Harney's enterprise made it appear that the United States was doing the same. The American authorities of Whatcom County were taking all the measures of American jurisdiction by assessing property, demanding tax payments, and establishing Henry R. Crosbie as magistrate, while the British authorities, by their agents, the Hudson's Bay Company, were in solid occupation of part of the island. The correct tactic, in Douglas's view, was to "cope with a small detachment rather than to wait until reinforcements from Washington Territory should make the dislodgement impracticable with our present force." Unfortunately, Douglas was prepared to go even farther, for he was ready to drive Pickett's forces off the island, which would certainly have precipitated active hostilities.[35]

To the end Douglas believed "that vigorous measures on our part would soon dispose of the question in our favour; a policy of national concession is always mischievous and in the case of these colonies dangerous."[36] And when he spoke thus he was iterating the almost unanimous view of the British colonists to whom he had to pay some attention as their governor. He was inflexible in the opinion that his initial policy would have forced the Americans to withdraw or to leave only a nominal occupation body of troops. It is difficult, however, to reconcile this view with his knowledge of the motives and character of General Harney. He had seen Harney at Victoria on July 8, that is, shortly before the general had sent Pickett to occupy San Juan, but Harney had made no mention of his intention or indeed of the alleged motive behind his decision to "protect" American citizens on the island which he visited on the following day. Douglas must therefore have realized Harney's true character of extremist and the danger of matching forces with such a man.

Vancouver Island had been conveyed to the Hudson's Bay Company by Crown grant on January 13, 1849, and the company agreed to promote settlement there by British colonists within five years. Douglas, who insisted that he was treating the island as a "de facto dependency" of Vancouver Island (a clever if illegal Douglas euphemism), was therefore conforming with instructions in establishing a company settlement on San Juan in December, 1853, under Charles J. Griffin. Accordingly, he was carrying out company as well as government instructions in promoting settlement on San Juan and other islands, though it is not certain that the royal grant to Vancouver Island comprehended the islands of the archipelago.

Sir George Simpson, chief officer of the Hudson's Bay Company in America, a keen judge of character and a man possessed of enormous experience of human frailty, who knew and understood Douglas probably better than any other, said of him that he was "well qualified for any service requiring bodily exertion, firmness of mind and the exercise of sound judgment, but furiously violent when roused."[37] There is no doubt about his being thoroughly roused by Harney's action, and his natural inclination impelled him to meet force with force. His position had never been easy, for upon him had been imposed a protracted, onerous task never, as he complained, "free from alarms." For his pains, he asserted that he had been calumniated in the American press where he was denounced for having let loose the Indians and for having maltreated the American collector of taxes. Actually he had on three occasions successfully resisted attempts by collectors to levy county taxes in 1854; "as we always managed to have a superior force on the ground they completely failed in the object intended."[38] In addition, he had survived the arrival of an armed revenue cutter as well as the visit of the acting governor of Washington Territory who told him that he was tempted to seize the island for the United States. To keep possession of the islands and maintain them as what he called a "de facto dependency" of Vancouver Island by means of hired labourers was a task of great magnitude, and he was proud of the fact that the government had commended him in 1854 for unostentatiously and peacefully dispossessing potential American settlers.

Douglas had convinced himself that the treaty of 1846 meant the boundary to follow Rosario Strait and not Haro, for in his view neither the letter nor the spirit of the treaty substantiated the claim of the United States and, knowing the area like the palm of his hand, he made much of the undeniable fact that at least up to 1853 Rosario was the route invariably taken by sailing-ships. Further, he argued, only this strait ran continuously in a southern direction as the treaty demanded.[39] He contended that the only possible object the framers of the treaty of 1846 could have had for leaving the whole of Straits of Juan de Fuca free and open to British vessels as far east as Whidbey Island was to secure a line running along Rosario channel. In August, 1858, the Colonial Office had asked him for his views on the boundary, and in his reply he insisted that "a safe and accessible Ship Channel to the British Possessions" was essential "for securing a ship communication with the most valuable and extensive portion of British Columbia."[40]

The governor had always before him what he considered the unfortunate example of Oregon where the American settlers had, a year or so before the negotiation of the final treaty, swarmed into the area south of the Columbia River and, when there were enough of them, had erected a provisional government with an undoubted American bias. If ejection or, alternatively, joint occupation were not adopted as British policy in the San Juan Archipelago after the advent of Harney, San Juan would have exactly the same fate. He was certain that delay in adopting a positive policy would have a bad moral effect, would lead to San Juan's "unavoidably slipping from our grasp," and to "ignorant American squatters" forming a *de facto* government.[41]

There can be little doubt that hostilities would have followed the literal implementation of Douglas's orders to Hornby. Harney anticipated a clash, and his instructions to Pickett make that clear. Pickett was "to afford adequate protection to the American citizens . . . and to resist all attempts at interference by the British authorities . . . by intimidation or force." Moreover, Pickett had made it clear to Hornby at their meeting on August 3 that he could not "allow any joint occupation until so ordered by my commanding general and that any attempt to make any such occupation as you have proposed before I can communicate with General Harney will be bringing on a collision . . ."[42] On August 6 Harney ordained that "no joint occupation or any civil jurisdiction will be permitted on San Juan Island by the British authorities under any circumstances."[43] Douglas had met the challenge by instructing Captain de Courcy to prevent the landing and to stop the erection of fortifications. There is no doubt what Douglas wanted to do. "I would have taken immediate steps to drive them from thence, had it not been for the opposition of the Civil and Military Authorities of this Colony," he told Lyons in Washington. There is no equivocation here and equally there is no doubt what would have been the result of his attempt to drive out the Americans; the reaction would have been that of any trained military men called upon to surrender. We know the temper and the instructions of the American officers; we know that they certainly would have resisted, as Harney desired, and that a merely formal occupation was not acceptable to them. It was therefore fortunate for the cause of peace that Admiral Baynes found the reasons against joint occupation overwhelming.

Douglas looked at the San Juan occupation from an angle different from that of the naval officers, who were much more detached, unfamiliar with the local atmosphere, and from their vastly superior strength inclined to be complacent and detached in their attitude. Both the governor and the naval officers believed in the efficacy of force but, whereas Douglas wanted to make positive use of his superior strength, the officers were content merely to display it and to secure their ends without the actual use of force. Douglas's position was infinitely more difficult because he was answerable for his actions to two masters—to the clamant, unreasoning, biased Legislative Assembly and to the remote, Olympian Colonial Office in London. In addition, he was being importuned by A. G. Dallas of the Hudson's Bay Company to secure redress from the United States because their forces were alleged to be destroying the Company's sheep and cattle at pasturage on their stock farms. Dependent as he was on the naval forces to carry out any policy of decision, he was being compelled to pursue a policy in which he did not believe.

The naval officers refused to carry out Douglas's orders because their conception of the legality of the situation was different from, and at the same time, more correct than his. It was their view that "in consequence of the territorial right of the Island of San Juan being still in dispute between the two nations," and the question of sovereignty being actually under discussion by commissioners of the two countries, they must at all costs obviate trouble; until the boundary was settled neither side could claim sovereignty and both Americans and British had the right of free access to the archipelago. The Americans, it is true, had made a false move in occupying the island and thus exercising exclusive sovereignty of a kind, but it would be folly to imitate their example and so complicate the boundary dispute still more. On the other hand, Douglas was determined to obey his orders to treat the islands as British, and in that view the United States military forces were trespassers who must be evicted, by persuasion if possible, by force if need be.

Douglas had been used to getting his own way for many years, and the opposition of the naval officers was therefore most irksome to him. He had been in a position of responsibility and power for so long that he had become notoriously autocratic, a characteristic which had been developed by his marked success in controlling American immigrants the previous summer, especially when some of the more exuberant had sought to fly the Stars and Stripes over Victoria. Now he had to contend with the lack of cordiality and apparent hostility of the naval officers, particularly of Rear-Admiral Baynes whose despatches to the Admiralty reveal a carping, hypercritical spirit not in keeping with his other gifts. In his official reports home Baynes mentioned the governor's failure to achieve complete success in keeping out squatters, even a deputy collector; he submitted a false, unsubstantiated report that Douglas had appointed Magistrate de Courcy *after* he knew of Harney's intention to occupy San Juan; he showed his lack of real understanding of the local situation by criticizing the "confined and narrow views of the Hudson's Bay Company" and inferentially also of the governor, for keeping British settlers away from the island; he blamed Douglas for stirring up the Legislative Assembly by assuring them that a military force would be landed on San Juan, an assurance which, he alleged, inspired "irritating expressions" against the United States and—again Baynes exaggerates—it was this circumstance which had been a cause of the reinforcements being sent to San Juan by the Americans.[44]

It is true that Douglas was adept at suiting his tone to his listeners' tastes, and this must give rise to a certain suspicion of his sincerity. To his government superiors he was usually all sweet reasonableness, sometimes almost sycophantic, but to Lord Lyons, a sympathetic listener and supporter, he was all fire and brimstone: "I would have driven them from thence had it not been for the opposition of the Civil and Military Authorities of this Colony." To the Americans he could be soothing and temperate: his clever reply to Harney's apologia to him is a masterpiece of litotes and plausible argument: he had always acted "out of consideration and respect to the friendly government to which the alleged offenders belong" and "how anxious I have ever been to cooperate to the utmost of my power with the officers of the United States." And this was succeeded by: "Following the dignified policy recommended in that despatch [that of Marcy to Stevens of July 14, 1855] I should, in any well-grounded case of complaint against an American citizen, have referred the matter to the federal authorities in Washington Territory, well assured that if wrong had been committed reparation would have followed;" but he omitted to explain how this statement could be reconciled with the appointment of Griffin and de Courcy as magistrates on the island.[45]

The British government had to make up their minds about the proper course to be followed by their representatives on the northwest coast and they had to choose between approving the policy advocated by Governor Douglas in the Harney affair and that followed by the naval officers. Bombarded as they were by correspondence from all sides, particularly from Baynes, Douglas, and Lyons, their decisions was not easy to take, and a memorandum which was the basis of discussions between the colonial and foreign secretaries illustrates this. This document was drawn up on November 1, 1859, by the Duke of Newcastle, colonial secretary from June, 1859, to April, 1864, in the following terms:

Whatever may be the eventual decision as to the Isld. of S. Juan, no British Govt. *ought* to be in the slightest degree influenced by this lawless occupation, and if so the fact of Govr. Douglas having been overruled by the Naval and Military Authorities can have no affect upon the ultimate result of diplomatic negociations. It is however quite open to question whether Govr. D.'s plan would not have been the best—but it was not open to question whether, when his plan had been abandoned, the Govt. at home should hesitate to share the responsibility of and approve that which had been adopted. If unhappily our Force had been inferior we could hardly have taken the course we did with honour—it being greatly superior, the act was one of generous forbearance, not of timidity.[46]

The final judgment of the British government proved therefore to be decisively on the side of the naval officers, and Newcastle told Douglas: "In consequence of the opposite views ... being entertained by yourself and Admiral Baynes ..., I must point out to you that the fact of the overwhelming force of the British Navy, which was so rapidly summoned to the spot, as compared with the force of the United States, removed any possibility of misunderstanding the reasons of Her Majesty's Government for adopting the moderate course of remonstrance instead of other measures."[47] Ironically, Douglas had also been commended a month earlier by the Foreign Office when they told him that they were glad he had not sent troops to San Juan for a joint occupation with Pickett because a collision might have followed; in future, he was to do nothing except to protect British lives. Douglas therefore had the satisfaction of receiving this unearned commendation plus later vindication when the ultimate solution adopted was joint occupation.

CHAPTER FIVE

HARNEY RETIRES FROM THE SCENE

WHILE the British naval officers debated the issues involved and Governor Douglas expressed his exasperation and frustration, General Harney was not inactive. To the Douglas protest he replied that he had sent Pickett to protect "American citizens residing on the island from the insults and indignities which the British Authorities of Vancouver Island and the Hudson's Bay Company officials had recently offered them" by sending a British warship from Vancouver Island to convey the "chief factor" of the company to San Juan for the purpose of "seizing an American citizen" and transporting him by force to Vancouver Island to be tried by British laws. "I shall not permit a repetition of that insult."[1]

Meanwhile Commissioner Prevost was seeking out Archibald Campbell, whom he ultimately found at the American Boundary Commission headquarters at Semiahmoo Bay, but he failed to induce the American to do anything. To Prevost his replies were unsatisfactory and "little short of being insulting in their tone"; he showed resentment at Prevost's efforts to "catechize" him, probably with justice, "as the supervision of the movements and operations of the military forces of the U.S. forms no part of the duties of the Joint Commission . . ."[2]

Harney followed up his explanation to Douglas next day (August 7) with one to the United States adjutant-general. An account of the origin of the dispute is given, this time stress being laid upon the fictitious threat of the Hudson's Bay Company to turn the Indians upon the innocent American settlers, an old *canard* that could always be relied upon to rouse a certain type of American. Mention was also made of the "overbearing, insulting and aggressive conduct" of the British executive officers. In conclusion, the adjutant-general was reminded that it would be well for the British government to be made aware that the American people of the Pacific coast would never sanction any claim the British might assert to any island on Puget Sound other than Vancouver Island.[3]

Although the affair had not progressed exactly as the gallant general had intended, the tactful, dilatory policy of the British naval officers being calculated to offset and nullify Harney's plans, he nevertheless remained undaunted. Consequently, he decided to increase his numbers on San Juan, and he followed up his explanatory letter to the British authorities and his apologia to his superiors in Washington by ordering Lieutenant-Colonel Silas Casey to proceed from Fort Steilacoom to San Juan with reinforcements. "Take with you all the ammunition you have on hand as well as your field guns . . . the British Authorities threaten to force Captain Pickett's position and they greatly outnumber him at present." If necessary he is to call out volunteers to defend the island. He is not to allow any joint occupation "either civil or military, and [to see] that the rights of our citizens on the Island will be respected as on American soil."

Casey duly arrived with nearly two hundred men, and at once called upon Captain Hornby. Not satisfied with that, he determined to go straight to the chief authority, and on the following day made the twenty-mile journey to Esquimalt in company with Captain Pickett and Commissioner Campbell for the purpose of discussing matters with Rear-Admiral Baynes who commanded the British fleet in the Pacific Ocean. Baynes, however, recognizing the fact that Casey was only a subordinate officer and mindful of the fact that "the port was a British one," declined to visit the American though he was quite prepared to receive him on board his flag-ship, the *Ganges*.[4]

Hornby found the new developments most menacing. He had accepted at its face value the early American statement that the first landing-party of fifty men had been sent to protect the American civilians from the Indians. But now there were four hundred Americans, continually landing supplies, with formidable heavy ordnance based on a protected hill overlooking the harbour. In other words, a mild innocuous position had been turned into one of positive threat. The situation that Governor Douglas had prophesied would develop had indeed arisen. Hornby feared "lest they should hereafter construe our tacit observance of all their operations into an admission of their right to the Island; and say that we had without dispute allowed them to exercise every sovereign right from administration of law to fortifying the Island."[5] The situation was so perilous that Hornby perceived that attempts to liquidate Magistrate de Courcy, even to the point of forcing him to hand over his flag, were imminent; that could have only one result—open hostilities.

Baynes, however, remained firm; he himself decided to remain in the area until the atmosphere cleared. His orders, on being advised of Hornby's fears, were specific: "It is now my positive order that you do not, on any account whatever, take the initiative in commencing hostilities by firing on them or on any work they may have thrown up."[6] In his report of August 19, 1859, to the Admiralty, Baynes made his position clear. He had been faced with two alternatives: to eject the Americans from the island by force or, "having protested against the occupation pending the decision on the Water Boundary, and on which the sovereignty of the island would rest, to await the issue of the event from England, keeping in the meantime a ship-of-war in Griffin Bay to watch over British interests." To use force to expel the American Federal troops from the disputed island would lead to open hostilities and war, Baynes was convinced. He was also opposed to the notion of joint military occupation as being too likely to lead to a collision; moreover, the Americans were increasing their forces on the island so substantially that there would soon not be room for a rival force. Though the British forces at the moment were preponderant, it would be difficult to increase or even sustain it with the forces available in the area. The Americans had 400 men on the island plus about 150 armed with rifles plus 400 at Fort Steilacoom ready to embark. If hostilities came, Vancouver Island and British Columbia, with a large American population, would be completely isolated.

Douglas's answer to Harney's new moves, and more directly to the general's explanatory letter to him was his clever and temperate letter of August 13. The letter begins with a courteous if slightly sarcastic expression of thanks for the general's "frank and straightforward manner" of explaining why his troops had occupied San Juan. An unhesitating and unqualified denial of the statement outlined by Harney is given, for no British man-of-war had ever been sent to convey the chief factor or any officer of the Hudson's Bay Company to San Juan for the purpose of seizing an American citizen. He denied that the company's officials had any government connection on Vancouver Island. If he had acted illegally, the governor reminds Harney that all his actions have been in accord with Secretary of State Marcy's despatch to Governor Stevens of July 14, 1855, wherein it is stated that "the title ought to be settled before either party should exclude the other by force, or exercise complete and exclusive sovereign rights within the fairly disputed limits."[7] If he had overstepped the bounds laid down in that letter, surely, insists Douglas, the most sensible step for Harney to take would have been to communicate with him and to seek redress before making the precipitate and extreme move of military occupation. Harney had very recently, on July 10, seen him personally in Victoria when he had not even mentioned the Cutler incident. "A few words from me would, I am sure, have removed from your mind any erroneous impressions ..." and assurance of desire to co-operate. Concluding, the governor expressed the view that the first essential to resumption of the status quo is the withdrawal of the United States force whose presence on the Island of San Juan is a "marked discourtesy" to Great Britain.[8]

In spite of its temperate nature and logical argument, Douglas's letter made no impression on General Harney, and the Americans continued with the erection of military works on the island until by the middle of August they had a formidable fort manned by over four hundred men together with a considerable number of artificers and labourers, in all five infantry companies and four artillery companies. In the governor these preparations still excited an impulse to retaliate, and events merely strengthened his feeling that the wrong policy was being pursued. "I confess with regret that my views differ essentially from those expressed by Rear-Admiral Baynes.... I feel assured that a bold and resolute stand, as I proposed in the first instance, would have nipped in the bud the project, increased the influence and dignity of this Government, and prevented collisions which a policy of concession may precipitate"; thus he wrote the Colonial Office.[9]

Indeed the manner in which the United States was strengthening its position daily must have created doubts and misgivings in British official circles, for it would obviously be a difficult matter to dislodge them from the island once the Americans were firmly established there. On the other hand, in British eyes the occupation of San Juan was quite an illegal act,[10] and their confident hope that justice and common sense would prevail convinced the Colonial Office and the Foreign Office that there was no need for alarm. The great danger, as they saw it, was that Harney and Pickett would reject, and forcibly resist, attempts at a joint occupation, in which case, as Douglas argued, the vast superiority of the British forces, at least initially, might prove an effective deterrent. We know that Captain Pickett was well aware of the weakness of his position, for he reminded Harney that "they have a force so much superior to mine that it will be merely a mouthful for them."

Governor Douglas, in an attempt to enlist the aid of an additional important agency, wrote to the British minister in Washington, tracing the origin and development of the whole Harney episode. Lyons, receiving the account on September 3, 1859, acted with alacrity. He telegraphed details home and personally broached the matter that day to General Cass, the United States secretary of state. The secretary assured the minister that he had heard nothing of General Harney's attack on San Juan. To Lyons's subsequent suggestion that Cass should send a positive injunction to the American troops on the island the general retorted that Harney's action did not affect in any way the diplomatic progress of the settlement of the dispute, inasmuch as he was prepared to guarantee the immediate evacuation of American troops if the island were awarded to Great Britain. Lyons was particularly careful to avoid raising any collateral point of debate which might have added to the difficulty of inducing the American government to replace matters at San Juan on the footing which had been so disturbed by General Harney.[11]

From Lord John Russell, the foreign secretary, the report evoked the angry "It is of the nature of the U.S. citizens to push themselves where they have no right to go, and it is of the nature of the U.S. Government not to venture to disavow acts which they cannot have the face to approve."[12] The formal answer of the Foreign Office to Douglas's account of the Harney episode told him that the proceedings had caused "much concern but his message to the Legislative Council was approved" and his decision not to send troops for occupation was applauded, for it would have caused a collision. He must do nothing "except to save British lives."[13]

There was no doubt that Cass was intensely irritated by the information he had received from Lyons, and he acted with despatch in silencing Harney. On the very day of Lyons's protest Acting Secretary of War W. N. Drinkard wrote to the general intimating that "the President was not prepared to learn that you had ordered military possession to be taken of the Island of San Juan or Bellevue. Although he believes the Strait of Haro to be the true boundary ... he had not anticipated that so decided a step would have been resorted to without instructions." In addition, Harney was instructed to inform the British officials on San Juan that he had not been attempting to prejudge the question as to whom the island should ultimately belong.[14]

A fortnight later the United States government gave further evidence of the concern with which they viewed the situation when they sent orders through the War Department to Lieutenant-General Winfield Scott, commander-in-chief of the United States Army, to take personal command of the San Juan position. The letter of instructions to General Scott reviews the whole controversy and advises that much will be left to his personal discretion. He is reminded that the president's main object is to preserve the peace and prevent collision until the question of title can be adjusted by the two governments. The president abhors the possibility of the two nations' being thrown into the calamity of war over the possession of a small island and only in the remotely possible event of Great Britain's seizing and occupying the island would it be necessary to defend the national honour by an appeal to arms.[15]

General Scott arrived at Fort Vancouver on October 25, and immediately communicated with Governor Douglas. He suggested the establishment of a joint military occupation of San Juan, each country with a hundred men, but the governor, after consultation with Admiral Baynes, in a friendly note declined, suggesting in turn that there be a joint civil occupation composed of the resident stipendiary magistrates, complete withdrawal of the military, and return to the status quo obtaining after Marcy's despatch to Stevens of July 14, 1855. Douglas made the pertinent observation that "the principal protection that may be required is from dissensions amongst themselves, and not against hostile Indians, from whom I do not apprehend there is the slightest danger of molestation." Baynes, who forwarded copies of the Douglas-Scott correspondence to the government, gave as his reason for his action the palpable one: "It was ridiculous to suppose they had been placed there to protect a few American squatters from the hostile attacks of northern Indians. They were evidently there as a menace to us and until they were withdrawn I thought it impossible to treat." In any case to land a force "would be to acknowledge that protection was needed for British Subjects . . ." when it had been consistently denied that it was needed for Americans.[16]

Objecting that civil magistrates could hardly prevent collisions and give protection, and pointing out in the friendliest possible manner that Lord Lyons had made no such demand of General Cass, General Scott found himself unable to subscribe to Douglas's plan and, insisting upon the adoption of his own proposal, he enclosed a project of settlement whereby the two countries should agree to joint military occupation with one hundred men each. Douglas, besides finding such an arrangement incompatible with his original emphatic opposition to the Harney-Pickett occupation, had no instructions to agree to joint occupation, and he advised Scott that, pending the receipt of further word from London, he would be unable to proceed with the negotiations.[17] Scott proved thoroughly conciliatory. He reduced substantially the number of American troops on the island; he transferred the heavy artillery; he instructed the Americans not to interfere with British subjects, reminding them that British subjects possessed equal rights with Americans on the island.

Both Douglas and Scott had perfectly sound reasons for their respective positions. If joint civil occupation were established, the status quo would thus be resumed and the incident would close with complete United States surrender, for the evacuation of their troops would be deemed tantamount to public repudiation by them of Harney's actions. It would mean not only humiliation but also the possible misconception that the claim to the island was being surrendered. Scott realized too that, if the Americans were to have a good claim, San Juan came within the jurisdiction of Washington Territory, not yet constituted a state of the Union but possessing considerable independence of the federal government with a legislature and laws of its own, and to withdraw federal forces would be to risk leaving the future in the hands of irresponsibles far removed from the control of the executive in Washington. Joint civil occupation would mean occupation, on the United States side, by the officials of Washington Territory who were much more likely to provoke a collision.

Vancouver Island stood in somewhat the same position with respect to Great Britain. The colonial government, somewhat similar to a territorial body in the United States and having considerable independence from the distant imperial executive, had not acted imprudently in the recent controversy, but this was because the advice of the Legislative Assembly which had shouted "Why were troops not landed?" had been ignored. Nor was there any guarantee that in the absence of pacific men cognisant of the larger issues in jeopardy, men like Hornby and Baynes and Prevost, whose presence during the Harney affair had been more or less fortuitous, the firebrands of Vancouver Island and British Columbia, and the men with private axes to grind would remain in the background. Perhaps the best arrangement would have been to set aside both military and civil occupation and to leave the island unoccupied by both countries until the question of title was settled. But Scott's mission was by its very existence sufficient repudiation of Harney, while withdrawal of all troops from the area might have seemed to the American public absolute submission to British dictation.

Great Britain could be completely satisfied with joint military occupation because the Americans, by peacefully accepting the arrival of British troops, would be admitting their denial of any claim to exclusive sovereignty. The British government considered joint occupation with equal forces as eminently suitable. While there was always the risk of a local collision, the quality of forces and their command of the sea gave the British a feeling of security which would not have obtained under other circumstances. Their experience of the Oregon controversy had taught the British the danger of the disputed area's becoming filled up with American squatters. Joint military occupation would keep out squatters and would therefore prevent a repetition of the Oregon settler problem. As a matter of fact, one of the phenomena attendant upon the American occupation of San Juan was the celerity with which American squatters established themselves there. Appreciable numbers of immigrants arrived daily until within a few weeks there was a small town at Griffin Bay. Since Scott was instructed to act upon the terms of the Marcy letter of July, 1855, there was adequate guarantee that the United States was not claiming exclusive jurisdiction. The British government, therefore, as soon as they learned from Lord Lyons of the impasse on San Juan, decided to instruct Douglas to concert with General Scott and to act upon any proposition he might make for joint occupation of the island, each to place the same number of troops there. A despatch with these instructions was forwarded by the Colonial Office on November 16.[18] Douglas received this despatch on January 26, 1860, but he and Baynes decided not to carry out the instructions until they had heard something of the progress of the San Juan negotiations in Washington. Besides, Scott's absence retarded their progress.

Meantime General Scott had sought to remove from the scene a more concrete cause of British irritation. On November 15 he intimated to General Harney that "it might be a great relief to the President to find you, by your own act, no longer in your command."[19] Harney, however, refused to accept the proffered command of the Department of the West (Oregon and California), professing his belief that Scott was acting wholly on his own responsibility, and not under government instructions.

On March 21, 1860, one hundred British troops under Captain George Bazelgette were landed on San Juan, taking possession of the northern end of the island about fifteen miles from that occupied by one hundred American troops under Captain Hunt, an officer "remarkable for firmness, discretion and courtesy." Bazelgette's instructions forbade him to interfere in any way with American citizens on San Juan; he was to recognize American and British as possessing equal rights; he was to keep in frank and open communication with Captain Hunt.[20]

Calm was now restored and the Harney episode appeared about to become no more than a memory. But the general, though thus unceremoniously thrust into the background, did not remain there long. The limelight exerted a too powerful influence over him, and this time his love of ostentatious display proved fatal to the success of his career. His action in 1859 had very nearly precipitated war, but his efforts in 1860 did not prove nearly so formidable. He despatched orders to Captain Pickett to replace Captain Hunt in command on San Juan. General Scott, he said, had left no instructions about a joint military occupation of the island, nor had the government given him authority to do so. Douglas had rejected Scott's offer, and consequently that "concluded the transaction." By Act of Congress San Juan is part of Whatcom County of Washington Territory, and the jurisdiction of that area must be respected "in the discharge of your duties on San Juan." If Captain Bazelgette ignores this, there will be "deplorable results."[21] A copy of these instructions was sent to Governor Gholson of Washington Territory and Pickett was also to give one to Bazelgette. It is obvious that if Pickett carried out these orders literally, all the pacific work of Scott and Baynes would be nullified, for Scott had advised Hunt that he was to remember that no officials of Washington Territory were to interfere in any way with British subjects on San Juan so long as the title remained unsettled. Douglas and Baynes had given exactly similar orders to Bazelgette in respect of American citizens.

When he landed on the island on the last day of April, Pickett's first act was to send a copy of his instructions to Captain Bazelgette,[22] and the latter, as soon as he realized their significance, hastened to report the facts to Admiral Baynes. That officer, after consultation with Governor Douglas, deemed it speedier to achieve something by acting through Washington, and he accordingly communicated the details to Lord Lyons there. The minister requested General Cass, the secretary of state, to take immediate measures to avoid a clash. Cass, having read the orders of Harney "with surprise and regret," was obviously perturbed and extremely angry, and he undertook to give a written answer "completely satisfactory" to Her Majesty's government. He assured Lyons that his government absolutely rejected and disavowed General Harney, and the commander of the United States forces in that region would be instructed accordingly.[23]

When Governor Douglas heard of the extraordinary nature of Harney's latest instructions, he concluded and wrote home to the effect that until the question of title was settled, the best move would be to draw up a convention and to withdraw the civil magistrates of both sides, as no civil jurisdiction could properly exist within the region as long as its possession remained in dispute.[24] This advice had not reached London when the foreign secretary, acting immediately upon receiving news of the new *contretemps*, instructed Lyons to make a convention with Cass in the sense of General Scott's proposition, that is, a temporary and provisional arrangement with magistrates withdrawn or with defined limits of jurisdiction.[25] Douglas was duly informed of this development, and he and Scott proceeded to provide for joint military occupation of San Juan. In agreeing to this the British government were amplifying their earlier order to Douglas, which did not authorize his consenting to a joint occupation; they agreed to joint occupation, the foreign secretary asserted, because of the embarrassment Harney had caused the United States government by his latest sally.[26]

On June 8, 1860, the United States government, angered by General Harney's latest outbreak, relieved him of his command in Oregon and summarily ordered him to report to Washington. And so faded from the scene, in not very dignified or graceful fashion, the man who had almost succeeded in making possession of the apparently unimportant little island of San Juan the cause of a war between two great nations.

This extraordinary, anachronistic, Ruritarian figure, more like a character from grand opera than a sober, responsible, senior military officer, had held the stage for over a year. He had shown himself to be either very naive or rashly malicious and reactionary. The fact that a mischief-maker of his calibre could almost precipitate war between two great countries over possession of a small island is an indictment of the immaturity of the system which allowed him to come to the front and remain there for so long. His proceedings had had the tacit approval of the War Department because of a want of system in the conduct of business. The whole situation, with its customs officers having no taxes to collect, with its magistrates having no offenders to apprehend and try, with its characters so extravagantly punctilious, can only be described as deliciously, if dangerously, Gilbertian. Harney had attempted to prejudge the San Juan water boundary issue because of his assessment of the military importance of the island; if indeed he really had any motive other than zeal for the limelight.[27] To achieve his purpose he had shamelessly lied and had not hesitated to misrepresent the facts. He had magnified and distorted the nature of the Dallas-Cutler incident because it had suited his purpose to represent Dallas as a foremost government official transported to San Juan on a government vessel for the purpose of arresting an innocuous American citizen to be tried in a British court at Victoria in the British colony of Vancouver Island. He had made no attempt to investigate the veracity of Cutler, which ought to have been his very first step, and he conveniently ignored the fact that Cutler had still not been tried six weeks after the "pig battle." In the face of comprehensive denials and factual corrections from official sources on both sides he had persisted in his mendacity and misrepresentation.

Harney's initial instructions to Pickett had been designed to invite trouble, for Pickett was told to assert exclusive sovereignty and, inferentially, oppose a British landing on the island. In defence of his action he had given the extraordinary excuse that Commissioner Campbell had "always assured him that there could be but one solution of the boundary question ... Haro." His pretext that his action had been inspired by the necessity to protect a handful of American settlers from hordes of what he called "British Indians" who, he averred, had been "instigated by" the wicked Hudson's Bay Company to acts of murder and pillage, was supremely inexact. He had consistently exaggerated the peculiarities of the situation, telling Governor Gholson, for instance, that the British authorities of Vancouver Island were "becoming more and more oppressive." Harney had made reckless charges against Baynes, Hornby, and Prevost, accusing them of "wilful falsehoods ... to advance the sinister designs of the British government in obtaining territory that rightfully belongs to the United States." He had allowed and encouraged all with whom he came in contact to think that the United States government was behind all his orders, and that is probably the most damning thing to be said of him. Pickett had obviously been certain that Harney was acting on government instructions and in his letter to Douglas he talks of remaining in command on San Juan "until I receive further orders from my government." He had taken it upon himself to assure the American settlers that the United States government would never tolerate a joint occupation of San Juan. He had whipped up war fever by demanding naval assistance from Washington and he had sought to spread the trouble by enlisting the aid of volunteers in Washington Territory. In spite of the fact that he had directed Pickett to allow no joint occupation, he told the adjutant-general on August 29 that he had no intention "of asserting any sovereignty over San Juan beyond that which the necessity of the case had demanded." [28]

Harney had acted against the advice of Commissioner Campbell with whom he ought to have communicated because Campbell's commission was still in existence; in addition, he was near at hand. He had lied when he said that he had never heard of the Marcy-Crampton agreement of 1855 which governed Anglo-American relations in the archipelago and he lied again when he told Colonel Casey that his troops were being sent to San Juan as reinforcements because the "British had threatened to force" Pickett's position. He had countermanded the orders of his superior, General Scott, a heinous crime in military eyes and he had ignored his government's injunction to leave the area. Yet after being quashed he had returned to the fray without advising his superiors, so that Secretary of State Cass had the doubly humiliating experience of first hearing about Harney's latest misdemeanour from Lord Lyons and then having to disavow it.

He had remained intransigent in the face of correction, and after declining General Scott's tentative order of November 18, 1859, promoting him away from temptation to mischief-making, he had proceeded to do all he could to nullify and revoke Scott's remedial steps of the same month. He had rejected and ignored his superiors' assertion that the sovereignty of San Juan was not yet settled, and he had flagrantly overturned first of all the Marcy-Crampton agreement of 1855, later the Cass-Lyons agreement of August, 1859, and still later the Scott arrangement which had been formally accepted by the president and the British government.

It has been suggested that the incident of 1859-60 was used by Harney, Stevens, and Pickett with a view to precipitating a war between the United States and Great Britain in the hope that such a war would rally to the American flag and unite in battle the diverse sections which could not agree on the issue of slavery. As Pickett put it, it was believed that "the first British gun that should launch its thunder against the Pacific coast would echo and re-echo across the continent and send its reverberations to the remotest limits, North, South, East and West." [29] There seems to be more than a grain of truth in the suggestion that Harney's southern sympathies made him a war-monger, and it is perhaps significant that he initiated the whole affair shortly after word came to the Pacific of the war in Italy. The chaos of the Crimean War and the recrimination that followed it had lowered British prestige, and the position was not improved by the Indian Mutiny. The year 1858 seemed certain to find England involved in a continental war, and many outsiders, Harney among them, thought she would find it impossible to keep out of the war in Italy. [30]

The Harney incident, though signally failing in its purpose, left a certain amount of bitterness and suspicion in its wake. This was especially true of the area immediately affected where the opinions of the British inhabitants were not unnaturally prejudiced and strongly held. The temper of such people was as short as their memory was long, and it was they who had so strenuously urged Governor Douglas to meet force with force when the Americans had landed on San Juan.

The Hudson's Bay Company must take some of the responsibility for the bad feeling that existed in the disputed region. Their agents had done everything possible to discourage American squatters—a policy which had had great success in keeping American settlers south of the forty-ninth parallel before the Oregon Treaty—and, by doing so, they were, perhaps negatively, exercising exclusive sovereignty, which they had no right to do while the title to the archipelago was in dispute. The company's direct connection with the Harney episode was an innocent one. Their very presence in the northwest was obnoxious to super-patriots like General Harney, and the latter's attempt to identify the Hudson's Bay Company with Indian attacks was an astute, though totally unworthy, move to embroil the company and to secure support for his action in sending troops to the island.

CHAPTER SIX

DIPLOMATIC NEGOTIATIONS: 1859-61

WE HAVE ALREADY NOTED the terms of Lord John Russell's San Juan boundary proposal made in August, 1859.[1] On November 12, 1859, the answer of the United States government was communicated by the American minister, Mr. Dallas, to Russell. The Foreign Office thought it important enough to have it printed in order that each cabinet minister might have a copy. It was drawn up on October 20, that is, significantly, immediately after the Scott-Douglas agreement, so that the United States government had had plenty of time to consider the terms of their answer and after consideration of all the latest developments.

General Cass began his reply with an assurance of the president's desire for a settlement of the dispute, but followed up with what seems to be a justifiable objection to the foreign secretary's declaration that the British government were determined, under any circumstances whatever, to maintain their right to the Island of San Juan; on that they would accept no compromise. "If this declaration were to be insisted on, it must terminate the negotiation at its very threshold, because this Government can permit itself to enter into no discussion with that of Great Britain, or any other power, except upon terms of perfect equality...." Cass felt sure that Britain would withdraw or explain the offensive statement and he went on to examine the arguments on the water boundary without adducing any new material. In view of all the evidence, how could Russell maintain that Rosario Strait alone was intended by the negotiators of the treaty of 1846? Britain was prepared to accept the Middle Channel which Lord John admitted to be inferior, and he was pressing his argument because Britain needed San Juan, which he deemed of no value to the United States. Cass denied this latter statement and, while admitting that both Great Britain and the United States had made concessions in 1842 and in 1846, he could not agree that there was in this case any need for a policy of mutual convenience.[2]

This despatch of General Cass became "the subject of serious consideration by Her Majesty's Government" and, pending preparations for a comprehensive answer, Lyons was instructed to remove from the president's mind the unfavourable impression created by the Russell despatch of August 24, 1859. When the meaning of a treaty is clearly in favour of a certain interpretation, lamely argued Russell, but the interests at stake are unimportant, a point may willingly be yielded for the sake of peace; when the interests are high and the meaning is clear, concession cannot be expected.[3]

The British answer to the Americans was finally composed by December 16, 1859, and a copy sent to the secretary of state. Russell started off by hastening to assure the United States government that his instructions of August 24 were forwarded many days before news of the Harney incident had reached London.

Had Her Majesty's government been aware of the proceedings at San Juan, it would have been impossible to propose a friendly compromise of the question in dispute until the United States had repudiated the "proceedings" of General Harney. After this reprimand the foreign secretary affirmed that the nature of the American instructions to General Scott made it possible for Great Britain to continue negotiations.

Russell proceeded to answer Cass's arguments, the burden of his contention being that the expressed intention of contemporary negotiators, upon which the Americans placed so much stress, was as strong for the British as for the American position. If the United States got San Juan she would control both Rosario and Haro channels; San Juan was therefore a defensive position, asserted Russell most inconclusively, if in British hands, but an aggressive one if in American hands. And the United States might fairly be called upon to renounce aggression, but Great Britain could hardly be expected to abandon defence.[4]

Cass quite correctly did not find the British explanation satisfactory, and his answer of February 4, 1860, made this clear. He protested that Russell had not withdrawn his demand that Britain must have San Juan. Since he had abandoned the claim to Rosario as boundary for that of the Middle Channel, the issue was narrowed to possession of that island, and to declare that it would not be ceded under any circumstances was peremptorily to end discussion. Britain had attached too great importance to this island, suggested the secretary of state; she had overrated its military value; it did not command Haro Strait; no fortifications erected upon the coast of the channel could ever control its navigation. There was no need for further discussion, and the president could only decline to continue negotiations.[5]

If negotiations were to continue after this snub, it was clear that Russell must apologize for his injudicious ultimatum that the Island of San Juan was British and not to be negotiated for. Fortunately he had the grace and good sense to do this. He assured Cass that the United States had entirely misconceived the purpose of his declaration. Great Britain, he said, had proposed compromise without prejudice to her claim to the Rosario channel; in effect, she maintained that either Rosario channel or the Middle Channel answered the phraseology of the treaty, but never Haro channel.[6] Cass found this explanation acceptable, and on April 2 he expressed his willingness to proceed with negotiations.[7]

Accordingly, on April 23, General Cass forwarded to Dallas another despatch on the San Juan controversy. For the first time he pointed out how the British had weakened their position by proposing the Middle Channel as boundary. In the previous August Russell had demanded the Rosario boundary, but in substantiation of his claim he had quoted from Aberdeen and Pakenham, both of whom were firm in their view that they had meant in 1846 to establish a line midway along the whole space intervening between Vancouver Island and the mainland. Yet in December Lord John had plumped for the Middle Channel, that is, for the channel of Aberdeen and Pakenham. To increase the confusion, Russell in March, 1860, had declared his readiness to accept either Rosario or the Middle Channel. In other words, argued Cass, he had proposed three different lines omitting one only—Haro channel—which American negotiators of 1846 like Benton, McLane, and Buchanan had mentioned so distinctly. "The whole subject in question," concluded Cass, "is the Island of San Juan ... and a proposal which gives the Island to Great Britain is a proposal to surrender the whole American claim, and not, in any sense of the term, a proposition for compromise."[8]

The summer of 1860 seemed propitious for a settlement of the San Juan controversy for, after Villafranca, Great Britain had her hands free, and there was nothing in foreign or domestic politics to suggest that she might be involved in war. Conditions in America also favoured a settlement. The presidential election campaign was under way and, almost for the first time in history, no party sought to make political capital by stirring up Anglo-American hatreds. The peaceful settlement of the Central American controversy by which the British agreed to withdraw from the Bay Islands and the protectorate around Greytown, intimated to the Americans in August, 1860; a quiet Canadian-American border after Reciprocity; the surrender of British maritime claims after the law officers of the Crown had in 1858 given it as their "decided opinion by the international law in time of peace we have no right of search or visitation whatever": all these were factors in smoothing ruffled feelings and in producing the calm necessary for successful negotiation. The approaching visit of the Prince of Wales to Washington, on the invitation of the president, was also bound to produce and foster amity between the two peoples.[9] But despite these favourable circumstances, no settlement was attempted in 1860.

On the water boundary the British government felt that their offer of 1859 had been reasonable, and they seemed to be surprised at the American rejection of their line of compromise. They realized too late that by suggesting this line they had irretrievably weakened their position. The rejection of their offer made it difficult to know what new proposition ought to be presented. Neither country favoured the principle of arbitration, and even if a third power were appealed to, upon what was it to arbitrate? It would be ironic if the two nations had to call upon a third to tell them what their negotiators had meant in 1846. Yet the attempt to settle it by commissioners had failed completely.

The officials at the Foreign Office were aware that the words of the treaty of 1846 were their vantage-ground, just as the Americans were convinced that their claims were based mainly on contemporaneous evidence. To lose sight of the treaty was to lose sight of San Juan too. The deliberations of the British government finally reduced themselves to the single question as to whether it would be wise for Great Britain to suggest arbitration at all. Arguments had been exhausted on both sides and, while Cass had written last and an answer to his proposal was necessary, he had made no proposal counter to the British offer of 1859. The British thought, therefore, that it rested with the Americans to submit a proposition. Arbitration might not be an impossible method of settlement, but the British were not disposed to suggest it; that the United States could propose it if they wished seems to have been the attitude of the Foreign Office.

The truth is, of course, that unanimity of purpose was absent from British counsels. The Colonial Office, acting on the advice of Governor Douglas and its other agents in the Pacific northwest, that is, on the advice of men living in the disputed territory, declared the retention of San Juan to be essential to the safety of British Columbia. But the views of these men were coloured by their attachment, present or past, to the Hudson's Bay Company, which had for some time been at loggerheads with the American authorities in the West. Supporting this group were the influential "true blue" ruling English hierarchy who glorified everything that was English and despised all things American. The Harney incident, though signally having failed in its purpose, left bitterness and suspicion in its wake and, as long as the circumstances of American politics allowed men like Harney to act on their own initiative in matters of international concern, there was real danger to San Juan, to Vancouver Island, and to British Columbia. The company's agents could never forget that the whole area west of the Rockies even below the Columbia River had once been their *locus operandi* and to many of them, notably to those of the older generation, the Americans were no more than interlopers. This view of the controversy held by the Colonial Office was supported by the Foreign Office, probably more from a desire to co-operate than from any sense of real conviction.

The lords of the Admiralty, who were the experts on the matter, did not consider the retention of San Juan to be essential to the safety of Vancouver Island; their conclusion was that, if free navigation of the various channels were secured, Vancouver Island would not be in jeopardy. The officials at the War Office did not consider the militia of British Columbia sufficient to cope with the considerable American population in British Columbia, in some of the adjacent islands, and more particularly in the neighbouring parts of the United States. This population was very mixed and included numbers of fugitives from justice who were ready for any opportunity to attack the civil power. Ultimately, to offset the influence of these people, the Colonial Office in January, 1861, at the instigation of the foreign secretary, asked the War Office to release a battalion of troops from China for service in British Columbia.

It had become obvious by the winter of 1860-61 that the United States would not make a proposition to end the dispute, and on November 22, the British government decided to instruct Lord Lyons to proceed with arrangements for arbitration. The subject matter of the arbitration was to be the true meaning of the words of the treaty of 1846 or, "if the precise line intended cannot be ascertained, is there any line which will furnish an equitable solution of the difficulty, and is the nearest approximation that can be made to an accurate construction of the words of the Treaty?"[10] For arbiter, the United States might choose the king of Norway and Sweden, or the president of Switzerland.

This instruction to Lyons was followed, two months later, by a copy of a convention from the Foreign Office covering reference of the dispute to arbitration. Article 1 recapitulates the terms of the treaty of 1846 and mentions the failure of the commissioners in 1857-9 to reach an agreement. It calls for reference of the controversy to an arbitrator within three months of ratification of the convention. Article 2 empowers the arbitrator, if he rejects both Rosario and Haro channels as boundary, to choose the channel most nearly approximating to that meant by the words of the treaty. Article 5 calls for the payment of 500,000 dollars to the Hudson's Bay Company as compensation for the surrender of the latter's rights.[11]

Circumstances were against immediate acceptance of the convention by the United States because a new government were due to assume office in March, 1861, and the Senate were unlikely, with such a short time remaining, to vote such a large sum of money. Judge Black, who had succeeded General Cass as secretary of state, promised however to ask the Senate if they considered arbitration desirable, and if they would empower the arbiter to draw his own line. This meant that the claims of the Hudson's Bay Company were not to be put to the Senate, though Black should have secured Lyons's consent to this omission. The Senate duly considered the matter, but nothing was done. The secretary of state expressed himself as sanguine, however, that the incoming administration could secure, if they chose, a positive and favourable answer to the questions asked, and he added that, in giving up his charge to his successor, he would affirm that he had never seen a case, during his whole experience of public affairs, in which arbitration was so properly applicable or so "imperatively called for." [12]

The new Lincoln administration, which took up office on March 4, 1861, had William H. Seward as secretary of state. Seward's record, to say the least, did not suggest that he would be very anxious to settle any outstanding difficulties with England. He belonged to that class of American politician which sought to make political capital out of Anglo-American relations. Lyons, who distrusted him, while he did not think that Seward would go to war, considered that he would be disposed to "play the old game of seeking popularity by displaying violence" towards Great Britain. [13] Lyons found himself in something of a dilemma because he was anxious to settle the San Juan controversy before another Harney might appear; but his instructions made settlement contingent upon a satisfactory agreement upon the Hudson's Bay Company claims. The company could be exacting and clamant, and the directors of the company might feel that, if their claims were separated from the water boundary discussions, their cause was being wantonly abandoned by the government. [14]

Contrary to expectations, Seward appeared willing enough to enter upon negotiations on the water boundary, but he was not so willing to discuss the Hudson's Bay Company claims. He decided to lay the matter before the Senate, but that body adjourned on April 1 without having answered his questions. The obstacle in the way of acceptance of the convention was the proposal to allow the arbitrator to draw a line of his own, and the Foreign Affairs Committee absolutely declined to recommend the adoption of this proposal. Yet this clause in the proposition for arbitration was so vitally important to the interests of Great Britain that to abandon it would almost constitute surrender of the whole British claim.

There still existed a feeling in some quarters in the United States that the bargain made by them in 1846 was not a good one, and the new generation of Senators, remembering the "Fifty-four forty or fight" campaign and the subsequent withdrawal to the forty-ninth parallel, however obvious might be the advantage of the settlement arrived at in 1846, could reach only one conclusion, namely, that Great Britain had scored a diplomatic victory in that year. There was therefore slight hope of ratification by the Senate, while so disposed, of any convention which would allow an arbitrator to draw a new line of compromise. Should the arbiter be unable to determine the line, Britain would be thrown back upon her claims as they existed previous to 1846, which would allow the United States to make effective use of their argument that the Oregon treaty prescribed a line which deviated from the forty-ninth parallel enough only to give Vancouver Island to Great Britain. The latter, therefore, had to choose between submitting the question to arbitration at the risk of losing San Juan and, on the other hand, allowing the continuance of the joint occupation of the island with all its attendant risks and inconveniences. But there was no doubt about the finality of the Senate's decision: they expressed themselves as in favour of arbitration, "but without power to establish any line but that provided for in the Treaty."[15]

Unfortunately, the American Civil War intervened to prevent any further progress on the San Juan question. The Senate, due to convene on July 4, were then expected to vote upon the questions submitted for their consideration; but when both houses met they decided to postpone discussions of all business not connected with the Civil War. Lyons had to be content, then, to remain in the background with his scheme of arbitration till a favourable opportunity for its presentation should arise.

Britain had always been afraid that the joint occupation of San Juan might produce an eruption—Lord Lyons had spoken more than once of being "a little nervous about our company of marines on San Juan."[16] But the Civil War brought in its path a solution of this difficulty. Captain Pickett was ordered to withdraw his troops from San Juan but, before completing arrangements for evacuation, his orders, owing to threats from the Indians, were countermanded, though the number of his men was reduced by half, and a force inferior to the British was left on the island.[17]

Advice was sent to Lyons on December 14, 1861, to take no steps to hasten the negotiations about San Juan because Great Britain was too deeply involved in incidents arising from the Civil War, and the safe course was obviously to prevent questions arising if possible. It was realized, too, that the arbitrator, if and when appointed, might find no line that fitted the words of the treaty; that consequently the principal point in dispute might after all not be brought to a settlement; further, in the subsisting state of affairs in the United States, the questions concerning this treaty were hardly important enough or exciting enough in the eyes of the American people to be made the grounds of a quarrel with England. American opinion was totally opposed to war, and even the anti-British Seward was on the side of peace after the *Trent* incident and, as Lyons had it, did not like "the look of the spirit he had called up. Ten months of office had dispelled many of his illusions."[18] Lyons' prescience at this stage was praiseworthy: "While Canada, in particular, is apparently defenceless, the Americans will never believe that we contemplate the possibility of war. And it must never be forgotten that when they make peace with the South, they may have a large army to provide with employment, and an immense amount of popular dissatisfaction and humiliation to find a safety valve for."[19] In these circumstances there was only one safe policy to follow: to prevent questions arising if at all possible.

With the possibility of war's being precipitated by the United States thus most remote, there was also little fear from the British side, for Great Britain was confirmed in a policy of neutrality, the maintenance of which produced more than one "incident." She had no economic motive for intervention because, though the cotton operatives of Lancashire suffered greatly, adjustment and compensation were obtained from war profits. Her governing classes favoured southern aspirations but sympathy was not profound enough to justify war; indeed, it was thought to the end that the South would achieve independence without outside aid. Moreover, at this time of paramount importance to Britain were fear and suspicion of Napoleon III, whose star reached its zenith between 1860 and 1866.

The importance of San Juan during the Civil War lay in the danger of trouble arising there and spreading, to complicate settlement of one of the several provoking incidents produced by the war. It was the *Trent* incident that "cleared the air. Seward now appeared in the new role of conciliator; an Anglo-American war had been faced and found disagreeable to both Governments; and the British Cabinet was stiffened in its policy of neutrality."[20]

CHAPTER SEVEN

PROGRESS IN THE POST-CIVIL WAR PERIOD

THOUGH SAN JUAN was of too minor importance to receive much consideration during the early part of the Civil War, it was not allowed to fall completely out of sight. In March, 1863, for instance, a member of Parliament named Longfield wanted to know what progress had been made towards a settlement of the dispute. He was rewarded with a brief review of the controversy, but it was explained to him that, since the question was not yet settled, the relative correspondence could not be made public. With respect to the island itself the attitude of the British government was that, pending agreement on the question of its possession, they must decline to sell any land on it and must continue to dissuade their subjects from settling there.[1]

Lord Lyons began to feel that the difficulty might be cleared up in spite of the interference of the Civil War and, writing optimistically on the subject in the same month that Longfield posed his question in Parliament, he wrote home for instructions. Though there had been no great change in the feelings of the Senate, they might be induced to consider the second draft convention sent by Lord John Russell, a draft which they had not seen and wherein it was stipulated that an arbitrator should determine only the line meant by the treaty of 1846.[2]

The home government were not very enthusiastic about originating a proposition on San Juan, though they were prepared, if Secretary of State Seward mentioned the subject, to stand out for the demarcation by an arbiter of what they termed an "equitable" line. Thus matters stood throughout 1863, until the friendly nature of the president's message of December 8, 1863, prompted them to instruct their minister once again to ask Seward if he thought the time propitious to settle the controversy by means of arbitration.[3] The secretary of state when approached welcomed the mention of arbitration and expressed the hope that the Senate would agree to this method of adjustment. He undertook to moot it as soon as the Hudson's Bay Company's claims were settled, a joint commission having been arranged for in July, 1863, to settle the claims question.[4]

Following this development Lord Lyons was instructed to insist "as much as possible" that the arbitrator should have power to fix a line as nearly as possible in accordance with the description in the treaty, if he found himself unable to find a line strictly meeting its terms. Lyons was not to sign any convention which did not give this discretionary power to the arbiter. As arbitrator Lord John suggested the Swiss president, or the king of Holland, or the king of Sweden, or the king of Italy; in short, almost any ruler except the czar of Russia.[5]

To explain the term "equitable boundary," Lyons furnished Seward with a copy of Lord Russell's despatch of January, 1861. This was to the effect that the arbitrator should not depart from the true meaning of Article 1 of the treaty of

1846, if he finds himself able to deduce that meaning from the words of the article, for these words had been agreed to by both parties and had been inserted in a treaty ratified by both governments. No matter whether the referee gives a positive decision for one of the lines or, "being unable to give such positive decision," chooses a line as the nearest approximation to an accurate construction of the Treaty "and as furnishing an equitable solution of the difficulty," his decision is to be accepted as final and conclusive.[6] It is noteworthy that this definition of policy was to remain the basis of British views until the final stages of the controversy.

Seward consulted leading senators before making any attempt at formal presentation of a convention to the Senate, and he found the views of the senators adverse, mainly because there had developed, as the outcome of England's attitude during the Civil War, a revival of the feeling of irritation in the United States against Great Britain. Whereas at the beginning of the Civil War, with all boundary disputes except that of San Juan removed, relations between the two countries had been more cordial than for some time, by the end of the war a strong anti-English sentiment had developed in both North and South. The former could not forgive Britain for appearing to favour the South, for allowing the *Alabama* to escape, for the frequently manifested sympathies of her upper classes for the South, for the humiliation suffered in the *Trent* affair. The South, on the other hand, resented Britain's refusal to recognize southern independence, though nearly gained, and her refusal to interfere in the war. In the summer of 1864, Lyons wrote home that the United States was preparing for a foreign war and Canada might be suddenly attacked. Thus he was instructed to visit Lord Monck in Canada and discuss defence with him.[7]

Events in the immediate postwar years did nothing to improve relations. To the Americans British prestige in Europe seemed at a low level, and after her conduct in the Danish dispute American newspapers reiterated in strong terms their old conviction that Britain would never fight again. After the Civil War the American merchant marine failed to flourish, and Great Britain was blamed for this, although the truth was that, because of the American protective tariff, Britain could build iron-clads much more cheaply than the Americans. The rival Civil War protagonists blamed the British, believing that Britain had assisted their enemy. In short, there existed in the United States a rankling resentment similar to that felt by Englishmen during the First World War, and again during the Second, when the United States delayed entering hostilities.

Once again, therefore, attempts to settle the San Juan dispute ended in failure, and the controversy languished for an appreciable time thereafter. Fortunately, the relations between the British and American occupation forces on the disputed island were of the friendliest, though the danger of local trouble precipitating an international struggle remained real. One or two minor incidents which seriously tried the patience of the officers in charge did arise, it is true, but on the whole remarkable forbearance was displayed by both sides when trouble seemed to be imminent.[8]

The prospect of settlement did not improve with the passage of time, because the delay in settling the dispute had served to introduce a number of additional thorny problems, some of which were deemed more pressing and dangerous. The celebrated *Alabama* claims question, for instance, was considered the most clamant, while the rights and position of naturalized citizens and the longstanding fisheries question were officially given equal prominence with the San Juan dispute. The naturalization question, which the United States now decided to link diplomatically with San Juan by insisting that it was to be satisfactorily settled before the water boundary dispute was tackled, was particularly difficult because it was directly concerned with Ireland. As Seward told Reverdy Johnson: "It happens that every considerable surge of popular discontent that disturbs the peace of Great Britain affects that portion of our people who have derived their descent from Ireland, and this emotion, in no inconsiderable degree, affects by sympathy the whole population of the United States."[9] After the Civil War many Fenians who had taken part in the fighting returned to Ireland. Some became involved in the Fenian Brotherhood campaigns of 1866 and 1867, and when the Habeas Corpus Act was suspended in February, 1866, among the number arrested for seditious activities were many naturalized Americans. The activities of the Fenians, their drilling in the United States, their periodic attempts or threatened attempts to invade Canada, and the apathy of the American government in suppressing this organization's work concurred in endangering the peace which nominally existed between the two countries.

The Fenians hoped to involve the United States and Great Britain in war, and they intended to use the fact that in some parts of the country they held the balance of political power between Johnson's party and the Radicals. Fortunately, Charles Francis Adams, the United States minister in London, and Lord Clarendon, the foreign secretary, were on terms of good mutual understanding, and the release of some of the Fenians was obtained. When these men returned to the United States they spread accounts of their arrest and maltreatment to sympathetic audiences. The sequel was a series of resolutions of sympathy for Ireland and a public opinion inflamed against England. Moreover, the Fenian agitation proved a costly business for Canada, "even with generous aid from Great Britain, for the provinces to guard their frontiers for seven years while American federal and state authorities, ever mindful of the Irish vote, behaved in a conspicuously dilatory and tender way towards the Fenians."[10]

Briefly, the position of the United States government on the question was that they asserted their belief in the absolute right of expatriation and maintained that, with the exception of eligibility for the presidency, their naturalized citizens were on terms of complete equality with native-born Americans. Seward insisted on "the right of every human being who is neither convicted nor accused of crime to renounce his home and transfer his allegiance to any other nation that he may choose . . ."[11] Great Britain, on the other hand, based her views on the dictum "once an Englishman, always an Englishman," and refused to recognize as American citizens those Irishmen who had become naturalized subjects of the United States.

The problem became a matter of discussion in English newspapers, and the government were speeded to action by the introduction and acceptance by 104 to 4 votes in the House of Representatives of the Banks Retaliation Bill at the end of 1867. This drastic measure provided that when a naturalized American was arrested by a foreign government upon the allegation that "naturalization in the United States did not operate to dissolve his allegiance to his native sovereign . . . , the President should be empowered to order the arrest and to detain in custody any subject or citizen of such foreign government who might be found within the jurisdiction of the United States." It is obvious that, had this extreme bill become law, the prospect of amicable adjustment of the outstanding disputes between the two countries would have been dim for an appreciable time. Edward Thornton, successor of Lord Lyons at Washington after December 6, 1867, was alarmed, and cabled home advising speedy settlement of both the San Juan and naturalization problems: "you know how impulsive these people are," he exclaimed.[12]

There was a more promising side to the situation, however, and this lay in the fact that Secretary Seward really desired to settle outstanding matters of difference—the *Alabama* claims, San Juan, the fisheries, extradition, naturalization— between Britain and his country because he realized that any of them, the naturalization one particularly, might at any moment become a subject of "exciting controversy."[13] The water boundary position was not now so quiescent, for the legislature of Washington Territory had in January, 1866, asked him to hasten settlement of the boundary question "in order that the said Islands may be surveyed and the laws of the United States and of Washington Territory extended thereon." He was reminded that there were over a hundred American settlers on San Juan, "whose persons and property have been for the last five years at the caprice of a Military Officer who states officially that his instructions set forth that no functionary of Washington Territory shall exercise any authority on San Juan during the Joint Military Occupation. . . ."[14]

Seward was prepared to conclude a treaty with Britain which would settle the naturalization problem on the lines of a similar arrangement concluded with Prussia in March, 1868, and he instructed Adams in London to seek a "conference" with Her Majesty's government for discussion of all outstanding matters of difference. At the same time Seward suggested to Thornton at Washington the lines of a possible settlement of the two most pressing problems. The occasion was most propitious, he said, and it was the first time in his experience that Congress, in a year preceding a presidential election, "did not want to make capital out of a war cry against England." An adjustment of the naturalization question on the lines suggested above, and reference of San Juan to the arbitration of the Republic of Switzerland would dispose of these problems.[15] Then, later, would come a proposition on the *Alabama* claims. Though Lord Stanley, the foreign secretary, professed his keenness to acquiesce in any plan likely to produce success, he did not understand what exactly was meant by a "conference." He telegraphed powers to Thornton, however, on March 11, 1868, to conclude a convention settling the water boundary question on the basis of arbitration, that is, on the basis of the British government's proposal of 1861 to Lord Lyons.

Developments on San Juan itself had something to do with Seward's determination to get the water boundary dispute out of the way. On November 18, 1867, Major-General H. W. Halleck, commanding the Military Division of the Pacific, wrote to the secretary of state, through the secretary of war, to the effect that General Scott's arrangement with Admiral Baynes had not the sanction of law and was repudiated by the civil authorities of Washington Territory. "They therefore continued to claim the right to collect taxes, execute political process &c. in the disputed territory. Moreover, the United States officers of Customs claimed the right to enforce our revenue laws on the same Island." These were incompatible with military occupation, and the military were resisting all attempts at the exercise of civil authority. Hence there arose an anomalous position. "The military officers of the United States are required to prevent the exercise of civil jurisdiction on the disputed Islands, while the civil officers of the same government insist upon its execution, and proceed to punish the former for the very acts which are required of them by the War Department." Halleck proposed any of four possible remedial measures: (1), stop the exercise of all civil jurisdiction in Washington Territory; (2), change the northern boundary of Washington Territory by Act of Congress to exclude the disputed islands which would remain under military control; (3), revoke the orders requiring the military to resist civil jurisdiction; (4), buy out all British territory west of the Rocky Mountains, for it is of little value to Britain and can never be colonized by her. It is of greater value to the United States. In any case the people want annexation to the United States, trade is paralysed, the population is declining, agriculture languishes, the land has deteriorated in value, taxes are "enormous," and the revenue does not meet the cost of administration.[16]

This report by General Halleck concurred with a memorial to Congress by Washington Territory for an end to the joint occupation. In this document the history of the case is given and complaint made that the military deny citizens trial by jury for any offence and have punished many American citizens without trial, "depriving them of their real and personal property." "Your memorialists know of no law of the United States, nor of any treaty entered into in due form of law with any foreign power, permitting or justifying so anomalous a condition of affairs. ... They claim that they are bound only by the law, and know of none subjecting our citizens ... to either military rule or military caprice."[17] A situation which so disturbed the West must be emended at once, thought Seward, and a comprehensive settlement with Britain seemed to be the solution.

Of all the issues between the United States and Great Britain after the Civil War that of the *Alabama* claims was the most dangerous. The *Alabama* and other less famous vessels, built in England with English equipment, had made attacks on Federal shipping during the war. They had made so many captures that American insurance rates soared, for in all 260 ships were liquidated. To make matters worse, the marauders were allowed to purchase supplies, and even engage seamen, in British colonial ports. A panic to sell American ships ensued, with the result that the American merchant fleet was almost halved at the end of the war. The Americans never forgot Britain's part, or indeed that of her colonies, in all this, direct and indirect, fancied and real. It was their loss of merchant marine that was the most substantial, the most bitterly regretted, part of the so-called "indirect claims." Throughout the war Charles Francis Adams, the United States minister to Britain, had made many protests to the British government, and he engaged in a voluminous correspondence with Lord John Russell, the foreign secretary, on the American claims for losses suffered at the hands of the *Alabama* and her prototypes. Russell refused to pay compensation for the claims, nor would he agree to put the matter to arbitration. A situation had arisen which, it was soon apparent, could only be resolved by one side's giving way. The fact that it had as its concomitant varied interpretation of international law on neutrality made it all the more vexatious and explosive.

In July, 1866, the American House of Representatives unanimously passed a bill to revise the neutrality laws so that the fitting out of ships for belligerents would be permissible. The menace inherent in this was too substantial to be ignored by Britain, for it meant that if Britain were involved in war with another country and the United States were neutral, the Americans could build and equip the ships of Britain's enemy. The effect upon British commerce could well be disastrous. The British press began to discuss the *Alabama* claims freely, and the danger of the issue's becoming a running sore was soon realized.

In November, 1866, Lord Stanley, now foreign secretary, instructed the British minister at Washington, Sir Frederick Bruce, to suggest to Secretary Seward that the subject should be put to arbitration. He was not to admit liability and he was to remind Seward of the numerous British claims arising from the war. Seward's reply was positive enough. The United States would submit the whole controversy, without restrictive conditions, to the arbiter. The root of the trouble, he said, was the royal proclamation of May 13, 1861, which accorded the South belligerent status, "an act of wrongful intervention, a departure from the obligation of existing treaties and without the sanction of the law of nations."[18] Later, he insisted that the minimum form of satisfaction for the *Alabama* and other depredations must be indemnification of American citizens who had suffered from them. "We charged and we believed that Great Britain and her colonies had been the arsenal, the navy-yard and the treasury of the Confederates"; that was the gist of the American argument.[19] Here was a bitter issue which, as we shall see, was to be linked with the minor San Juan controversy.

When Reverdy Johnson sailed for England in June, 1868, to succeed Charles Francis Adams he carried with him instructions on the most pressing Anglo-American controversies: naturalization, the water boundary, and the *Alabama* claims. The British Liberal government of 1868-74 agreed on January 14, 1869, to submit to a commission both the claims and the question of the right of the British government to have recognized the Confederacy as belligerents; if the commission failed to agree, another arbitrator was to be called in. Johnson and Clarendon, the foreign secretary, were able to conclude a convention for the adjustment of the claims.

The progress of the naturalization agreement had meantime been halted, and on this occasion the obstacle to settlement came wholly from the British side. When the terms of the proposed naturalization agreement were submitted to the law officers of the Crown for their opinion many objections arose, and when they were instructed to draft a treaty they asked for an extended period to study the problem.[20] Seward was annoyed at the delay when Adams reported on March 28 that a change in the naturalization laws would affect the British law of inheritance and succession and right to property; consequently progress would be slow. He complained of the "entire inattention" of the British government to American promptings on naturalization, thus rendering "every form of expression in reply to complaints difficult and embarrassing for the Executive Authority." Seward had made it clear that the naturalization matter must be adjusted before any of the other subjects of discussion were to be considered, and San Juan had to languish once again. Fortunately, however, the delay for which the law officers were responsible was no longer dangerous because the naturalization question was becoming less urgent with the release gradually of Irish-American Fenians and with the alteration of the Banks Bill in the Senate so as to make the retaliatory clause more or less innocuous.

On October 9, 1868, Reverdy Johnson and Lord Stanley were able to draw up a protocol adjusting the naturalization question, and within a few days a protocol on the San Juan dispute, based on the draft convention of February 18, 1861, was also concluded. Article 1 of this San Juan protocol agreed to refer the dispute to some friendly sovereign to be chosen within three months,[21] while Article 2 contained the very valuable stipulation that Great Britain so strenuously insisted upon, namely: "If such Sovereign or State should be unable to ascertain and determine the precise line intended by the words of the Treaty, it is agreed that it shall be left to such Sovereign or State to determine upon some line which, in the opinion of such Sovereign or State, will furnish an equitable solution of the difficulty and will be the nearest approximation that can be made to an accurate construction of the words of the Treaty." Article 3 empowered the arbitrator to call for any correspondence he wished and to weigh it as to the intentions of the negotiators, but "the referee shall not depart from the true meaning of the Article as it stands, if he can deduce that meaning from the words of that Article. ..." Article 5 made agreement inoperative until the naturalization question was settled satisfactorily between the two governments.[22]

When on January 14, 1869, the protocol was converted into a convention to be ratified within a year, there remained only ratification by the Senate to allow the arbitrator to begin his task. There was however at this time a resurgence of anti-English feeling in the United States. Mass meetings demanding war were held in different parts of the country, and the *Alabama* claims became a subject of general discussion and agitation in the United States. The American government gave countenance to agitation for petitions seeking the release of Fenians. All this inevitably affected the attitude to the San Juan question, and inevitably also opposition to the idea of putting it to arbitration grew in volume. The opinion that Great Britain, largely because she was Great Britain, had outwitted the Americans in 1846 was now widely held, and it was argued that Article 5 of the agreement was merely a device to surrender American claims to the island of San Juan in return for a satisfactory adjustment of the naturalization question. The Pacific Coast senators and their allies made violent anti-English speeches with the result that, in spite of the efforts of senators favourably disposed towards England, decision upon the convention was from time to time deferred until eventually the time for ratification—a year—had expired without the subject's having been considered by the Senate.[23] This development was extremely disappointing to the British government, and the position was not made any easier when the old question of the military importance of the Island of San Juan (which had so bedevilled the problem since 1856) was reintroduced on March 10 when the Senate adopted a resolution asking the secretary of war about the military value of the island. This was sure to delay settlement.

The British government could, however, do nothing until a year had elapsed after the signing of the convention. When that time had gone, feeling that they had been shabbily treated, they had the foreign secretary draw up a very stiffly worded despatch, in which the Senate were denounced for their failure to cooperate, and Thornton in Washington was instructed to show it to the secretary of state. At the same time, J. L. Motley, the historian who had replaced Reverdy

Johnson in May, 1869, was told that the British government regarded the Senate's neglect to consider for ratification the San Juan convention before January 14, 1870, a frank and glaring discourtesy. Hamilton Fish, now secretary of state, was perturbed at the development, and he wrote at once to Motley on the matter.[24] His explanation for the failure to consider the San Juan convention was that it was linked with the naturalization question, and though Article 5 of the protocol had been omitted from the subsequently signed agreement, his government expected Britain to keep a promise which was a "solemn agreement not to be waived by implication or by inference." When Reverdy Johnson had been sent to England it had been made clear that the naturalization question came first, and he had been told to state frankly to Lord Stanley, with whom he negotiated, that until that difficulty was removed, any attempt to settle *any* of the existing controversies between the two countries would be unavailing. Great Britain, he pointed out, had agreed in the naturalization protocol of October 9, 1868, to introduce measures in Parliament for a speedy settlement. This had not been carried out in spite of the fact that Parliament had sat from February 16 to August 11, 1869. The United States had not pressed the matter because of Britain's preoccupation with the Irish disestablishment question.[25]

This in turn demanded an explanation from the British, and that also was forthcoming. Lord Clarendon pointed out that the claims convention and the San Juan convention were sent to the Senate without any reference to the naturalization question. The Senate had rejected one on its demerits, and had postponed consideration of the other. The British government had set up a Royal Commission to go into the intricacies of the naturalization problem and its report of an extremely complicated subject was not presented till February, 1869. Other engrossing matters took precedence over it, and so nothing had been done till the current month.[26]

A possible method of saving the situation would have been prolongation of the time for ratification, but Thornton was instructed not to ask or show desire for a prolongation of the term.[27] Charles Sumner, chairman of the Senate Foreign Relations Committee, and Secretary of State Hamilton Fish discussed the matter, and Thornton was told that they wanted prolongation. It was obvious that events had taken a new turn for the Americans, and it was now their policy not to settle differences between the two countries singly, but to wait till a simultaneous understanding could be achieved on all of them. This development was, as we shall see, connected with the United States' desire to acquire Canada.

A turning-point in Anglo-American relations had come with the speech of Sumner on the Johnson-Clarendon convention of January, 1869. In a vitriolic speech on April 13, 1869, besides reminding his listeners that Great Britain had made no mention of apology or regret for the "massive grievance" done his country, and stating that the British government had acquiesced in, if indeed they had not actually connived at, the escape of the marauding vessels, he recited the enormous "indirect" *Alabama* claims. Great Britain, he said, was responsible not only for the actual losses inflicted by the *Alabama* and her prototypes but also for half the cost of the war and for the ruin of the American merchant fleet. The increased insurance rates, the diminution of United States exports and imports, the increase in tonnage, and the additional cost of carrying on the war were all subject to claims. Serious objection was also taken to the form of arbi-

tration—two British and two Americans plus a neutral commissioner—proposed in
the convention. The staggering total of the indirect claims was calculated to
establish a claim so colossal that only the cession of Canada to the United States
could satisfy it. President Grant warmly approved of the speech, and details of
it were broadcast from Atlantic to Pacific.

Besides reflecting American public feeling, Sumner's speech seemed outrageous
to British minds of all political hues. The *ex parte* nature of the argument of the
speech and Sumner's failure to mention the not inconsiderable losses sustained
by the large British cotton trade arising from the operation of the American
blockade were widely noted in the British press. Indeed, the speech went some
way towards inspiring the new imperial policy fostered by Disraeli and the
Conservatives who, a year or so later, like explorers exulting in the discovery of
a new world, proclaimed the wonders of the Empire and denounced Gladstone
and the Liberals as "Little Englanders." The very extravagance of Sumner's
"indirect" claims and the realization that the senator sought to facilitate the
annexation of Canada by equating its worth with the enormous total of the
claims had an effect opposite to that intended. His demand that England should
publicly confess her wrong-doing was a severe blow to English pride, and instead
of frightening England into a hasty effort to loose the fetters which held Canada,
the speech simply drew attention to the Dominion's importance and made the
British government determined to retain the connection. Moreover, in view of
Sumner's office as chairman of the Senate Foreign Relations Committee, public
opinion wrongly saw the speech as the opinion of the administration, and it was
now being said that it would be cheaper to go to war than pay the American
price. Charles Francis Adams, on retirement in Boston, reminded his compatriots
that Britain would never confess her error "and sell Canada as the price of a
release from punishment,"[28] but the incongruity of seeking the cession of Canada
as expiation of the grievous sin of May 11, 1861, seems never to have occurred to
the Americans. The speech was supremely mischievous in its effect because it
raised in American breasts great expectations as to the terms to be demanded
from the British.

The Senate almost unanimously rejected the Johnson-Clarendon claims convention because it had no regard to national claims arising from the prolongation
of the war and arranged only for the settlement of individual claims. Fortunately
for the sake of peace the disastrous quarrel between President Grant and Charles
Sumner was imminent, and when Grant decided to show the chairman of the
Senate Foreign Relations Committee that he, the president, alone initiated foreign policy he saw that he required the secretary of state as ally. Accordingly,
he agreed with Fish that the British should be told that the American Administration was prepared to settle all outstanding questions between the two countries.

Fish was conciliatory and the tone of his instructions to Motley affecting
Britain was friendly, stressing the common origin, language, literature, interests,
and objectives of the two countries. He determined not to press the matter of
the declaration of belligerency of 1861, for he recognized the right of every
power to define its own relations with conflicting sides in another state affected
by civil war. There had been no need for the proclamation, but that fact ought
not to be laboured. It was the damage done by the *Alabama* and others that

counted. "The British people were too much irritated by the rejection of the treaty, and by Mr. Sumner's speech, and our people were too much carried away with the idea of paying off the cost of the war with the amount of damages that Mr. Sumner's speech had made out against Great Britain."[29] The best means to achieve a peaceful settlement would be to allow an interval of calm so that the public mind might recover from its excitement. "In short, this document was a brief, courteous, and precisely worded proposal for a mollifying delay."[30]

Motley, however, convinced of the righteousness of Sumner's attitude, ignored his instructions and described the proclamation of belligerency as "the fountain-head of the disasters which had been caused to the American people both individually and collectively, by the hands of Englishmen. Other nations had issued proclamations, but only in the case of Great Britain had there come a long series of deeds injurious to the United States as the fruits of the Proclamation." It was the proclamation which at a stroke had given the rebels the status of a friendly and established government.

Lord Clarendon, the foreign secretary, was nettled at the suggestion that British neutrality had not been fair or genuine, but he assured the minister that he regarded war with the United States as *"crimen non nominandum inter Christianos."* Motley, however, had thus ingeniously contrived "to inject into his speech to Lord Clarendon the ideas which Mr. Fish had carefully eliminated from his instructions." Both Grant and Fish were dismayed when they received Motley's account of his interview with Clarendon, and Grant told Fish to dismiss the minister at once. The secretary of state, however, advised delay because of Sumner's position and influence in the Senate and his extreme attitude on the Johnson-Clarendon convention. Motley's days as minister were numbered. He was told that negotiations or discussions on the *Alabama* claims would in future be conducted in Washington between Fish and Thornton, and it was expected that Motley would resign at this snub. In June, 1870, he had to be invited to resign, but he refused to do so. The State Department thereupon simply informed the world that General Robert Schenck had been appointed Minister to the Court of St. James's. When Motley still persisted in refusing to leave his post, Grant in December had to dismiss him, an indignity, he said, "to which no public Minister of the United States had ever before been subjected."

CHAPTER EIGHT

CHAPTER EIGHT

CANADIAN-AMERICAN PROBLEMS

THE SAN JUAN QUESTION might have been easily and summarily resolved in the post-Civil War years if the United States' ambitions in respect of Canada had been realized. When the Americans thought of acquiring British North America after the Civil War they meant not only Upper and Lower Canada and the Maritime Provinces, but also what are now the prairie provinces and British Columbia. Of course, if they acquired British Columbia, they acquired Vancouver Island, with which it was united in 1868, and the San Juan water boundary controversy disappeared.

Canada was deemed highly vulnerable from a military point of view, and it was a constant obstacle to good Anglo-American relations, for the current outstanding disputes between the two powers, except the *Alabama* claims, were essentially Canadian—the fisheries, San Juan, Fenian Raids, Reciprocity. Moreover, in the resurgence of "manifest destiny" ideas after the Civil War, Canada lay invitingly before the eyes of the expansionists and the Anglophobes, and it did not require much ingenuity to devise the plan that all difficulties could be resolved by the cession of Canada to the United States. Thus, within the half-dozen years immediately after the war, we see the Americans keen to annex either all or part of British North America. At one time they wanted all Canada as we know it to-day; at another they would have been content with Red River or with British Columbia; at still another, during the Treaty of Washington negotiations, San Juan would have satisfied them. A tremendous "swallow for territory" had developed among Americans, and the triumvirate of the early days of the Grant administration—Grant, Fish and Sumner—like Seward before them, shared this thirst, though that was perhaps all they had in common. This period therefore provides an excellent example of the interaction and clash of two nineteenth-century political philosophical ideas, American manifest destiny and British anti-colonialism, for the Grant administration represented the recrudescence of manifest destiny just as accurately as the first Gladstone Government represented the high-water mark of anti-colonialism. The Americans, perhaps naturally, misunderstood the warmth of the colonial feeling for the mother country, and they came to believe that, if Canada freed herself of imperial ties as British statesmen suggested so glibly, amicable annexation to the United States would speedily and inevitably follow. The Americans could also be excused for reminding themselves that international trends were then in their favour; Spain was about to withdraw from Santo Domingo, the French from Mexico, the Russians from Alaska.

The annexation aim was not new in American history, and most of the arguments which have been adduced to justify manifest destiny in the nineteenth century have been put forward more than once specifically to encourage the absorption of Canada: geographical predestination, political gravitation, inevitable destiny, true title, self-defence.[1] The Gladstone government were avowed subscribers to the view that the allegiance of colonies to the mother country was purely voluntary; the day of parting should be postponed as long as possible; when it should inevitably come, it should be made as pleasant as circumstances would allow; let the colonies be the judges of the duration of the connection.[2] The Gladstone government did not merely theorize; they put their theories into practice. British garrisons were withdrawn from Australia and New Zealand, while Edward Cardwell, who was at the War Office under Mr. Gladstone, was able to boast that, within his first two years of office, he had reduced the number of British soldiers in the colonies from 49,000 to 18,000 and the military expenditure on them from £3,400,000 to £1,000,000.[3]

The great weakness of the American aspirations in respect of Canada was that if annexation were rapidly to follow independence, as they hoped, the British government would reduce the speed of the independence movement because no British government, however apathetic and anti-colonial, could afford to look with equanimity upon the annexation of British North America to the United States. Philosophizing was one thing, action was quite another. Anti-colonialism was fashionable among the pseudo-cognoscenti and radicals so long as it remained an attitude of mind, but no British statesman would have dared to make it more then theoretical. Gladstone, with all his alleged anti-colonial enthusiasm, was certainly not keen to preside at the liquidation of the British Empire.[4] Lord Granville, till June, 1870, colonial secretary and thereafter at the Foreign Office, give his appraisal to Parliament: "I am of opinion that the ties which bind us together are loyalty to the Crown, goodwill between the colonies and the mother country, and a reciprocity of mutual advantages. When this state of things shall cease to exist, the idea of compelling by force any great and self-governing colony to remain connected with this country is an idea which no statesman would entertain; though no statesman should take too seriously any lightly expressed wish on the part of a colony for separation from this country."[5] The position simply was that separation from the mother country was sure to come when legislative supremacy and sole responsibility would supplant Colonial Office authority. But there was no existing question of this in the period under review, and this is the most significant feature of the whole anti-colonial agitation. Even the most bigoted anti-colonials subscribed to the view that Great Britain could never acquiesce in Canada's falling into the United States's hands by mere default. Fish, in common with most Americans, did not understand this phenomenon, for he made the simple mistake of accepting all the anti-colonial utterances of Liberals and Radicals as sincere and based on reality. The "Little Englanders" began to go out of favour in the declining days of the Gladstone government of 1868-74, and Disraeli and the Conservatives then seized the chance to make the Empire politically fashionable once more.

The eminent statesman, Charles Sumner, chairman of the Senate Foreign Relations Committee since 1861, declared pontifically that only the surrender of Canada would be adequate reparation for the *Alabama* claims. Ulysses S. Grant, who assumed the office of president in March, 1869, went a little farther by saying that Sheridan could take Canada in thirty days, while many Americans

shared the view of firebrand Senator Chandler of Michigan, chairman of the
Military Affairs Committee, that if Canada was not ceded to the United States,
the latter would have to take it by force. "The new policy of hastening and
compelling the annexation of Canada ... appeared in urgent requests for the
construction of the Northern Pacific Railroad as a valuable political measure in
relation to Canada, in special reports on commercial relations, and in House and
Senate resolutions."[6] The president himself believed implicitly that Great Britain
had been responsible for prolonging the Civil War, and after the cessation of
hostilities he was as keen upon territorial expansion as Seward had ever been.
He looked more hopefully to the south, however, to satisfy his territorial thirst.
Secretary Fish lay somewhat between his two colleagues, Sumner and Grant,
though he was genuinely anxious to settle all his differences with Great Britain
as a matter of general policy.[7] His intimate relations with Sir Edward Thornton,
the British minister, convinced him that annexation was unlikely to be a simple
matter. He came to understand the British Liberal position that Canada herself
must determine the duration of her connection with the mother country. Fish
hoped that Britain would grant independence to Canada, thus leaving the question of annexation to be settled between the Canadians and Americans. This
could only be achieved by the exercise of tact, patience, and conciliation.[8] He
wanted to adjust all disputes with England, await the latter's voluntary liberation
of Canada, and then move for annexation.

Sumner and Grant favoured a policy of delay; it was their policy to keep all
questions, especially the *Alabama* claims, in suspension until the British were
ready to give up Canada. Constant reiteration of claims took time to have effect,
and it was necessary thus to prepare the British public mind. Sumner believed
that Canada would then fall into the lap of the United States. In a speech on
September 22, 1869, at the Republican party convention he declared his conviction that the appointed destiny of Canada was within the Union, but annexation
must come peacefully and with the consent of the Canadians. The Sumner
policy of keeping all Anglo-American issues alive in order to create in the British
government a feeling of frustration and exasperation so confusing that they
would agree to cede Canada was dangerous, and required almost Machiavellian
skill to operate. Moreover, it was likely to have the reverse effect of that intended.

The Americans played their cards very badly. They were aware of the existence of the long-standing anti-colonial movement in Britain, and they ought
therefore to have encouraged the Canadians to look southward for sympathy,
appreciation, and understanding. But they over-estimated the strength of the
"Little England" movement in Britain, partly because Sumner's chief friends in
that country, like John Bright, were confirmed anti-colonials, and they believed
Canadian independence to be imminent when indeed it was very far away. They
ought to have cultivated Canadian friendship and offered solutions for the apparently insuperable differences among the provinces which were without a
common banking system, a uniform postal arrangement, or a uniform currency,
among other important things. The differences of the integral parts of the
federation and the racial and religious antagonism of Upper and Lower Canada,
for instance, were there to be exploited for the defeat of Confederation. The
Americans ought to have offered remedies for their multifarious grievances as
colonists and should have explained how their differences would have been

sympathetically resolved by their joining the "model republic" to the south. Instead, the Americans succeeded only in uniting their neighbours in attachment to, and enthusiasm for, Confederation, while the vehemence of the American attacks on Great Britain had the effect only of drawing the colonists closer to the mother country. The failure to renew the Reciprocity Treaty of 1854 when it expired in 1866 was considered unforgivable by the Canadians, especially when this was followed by the Americans' giving open countenance and encouragement to the Fenian movement in its plan to invade Canada. In other words, at a time when so many senior English statesmen were asserting that the colonists could take the initiative in seeking independence whenever they wished, the Americans seemed to be trying to starve the Canadians into surrender while bullying them by means of harassing border raids.

Added to this was the fact that top American statesmen and many responsible newspapers were proclaiming the inevitability of absorption in the Union. Reliance was placed upon sporadic manifestations of annexation feeling in Canada to build up an inaccurate picture of the Canadian scene. It is true that there was a certain measure of annexationist sentiment in parts of British North America like British Columbia and Nova Scotia (though the strength of the sentiment was much exaggerated,) and there was enough of it, especially if stimulated and encouraged to ally with a more widespread independence movement, to split the Canadians and make annexation possible. His Alaskan success, though "a lucky chance, the only fruit of his multifarious projects for expansion," fired Seward to heights of prophecy, in August, 1867, that is, a month after the achievement of Canadian Confederation: "Nature designs that this whole . . . shall be sooner or later within the magic circle of the American Union." The purchase of Alaska, he said, was effected in order to counter British influence and "to strengthen the American influence in British Columbia." When the Fenian attacks ended in chaos and farce, the Canadians not only acquired a new conceit of themselves but also a contempt for the Americans. The glaring contrast between the Fenian chaos and their own government's efficient prevention of the shipment of arms to the United States during the Civil War seemed to point a moral. The "irresponsible utterances" of the press "combined with those of the cheaper brand of American politician, to ensure that now, as unhappily at several other junctures in Canadian history, Canadian patriotism became in many minds synonymous with dislike and distrust of the United States."[9] The Americans were unable to assess accurately the measure of natural attachment for the mother country felt by Canadians which was as intense in many ways as their dislike of the United States.[10]

Canadians were convinced that the bitterness engendered by the *Alabama* claims induced the United States government to allow the Fenians to organize on American soil for their attacks on Canada because it was considered a salutary method of reprimanding the British.[11] The Fenian raids did irreparable damage to American-Canadian relations. The United States government stood still on the occasion of the first raid at a time when there was no war between the countries and no flag under which the Fenians could operate; they had made a pretence of punishing some Fenian leaders, a gesture which indicated recognition of the essence but not the degree of their responsibility. The contrast between the American attitude to the *Alabama* claims and the Fenian raids claims seemed indefensible to Canadians. "It may safely be said that the failure to detain a single vessel furtively built by a foreign power in time of war, and under all the difficulties incident to the maintenance of neutrality between passionate and unscrupulous belligerents, will bear no comparison in point of criminality with the deliberate permission and encouragement, through a series of years and in time of peace, of an organization openly levying war against a neighbouring and friendly nation." Thus wrote a respected Canadian publicist, C. Lindsey.[12] The Americans were so concerned with making the Canadians fear them that they failed to make them see that their salvation lay in union. American ambitions furnished a focal rallying-point for the proponents of Canadian Confederation and a transcontinental Canadian railway. Even the astute Hamilton Fish was not aware of the gross error of judgment and prescience inherent in his ingenuous answer to the British minister's protest about Fenian raids: that Britain should give up Canada and so remove all pretext for Fenian attacks.

Nevertheless, while the Americans generally persisted in greatly underestimating the strength of Canadian national feeling, just as they continued to misunderstand the varying nuances of anti-colonial thought in England, Secretary of State Fish was the first to comprehend that Britain had no real intention of handing over Canada. He began to see that the frequent British protestations that the Canadians must take the first move towards independence were devised simply to cloak anxiety lest they might in fact insist upon seceding. It was not therefore until he was able to let the British see that he understood this that negotiations with them were possible. Fish would do nothing precipitate. He saw that rejection of the Johnson-Clarendon convention had produced an impasse, but he determined to wait for a British proposition. "Better that the question rest some years even (if that be necessary) than risk failure in another attempt at settlement."[13] As for British anti-colonialism, here also he was beginning to see the light by the summer of 1870. He was becoming weary of Thornton's persistent reiteration of the myth that the British are "desirous" for separation, for he "did not see the evidence of this willingness."[14]

A letter of March 12, 1870, from Fish's assistant secretary of state, J. C. Bancroft Davis, to Sir Curtis Lampson, deputy governor of the Hudson's Bay Company, shows how the State Department mind was working at that time. "A new departure in this affair" is necessary because "past mistakes have complicated matters," and the example of a similar situation with Spain in 1819 seems to indicate a positive method of adjustment—a territorial cession. By the treaty of 1819 with Spain the United States had acquired Florida, and in the present case if Great Britain would "use her influence in favour of independence" the *Alabama* claims could be disposed of without any trouble. " . . . a large portion of the British empire on this continent would be glad to-day to come to the United States, and Great Britain would be richer and stronger for having them do so." The writer goes on to state that there is no doubt about British Columbia which "certainly" wants to come over, and Canada cannot hope to force the Red River settlement to join Confederation. "Temporary independence, followed by American annexation, will settle more questions than the Winnipeg war, and will give the Hudson's Bay Company a better payment than Canada." The dissatisfaction of Newfoundland, New Brunswick, and Prince Edward Island with Confederation is "well known," and the solution for their problems is independence or annexation to the United States. "And why could not this change be accompanied by a settlement of differences on which we now appear to be too far apart to adjust in any other way?" Davis goes on to indicate the basis of American policy. "I know that Great Britain can never consent to relinquish any territory on this continent, the settlers of which show a desire to remain with her; nor can she honourably do so in the face of threats or shows of force; but she certainly can, of her own volition, so shape things that the separation may come at the request of the colonists, without tarnishing her honor." This pregnant last sentence succinctly explains the views of the secretary of state. Both the United States and Great Britain are to do everything possible to facilitate independence and annexation of Canada, and only in an atmosphere of calm, peaceful Anglo-American relations can this be effected. Thus the Americans must give no more than passive support to the groups of annexationists in British North America, they must on no account interfere actively, and they must exhort the British government to do everything possible to prepare the way for Canadian independence and subsequent annexation; to grease the rails of annexation there was the ointment of an *Alabama* claims settlement.[15] Fish assured Thornton that he did not want Canada, but he desired it to be independent and not a "constant cause of dispute between the two countries, and to cease to be a thorn in our sides by smuggling and other practices. You may depend upon it that 24 hours after Canada is independent, you and I will be able to settle the Alabama Claims question as easily as possible."[16] Fish ignored Thornton's remark that "Independence means annexation. They are one and the same thing."

If Fish had at last divined the true nature of the British position vis-à-vis the colonies and Canada in particular, he was much less quick to assess the real strength of the annexation movement in Canada, though the explanation of this fact is simply that American special agents were giving their government exaggerated, and in some ways, false notions of the extent and ramifications of annexation movements in parts of British North America.[17] The vital mistake was made of thinking that the independence movement and the annexation movement were identical. It is true that one of the causes of the two movements was the effect of the conclusion of reciprocity on the Canadian economy, which was considered a political rather than a commercial expedient, but it did not follow, as most Americans believed, that all opposition to Confederation came from annexationists or that all the disaffected wanted to go over to the Union. Even Fish was dazzled by the manifestations of sentiment favouring annexation and independence in parts of British North America,[18] and he refused to accept Thornton's better informed opinion that there was virtually no annexation sentiment in Canada. He dismissed the British minister's view with the extraordinarily naïve statement that "their elections are not true expression of sentiment on the subject, for the bankers and wealthy employers overawe the humbler population." From the steady influx of French Canadians into New England he drew the erroneous inference that annexation feeling was strong in Lower Canada.[19]

One of the earliest moves Fish had made as secretary of state had been to appoint General Oscar Malmros as United States consul and leader of the American party in the Red River colony which was supposed to be keen on annexation. The United States had long coveted the Manitoba country, and their desire to have it increased with the development of railways. The traders of the colony had their chief markets in Minnesota, for their natural communication routes led southward rather than eastward to remote Upper Canada. Throughout the sixties there was a struggle between the Americans and Canadians for the Red River colony. The latter had a population of about 12,000 of whom nearly 10,000 were half-breeds and less than 2,000 whites.[20] Malmros gained favour with the provisional government of Louis Riel, failing to appreciate that the French half-breeds were merely using him for their own ends. In December, 1869, Malmros wrote to Bancroft Davis to the effect that "in a short time" annexation to the United States would be achieved.[21] Though Fish sent an additional agent to Red River at the end of 1869, it soon became apparent that Riel had his eyes more on Ottawa than Washington, and that he was simply using annexationist ambitions for bargaining purposes. On the very eve of the convening of the Joint High Commission at Washington, the secretary-treasurer of Red River, W. B. O'Donoghue, was canvassing in Washington for support for the rebels. President Grant accorded him an interview on January 28, 1871, during which he expressed sympathy with the rebels in their grievances and revealed his knowledge of annexationist sentiment in Nova Scotia, New Brunswick, and Prince Edward Island. If there was a widespread desire for annexation, manifested in a popular vote, the United States would give it a "thorough examination," declared Grant.[22]

Secretary Fish turned from his Red River disappointment to what seemed more fertile soil for the germinating seed of annexation—British Columbia. In July, 1866, Nathanial Banks, whom we have noticed in another connection, had introduced into Congress a bill for the annexation, "after Great Britain and the several British provinces in Canada accepted the proposition of annexation," severally, of what were to become after July 1, 1867, the constituent parts of the Dominion of Canada, including the "Territory of Columbia," that is, Vancouver Island and British Columbia. This failed, but another more oblique attempt at annexation was made at the end of the following year when Senator Alexander Ramsey of Minnesota moved for a treaty between the United States and the envied new dominion which attempted to anticipate British Columbia's entrance into Confederation by providing for its cession to the United States by Britain with the same rights as those held by Montana Territory.[23] In return for this acquisition the United States would pay six million dollars to the Hudson's Bay Company and, besides assuming responsibility for the debt of British Columbia, she would arrange for the building of a railroad from Lake Superior to Puget Sound. A group of Minnesota expansionists led by Ramsey and James W. Taylor, both of whom had given instructions to O'Donoghue, kept the annexation issue well before the public view.

Fish was much impressed with the British Columbia movement, and he attached unmerited attention to it. His Diary, quoted by Allan Nevins, reveals that a memorial from residents of British Columbia to President Grant requesting annexation to the United States was a matter of serious discussion by the American cabinet on January 4, 1870. A copy of the memorial was sent to Motley in London and another to Thornton, though the official attitude decided upon was to "keep our eyes fixedly on the movement," and to keep "our hands off." It is remarkable that a statesman of Fish's perspicacity could have attached serious importance to a movement virtually confined to one small part of the colony

(Victoria) and could have taken notice of a petition signed by less than one per cent of its small population. Further, the government of the colony was in the hands of British subjects whose traditions and outlook were entirely British. The British Columbia annexation movement, such as it was, had no hope of success after the summer of 1869 when Anthony Musgrave was appointed governor of the colony. The great weakness of the colony's British connection was geographical because the province lay nearly two thousand miles from Red River to the east and the nearest British settlement westward was Hong Kong. Not only that; the Red River settlement stood in isolation from Upper and Lower Canada. By sea, Britain was more than twelve thousand miles from the mother country. The Fraser River goldrush of 1857-8 had brought Americans to the colony and many remained, especially at Victoria. The population of ten thousand was one of mixed national origin, but all the controlling officials from the governor down were British or Canadian. The British element was formidable and predominant; the Church of England was the semi-official church; the government was on the British model; there was a British naval base at Esquimalt which had had naval vessels since 1844. It is true, however, that immigration from Britain had become negligible, and indeed the decline of the Cariboo gold-diggings forecast a population decline.[24]

It is also true that nearly all British Columbia's trade was with San Francisco, and the colony was on the verge of bankruptcy. American steamship companies controlled absolutely the sea trade of the area. American ships carried the mail and only American stamps could take letters outside the colony. In the light of all this the United States could perhaps not be blamed for believing that the colony's population was predominantly American, especially since even the English press stressed the fact that a large part of the population was of American citizens. Actually, on the other hand, according to the Victoria *British Colonist*, which was on the spot, less than one-fifth was American.

The memorial seeking annexation which was formally presented to the president on December 29, 1869 and which Fish brought before the cabinet had forty-three signatures and a later list had sixty-one additional ones. Mr. Willard Ireland, British Columbia Archivist, has examined the petition with analytical care and, after indentifying all but two of the signatures, he has found that more than half of the signatories were not even Americans but were German Jews; several were Americans, but few had British connections; further, the movement was confined to Victoria with no help on the mainland.[25] "In the colony itself the petition did not arouse a great deal of interest," and Governor Musgrave told the Colonial Office that not a single British subject signed the petition.[26] Mr. Ireland's conclusion is that "annexation may be considered to have been a forlorn hope in British Columbia, and the annexationists ... appear to have had little or no connection with the political life of British Columbia."[27] He was also shown that the most extreme opponents of Confederation in British Columbia favoured independence rather than annexation, and it was Fish's mistake to assume that the enemies of Confederation were *ipso facto* annexationists. The result of the struggle for Confederation was a foregone conclusion because all the decisive factors were with the federationists: the attitude and personality of the governor, Colonial Office pressure, and Canadian diplomacy.[28] The sale of Hudson's Bay territory between the Great Lakes and the Rockies to Canada was the deciding factor in the Confederation struggle. The British government came out on the side of Confederation and the new governor, Anthony Musgrave, former governor of Newfoundland, was appointed in June, 1869, with explicit instructions from London to promote the federation of British Columbia with the new Dominion.[29]

In September, 1870, the American consul at Victoria advised that British Columbia was about to join Confederation.[30] His annexation aims thus repulsed in Red River and British Columbia and now aware that Great Britain had no real intention of promoting Canadian independence of the mother country, the secretary of state came to realize that the annexation of Canada was a dream unlikely to come true. An important discussion with Thornton a few days after the bad news from Victoria showed the new trend: he must save what he could from the *débâcle*. On September 27 Fish told Thornton that he had lately received hundreds of letters from Canadians assuring him of their desire for independence; some were also for annexation. He showed Thornton a bulky report from a United States agent in British Columbia to the effect that four-fifths of the population of the colony were "anxious for annexation." Fish remained unconvinced by Thornton's reminder that this was surely inconsistent with the recently expressed wish of British Columbia to join Confederation. "I added that the late protests of the Canadians against the withdrawal of the Imperial troops proved how little they desired separation from the mother country," reported Thornton.[31]

A week later, Fish in his discussions with the British Minister went a step further. All in Canada, even the French, he said, wanted independence and only the government, the bankers, and the smugglers were opposed. He suggested that the British government should "allow and encourage" the taking of a referendum in Canada (President Grant's hobby-horse) as to the people's wish to be independent. Thornton's acid reply was: "If we were to propose to the United States Government, that a vote as to independence should be taken in Louisiana or any other of the Southern States, whose population were known to be disaffected and desirous of separation," what would the Americans say?; "whilst the inhabitants of Canada had but recently given many proofs of their earnest desire to continue the present relations with England."[32]

With their future so variously provided for and their destiny apparently to be decided by either Great Britain or the United States, it is interesting to note the views of Canadians themselves. The Toronto *Globe*, which reflected what were considered Radical views in England, had a large and influential circulation and could be deemed to reflect the ideas of a large section of Canada's two and a half millions at that time. It therefore spoke for many Canadians when it said:

We are, at present, an integral part of an empire which has no peer in the sisterhood of nations .... We glory in her renown. We feel flattered in sharing the fame of her past achievements in the arts of war and peace, and her present wealth, power and position. We cherish the name of Briton .... We should lose all this by joining the States and it would be a gratuitous sacrifice .... England's parental heart yearns over us with affection and kindness; why should we leave the parental home and rush into arms so uncongenial, into a family racked with feuds and quarrels? ... Our institutions and our traditions, our judgment and our sentiments all go against political union. If we joined the United States the radical democratic elements would soon swamp our present system and the whole character of our cherished institutions would become changed .... A fusion with the Americans would dispel from us the feeling of home and brotherhood and would make us feel strange even in our own land.[33]

With his Canadian dreams dissolving, Fish decided upon a supreme effort to get San Juan. He was prepared to adjust his demands on the *Alabama* claims to obtain the island, and he asked Great Britain to cede San Juan without arbitration; if they did so, the Senate would be sure to agree to arbitrate the *Alabama* claims. But Thornton perceived the fallacy in this, and he retorted that Britain would find it impossible to give up San Juan. Fish pleaded with him that San Juan was so worthless that Great Britain might easily give it up in order to be on good terms with the United States, just as in 1846 she had ceded the Oregon area between the Columbia River and the forty-ninth parallel.[34] A true, but not a palpable parallel in British eyes. Many Englishmen still winced when 1846 was mentioned, and the "argument" based on San Juan's alleged worthlessness could be viewed from two different angles.

The British had made it abundantly clear that, after the rejection of the Johnson-Clarendon convention by the United States in April, 1869, the next move must lie with the Americans.[35] Fish was fortunately not the man to stand upon punctilio, and he now sounded Thornton on a project of agreement covering all matters in dispute between the countries: the fisheries, the *Alabama* claims, the water boundary, and the others. The United States, which had up to now refused to arbitrate the claims, might "abandon their opposition," he told Thornton, if the British would settle the water boundary by agreeing to accept Haro Strait as the boundary. If the British would admit the Americans to the Canadian inshore fisheries, the United States would admit certain Canadian exports duty free. Thornton was suitably impressed by all this, though he made it clear that his government would be unlikely to give way on San Juan on a "point of honour."[36] It was this realization on both sides that there was a congeries of points of possible agreement that "marked the great turning point in the negotiations on the Alabama Claims."[37]

Professor Maureen Robson has adumbrated the agencies acting for peace in 1870-71: primarily, the "ugly aspect" of the fisheries dispute; the Franco-Prussian War; the grave warnings against war by financiers on both sides of the Atlantic, for "nothing would have been more fatal to her financial and commercial enterprises than an estrangement from Britain"; the importunities of insurance companies and claimants who had sustained losses from the *Alabama* and her prototypes; the Francophobia of President Grant; the realization that "a quarrel with Britain would mean death to many ventures in America which depended upon British capital and resources. America was the world's greatest debtor nation, for she had borrowed to fight the war, and was still borrowing to develop half a continent."[38]

CHAPTER NINE

EUROPEAN COMPLICATIONS

As HAS BEEN THE CASE so often, European affairs intervened to force the British to depart from their plan of "masterly inactivity" in order to effect an agreement with the United States. In 1870 the policy of reducing the army to minute proportions pursued by the Gladstone government of 1868-74 reached its nadir when the Army estimates fell to just over twelve million pounds for an army of 110,000. The Franco-Prussian War showed up this policy in all its folly, for Prussia had nearly half a million men under arms and British impotence stood out in sharp relief. Bismarck, with his genius for exploiting a situation to his own advantage, after advising the United States minister to urge his government to get Canada in return for a settlement of the *Alabama* claims, exhorted the Russians to denounce the Black Sea clauses of the Treaty of Paris which had ended the Crimean War and provided that the Black Sea be a neutral lake. In November, 1870, the Russian government acted on the advice and Britain was unable to do anything about it. Yet the previous year when the Russians had reached the borders of Afghanistan, Great Britain had persuaded her to sign jointly an agreement guaranteeing the independence of Afghanistan. Here was a fresh shock to Gladstone and to the Russophobe British public. Lord Granville, who succeeded Lord Clarendon at the Foreign Office in June, 1870, protested against this Russian form of unilateral pronouncement, and a protocol criticizing it was subsequently agreed to by the powers. Mr. Odo Russell was sent as special envoy to the Prussians, and he told Bismarck that unless the Russians withdrew their pronouncement "we should be compelled with or without allies to go to war."[1]

These were brave words, but Prussia clearly dominated Europe, and the British position was bleak indeed. To whom could Britain turn? Not to Prussia; not to Russia which had had the temerity to slap her face; not to France, now prostrate. The gigantic proportions of the armies involved, and the cataclysmic nature of the events in Europe struck the British public almost to stupefaction; the swift advance of the Prussians, the capture of the French Emperor; Sedan; the surrender of Metz; the siege of Paris, all stupendous and dramatic, far-reaching and awe-inspiring. Italian unity was achieved; Germany was also united; a German invasion of England was even hinted at. "Militarism had supplanted liberalism as a force in Europe."

In her grave European situation of isolation it behoved Britain to stabilize her relations with the United States. The drift which had developed since the beginning of 1869, when the Johnson-Clarendon convention had been rejected, had to be arrested, for there was much justification for Lord de Grey's estimate of the position at this time: "War with America had become almost a question of opportunity and the opportunity was ominously nigh." The new foreign secretary deplored the fact that "our present position cripples us in every way. Not only would it do so if we wished for war, but it impedes our pacific efforts, making people attribute to fear that which is prompted by sense of duty."[2] On top of that came the president's message of December 5, 1870, wherein he recommended that Congress should negotiate with Great Britain for a commission to establish the amount of the *Alabama* claims.[3] John Morley expresses well Gladstone's view: "With Mr. Gladstone the desire [for reconciliation] was not a consequence of the possible trouble with Russia. His view was wider and less specific. He was alive to the extent to which England's power in Europe was reduced by the smothered quarrel with America, but he took even higher ground than this in his sense of the blessing to the world of an absolute reconciliation in good faith between the old England and the new."[4] Though American policy was hamstrung by the financial drain of the Civil War and reconstruction, and war for them would clearly be folly, there was ever present the possibility that the United States might attack if Britain became involved in a European war, and the imperial troops based in Canada would be needed in Europe. Above all, the Canadian fisheries could at any moment furnish a *casus belli*, and Grant's December message, which sneered at the inefficient handling of the fisheries by the "semi-independent but irresponsible" Canadian government manifested a trend. The president felt compelled to seek powers "to suspend the operation of any laws whereby the vessels of the Dominion of Canada are permitted to enter the waters of the United States."[5]

It was official British opinion that Russia, in the event of war with England, would be sure to draw the United States into the conflict. Further, the knowledge that there was an unsettled cause of war with the United States emboldened European powers to believe that the Americans would seek revenge on Britain for her actions during the Civil War.[6]

It was fortunate that the State Department was in the hands of a patient, unvengeful secretary. Any one of the conflicting disputes could flare up to war level at any moment, and he was well aware of this. The very friendly relations that subsisted between him and British minister Thornton now played their part in promoting settlement. Thornton made it clear in his despatches home that the Americans wanted to settle all outstanding disputes and not to settle any of them singly. They wanted to "wait till a simultaneous understanding upon all of them can be arrived at." On occasions before, as in 1842 when Lord Ashburton was sent to Washington to settle the northeast boundary with Secretary Webster, it had been found a valuable expedient to send a special envoy to prepare the ground for an agreement. This seemed an occasion for repeating the expedient as a good way of overcoming the difficulty arising from the indignity inherent in formally making any proposition after the rejection of the Johnson-Clarendon convention. At this point E. H. Hammond, the permanent under-secretary for foreign affairs, Sir Frederick Rogers, colonial under-secretary, and Lord Tenterden, Hammond's forthright assistant, prepared a memorandum on the situation and advised the government that advantage should be taken of the American desire to settle all matters in dispute, and they suggested this should be done by means of a joint commission. Since Canada was so closely involved, it was deemed advisable to choose someone with accurate knowledge of Canadian affairs to sound out the Americans. It was realized that Thornton could not achieve much without committing his government, and thus the choice fell upon Sir John Rose who could ascertain from all American parties what the chances were of "simultaneously agreeing to some beginning of a negotiation" in the direction of a joint commission which, without being erected specifically to settle anything, might arrange how each of the problems could be settled.[7]

Rose was a Scots-Canadian, born in 1820, who came to Canada as a boy, trained as a lawyer in Canada, became solicitor-general in John A. Macdonald's cabinet of 1857. He served from 1864 to 1869 as a member of the commission settling Hudson's Bay Company claims arising from the Oregon treaty of 1846.[8] In 1869 he had been sent by the Canadian government to Washington to discuss with the United States government outstanding matters affecting the two countries: extradition, fisheries, navigation of the St. Lawrence. He met Fish through a mutual friend, Caleb Cushing, and the two corresponded. Professor Long says that he acted as intermediary in London between the United States and Britain. "Keeping in touch with Fish by letter and quietly making known in influential circles in Britain the American Secretary's views—a function which the American ambassador Motley failed to perform as he reflected the extremist attitude of Sumner rather than the moderate one of Fish."[9] Rose was a director of the English financial firm of Morton, Rose and Company, and he had left Canadian politics to become head of the English branch. He was an obvious choice for private negotiator and he was sent to Washington where he arrived on January 9, 1871.

The confidential instructions to Rose, "Seen by Mr. Gladstone, the Queen and the Cabinet," told him that inquiry must emanate from him as a private person engaged in commercial transactions in both England and the United States, and he has "no authority to speak in the name of Her Majesty's Government, still less to pledge them to any opinion or any course of action. . . ." The questions to be discussed are those "so pointedly alluded to in the recent message of the President to Congress." The fisheries are the "most pressing" problem because the president had spoken of "measures of retaliation." There could be a commission to discuss matters. On the *Alabama* claims he may be able to arrive at some definite conclusion as to public opinion, for it is perhaps "the most dangerous from the spirit in which it has been dealt with in the United States; and the exaggerated pretensions which have been put forward by the Government, Legislature and people." But any fair or reasonable opening which the United States should afford would be readily met in a corresponding spirit by the British government.[10]

Rose saw Thornton and later Fish by whom he was received most cordially. The secretary of state said that he was prepared to move by means of a commission. When he talked of territorial cession, Fish was told that "if such an idea entered his calculations . . . it would inevitably postpone a settlement."[11] At their next meeting Fish, on the subject of the *Alabama* claims, remarked that "if John Bull had only at first given some expression of regret at the escape of the ships instead of seeking to justify it, and refusing absolutely all arbitration," the matter would never have attained its present dimensions. Rose found the other members of the cabinet he consulted in favour of an agreement, and the only obstacle was the formidable figure of Charles Sumner, who was reported to be a "monomaniac" on the subject of the claims. When Sumner spoke of the advantages of the annexation of Canada, and in reply Rose pointed out that not a single Canadian constituency favoured annexation,[12] Sumner insisted that certain English statesmen favoured this device, and if he could only see Gladstone and Granville he would soon convince them that there was only one course possible. The American proposals will be very "embarrassing" to England. "If they should propose making the possession of San Juan a *sine qua non,* I feel pretty sure, from some expressions used during the negotiations, that they would recede from that rather than allow the idea of a commission to fall through."[13]

Lord Tenterden, assistant to the permanent under-secretary, E. H. Hammond, was entrusted with the conduct of the correspondence on the British side. On receiving Rose's reports of his progress, Tenterden was particularly wroth on two matters. He did not have much confidence in Rose except on Canadian matters, and he was convinced that Rose was not competent to achieve anything on the *Alabama* claims with which he ought not to "busy" himself. Rose had said that the unnamed Americans with whom he had consulted wanted a payment by Great Britain to cover the *Alabama* claims proper, the reference of claims in respect of other vessels to arbitration, and the cession of the Island of San Juan. Very pertinently Tenterden asked, "What are the Americans to yield in return?" Fish, he felt, "naturally wishes to secure the assent of the Senate and gain public applause by showing that England has made some great concession. He therefore asks that the Alabama Claims may be paid without arbitration and the Island of San Juan ceded by means of a packed Jury of Commissioners."

To Tenterden the issue of San Juan seemed clear, because the United States had on several occasions agreed to arbitrate the dispute; actually, he pointed out, the Senate Foreign Relations Committee had agreed to recommend ratification of the last agreement for arbitration. The suggestion by Rose that the United States might not be able to see their way to authorizing the commissioners to concede arbitration was no more than an attempt to ascertain Rose's "squeezability." To Tenterden the suggestion of cession of the island was ridiculous after the two countries had held it in joint occupation under a "confessedly disputed title" for over a decade, and he bluntly asked, "Is it meant that the British Commissioners are to make a sham fight on this also?"

Tenterden seemed to forget that Rose was reporting what Americans expected to gain from a joint commission and his function was almost solely that of symphathetic interrogator, listener, and reporter. He had no power to make any kind of offer on behalf of his superiors; therefore he became the recipient of the most optimistic American demands. Tenterden was angered by the American optimism, and he was extremely annoyed at the implicit assumption that the functions of the British commissioners "are not defined beyond the suggestion of their being used as dummies." He saw that the Fenian raids claims of the Canadian government and the ordinary British claims of the Civil War were to be ignored by the Americans.[14] It was obviously important to disabuse the minds of the Americans on their San Juan expectations. On the advice of Tenterden, therefore, the foreign secretary deemed it prudent at this point to telegraph Thornton in Washington on January 24, 1871, that no matter what happens "we cannot cede San Juan." Rose's American confidants had made it clear that the United States favoured a commission provided it was confidentially understood that Britain would admit liability for the *Alabama* claims, that liability for losses by other ships should be left to arbitration, that San Juan must be ceded. There was no equivocation about the attitude of the British Government. The telegram was expanded into a despatch of the same date: "Her Majesty's Government cannot cede the Island of San Juan."[15] Unfortunately for the British case, Thornton and Rose deemed it impolitic to pass the message on to the Americans because they feared it might interfere with the appointment of a Joint High Commission.

This was a *faux pas* of great moment because it would have placed before Fish the awkward alternatives of surrendering the island or surrendering the commission. There is little doubt which he would have chosen. Moreover, failure on Britain's part to report this determination in respect of San Juan induced the Americans to believe that San Juan would ultimately be ceded. Fish had asked Rose whether, if the United States declined to arbitrate San Juan, the British would give up the island. When that was reported to the Foreign Office by Rose, Granville had sent his unequivocal reply. In light of the fact that the two countries had twice agreed to refer San Juan to an arbiter, the British were in a strong position, and this dereliction on the part of Thornton and Rose went some way towards undermining it. Only the circumstance that Rose was a temporary government agent, and the fact that Thornton was "a very good fellow," as Tenterden put it, absolved them from severe government censure.[16] Thenceforward, Fish took up the attitude that the Senate would not pass a treaty containing a clause for arbitration of the water boundary.

On January 26 Thornton formally proposed a joint high commission to consider the chief problems, and acceptance was prompt because of "appreciation of the importance of a friendly and complete understanding" between Great Britain and the United States. Such a commission was deemed the best manner of procedure because three countries, Great Britain, the United States, and Canada, were all involved, and any agreement achieved must have regard to Canadian interests as much as to those of the two major powers. The memory of the rejection of the Johnson-Clarendon convention was still too fresh in British minds, and a formula had to be worked out to save British dignity. Accordingly, Fish and Rose agreed that Britain should formally propose a commission to settle all disputes except the *Alabama* claims. The United States would receive this with approval but would suggest the condition that the *Alabama* claims should be included, a condition which the British earnestly desired but felt they could not initiate.

Subsequent action was swift, with the choice of commissioners the next problem. The American choice was not difficult. Hamilton Fish was an indispensable, Justice Samuel Nelson came on as an authority on international law, E. R. Hoar, the attorney-general, was selected to see that the legalities were observed, General Robert Schenck, who had already been selected to replace Motley in London, was an obvious choice, and George H. Williams of Oregon represented the West. On the British side the greatest delay was caused by the selection of a suitable Canadian representative, for it was considered absolutely essential that a Dominion statesman should sit on the commission. Sir John Rose was asked to act, but he refused to do so; moreover, his choice was not acceptable to the Canadian government which preferred one of its own members to sit. When

Sir John A. Macdonald, the prime minister, was invited to take part, as the result of pressure from the governor-general, he accepted on February 8 after pondering the enormous difficulties of the position. Mountague Bernard, professor of International Law at Oxford, who had written on the *Alabama* question, brought legal expertise to the British side of the commission. Lord de Grey, later Marquis of Ripon, was chosen as leader of the British delegation. He was a "Christian Socialist" of considerable diplomatic experience—a former undersecretary, secretary for War, secretary for India, and Gladstone's president of the Council. The wise decision to include a prominent Conservative found expression in the choice of Sir Stafford Northcote, experienced member of commission and formerly governor of the Hudson's Bay Company, and Sir Edward Thornton, British minister at Washington, completed the British group. The assistant secretary of state, J. C. Bancroft Davis, acted as secretary to the American delegates, and Lord Tenterden was his counterpart on the British side.

CHAPTER TEN

NEGOTIATIONS AT WASHINGTON: 1871

THE COMMISSIONERS were given instructions on a comprehensive list of subjects: the fisheries, free navigation of the St. Lawrence, the transit of goods through Maine, the Manitoba boundary, the *Alabama* claims, the claims of British subjects arising from the Civil War, the claims arising from the Fenian raids on Canada, the revision of the rules of maritime neutrality and, of course, the San Juan water boundary. On the boundary, mention is made in the instructions of the British commissioners of the series of negotiations beginning with Lord John Russell's efforts in 1859 to the unfortunate Johnson-Clarendon treaty and the Naturalization Treaty. The latter "having been ratified some months ago, Her Majesty's Government trust that the Government of the United States will no longer hesitate to act upon the Water Boundary Treaty, which should in that case be appended to and form part of the General Treaty for the mode of settlement of all outstanding differences which you are empowered to sign."[1]

The Joint High Commission's procedure was by discussion. Lord de Grey and Hamilton Fish, the respective British and American leaders, decided each evening what should be the points of discussion for the next day and sometimes they arrived at conclusions for mere homologation by their subordinates. Daily protocols were drawn up by the two secretaries, J. C. Bancroft Davis and Lord Tenterden,[2] but these were kept extremely short, largely because Fish wanted to avoid written documents as much as possible, for everything written would ultimately have to go to the Senate. Moreover, it was felt that the daily protocol should not record all the daily happenings "so that, as negotiations went on, the process of give and take, in mutual concessions, should not be impeded by previous recorded action."[3] Indeed the protocols were so brief that the British permanent under-secretary of state for foreign affairs, E. H. Hammond, complained to Tenterden[4] that their brevity made them very difficult for presentation to Parliament. The British and American commissioners were kept apart in separate rooms while the respective leaders discussed opinions. The leaders then returned to their compatriots to explain their rivals' position and to advise and initiate discussion upon a plan of campaign. The leaders thereafter met to thrash out a settlement acceptable to both sides, all the commissioners subsequently convening to deal formally with the points they had agreed upon. Much delay was caused on a number of occasions by the British commissioners' need to refer home for instructions on specific points, and there were times when the Americans, who were virtually in possession of full powers of decision, were exasperated at the vexatious amendments introduced by the other side on instructions from London. The very slowness of the procedure, however, made for thoroughness.

The British in general favoured what de Grey called "unrestricted arbitration," and they would have placed nearly everything within the purview of an arbiter. Fish, briefed by President Grant, was more specific in his demands, for he was aware that the Senate would not agree thus simply to dispose of all the important issues to be tackled. For him there was always lurking in the shadows the menacing figure of Charles Sumner, the enemy of the administration who might secure rescission of any agreement Fish might conclude. Grant and Fish had still not given up hope of acquiring Canada and they would have used the manifest British desire to dispose of all outstanding difficulties between the countries to achieve the cession of the Dominion. Since nearly all the matters at issue related directly to Canada, it was insinuated that cession of the Dominion would settle all at one stroke. All prevailing disputes except the *Alabama* claims and the revision of maritime neutrality law could be summarily settled by the transfer of Canada to the United States. There was also reiteration of the hint that such cession could be used to liquidate the claims in spite of Thornton's emphatic assurance that "it is impossible to connect the question of Canadian independence with the Alabama Claims; not even to the extent of providing for the reference of the question of independence to a popular vote of the people of the Dominion." This last mentioned project was the solution favoured by the president.

The United States secretary of state felt that there was a certain lack of responsibility about the Canadian government which was apt to presume upon British backing and to hide behind the obvious British reluctance to implement the much vaunted colonial policy of letting the colonies go whenever they chose to detach themselves. Canada interposed a positive obstacle between Great Britain and the United States, and while Fish was politic enough to disclaim to de Grey any desire to annex Canada because, as he said, the United States already had enough territory, he did press at least for an independent Canada. To this de Grey was able to give the stock British reply that, if the people of Canada ever expressed a desire "in an authentic manner" to secede, it would be the duty of Great Britain to acquiesce. But, he was careful to add, a question of that kind could never form part of an international arrangement.[5]

The earlier discussions of the Joint High Commission, which began its meetings February 27, were concerned mainly with the *Alabama* claims and the fisheries. The British had accepted for reference to London the American proposal that they should purchase a right to the Canadian inshore fisheries while the *Alabama* claims should go to arbitration. It was not until March 15 that the water boundary was introduced. By that time the British commissioners had been forcibly reminded of Canada's stake in San Juan, for they had received from the Foreign Office copy of a despatch from Governor A. Musgrave of British Columbia to Lord Kimberley, the colonial secretary. Musgrave had forwarded copy of a resolution of the Legislative Council of British Columbia stressing the great importance of San Juan to the Dominion of Canada, though "Her Majesty's Government are already so fully informed with regard to the Island of San Juan that I need not offer any observations on this subject." The Legislative Council's resolution asked the government to make representations to the British government upon "the great importance of the Island of San Juan to the Dominion of Canada as well as the undoubted claim of the Crown to the same...."[6]

The British initiated discussion by proposing submission of the controversy to arbitration, that is, action on the basis of the Johnson-Clarendon convention, but the Americans refused to entertain this, asserting that there was no hope of the Senate's agreeing to submit the question to an outsider. They pointed out that by using one of the methods sometimes employed by Congress for rejecting a proposed measure, namely, by refusing to take the Johnson-Clarendon convention into consideration, the Senate had shown clearly that they were totally opposed to arbitration. Surely, it was argued, the British and American commissioners were as competent to come to a decision as any arbitrator.

The British representatives refused to agree that an adjustment could be arrived at without outside assistance, but they professed themselves willing to listen to the American arguments. This gesture produced a long, good-humoured, but barren discussion upon the intentions of the negotiators of the treaty of Oregon of 1846 and upon the meaning of Article I of that treaty which provided for delineation of the boundary line between the mainland and Vancouver Island. With the exception of some recently discovered letters of Edward Everett, United States minister at London 1841-5, neither side was able, however, to adduce any valid fresh evidence. Lord de Grey announced the next day that he and his colleagues had perused the new correspondence, but found that it could not alter their views. He went on to ask for an explanation of the United States' seemingly incomprehensible opposition to arbitration, which they had twice before agreed to use to settle the water boundary; further, it was a method of adjustment which was acknowledged to be fair and reasonable by eminent men in both countries.

This reiteration of the virtues of arbitration by the British demanded a vigorous and conclusive answer, and that was forthcoming. The British were told on March 16 there was a feeling in the Senate and in the United States generally that the American negotiators in 1846 had been deliberately misled; that Lord Aberdeen, the foreign secretary, after having conversed with Louis McLane, the United States minister in London, on May 15, 1846, when it was agreed that the Haro channel should form the boundary west of the mainland, had immediately thereafter sent for Sir J. H. Pelly of the Hudson's Bay Company and proceeded so to word his despatch of May 18 to Richard Pakenham, British minister in Washington, that the phraseology of the treaty could afterwards be strained to the interpretation put upon it in subsequent negotiations by the British government. It will be remembered in this connection that the words of the Aberdeen draft were incorporated *in toto* in the treaty of 1846. In view of this, said the Americans, the United States could not consent to refer the question to arbitration or to discuss it on any other basis than acknowledgment of their right.

This slanderous and grossly untrue allegation, so unworthy of the American negotiators, roused their British counterparts on the commission to high indignation. De Grey stopped the Americans at once in peremptory terms, and he rejected "unhesitatingly, positively and in the strongest manner" the imputation which was thus cast upon the integrity and good faith of a statesman notable for the high standard of his conduct and his unblemished reputation. The false allegation had the immediate effect of stiffening the attitude of the British commissioners and, instead of receding from their position, they now demanded that the United States should suggest a mode of settlement alternative to arbitration.

The insinuation was clear: if the Americans could not suggest a suitable alternative, the water boundary and perhaps even the whole negotiation, would be abandoned. When the British retired to discuss the affair, Sir Stafford Northcote, whom Tenterden had written off as "too conciliatory" before the commission actually met, expressed extreme anger and pressed for abruptly breaking up the conference. An unofficial representative of the Conservative opposition, Northcote had important status, for the Gladstone government had been most careful to secure the aquiescence of Lord Derby's Opposition in agreeing to the Joint High Commission.[7] Northcote was the natural champion of his eminent fellow Conservative and former political colleague, Lord Aberdeen, who had died in 1860. Till the conclusion of the commission Northcote remained resolutely of opinion that if the British delegates had left the room in protest at the moment of the false American allegations, and had thus abruptly broken up the conference, the Americans would have been convinced of the earnestness of the British and would have been shocked into seeking means to re-open the conference on a more satisfactory footing.[8]

The majority of the British commissioners, however, decided that a dignified protest by de Grey against the American line of argument, together with refusal to make any further British suggestion on the water boundary, would suffice. De Grey decided that the best course would be to go on with the other questions until they had brought them to the point of settlement and then appeal to the Americans whether they were prepared to lose all by being unreasonable on San Juan. Northcote was not convinced of the wisdom of this policy, for he was "afraid they may take our tameness now as an encouragement to believe that we are anxious to get a settlement, and that we shall at the last moment give up San Juan rather than fail, and this will lead to a game of brag in which I have no great confidence in our proving a match for them."[9]

The American reply to this stratagem could hardly have been more startling. The Americans proposed that, as it was clear that there was a misunderstanding about the proper interpretation of the treaty of 1846, the two countries should agree to abrogate it and negotiate afresh the whole question of the boundary line west of the Rocky Mountains. The British answered that they would have to take the proposal *ad avizandum*. Surprised at the shock his proposal had caused, Fish explained that the term "annulling" was too vague, and he and his colleagues had merely meant to suggest a rearrangement of the border line in whole or in part.[10] The hand of the secretary of state is apparent in this remarkable American proposition. Still mesmerized by the illusion of a British Columbia clamouring for admission to the Union, he was confident that a resettlement of the boundary would bring the colony under the American flag. The intention underlying his unusual proposal was to follow it up by an offer to secure the cession, by sale or otherwise, of the whole of British Columbia, leaving the Rockies as boundary.[11] Though Thornton might confidently assure him that not a single Canadian constituency wanted annexation to the United States, Fish thought he knew better about British Columbia.

In private conversation de Grey found Fish "very ugly" on the water boundary. The secretary of state made it very clear that the United States would never be party to any treaty which left the passage of the straits under the absolute command of Britain; she must have San Juan. As we have seen, in the negotiations leading up to the appointment of the Joint High Commission, Thornton and Rose had been instructed, both by telegram and despatch, in unequivocal terms, to make it clear to the Americans that Britain would never cede San Juan. But both had omitted to convey this to the American representatives. Rose's failure was most unfortunate from a British point of view because Fish came to the commission quite unaware of the intractable nature of the British attitude on San Juan. Now no amount of threat by de Grey to Fish "in the strongest terms" that insistence on their attitude by the United States would lead to breaking off the whole negotiation had the slightest effect.[12] De Grey, therefore, without even referring the latest American proposition to his government, rejected the proposal to abrogate the Oregon treaty of 1846.

Fish's uncompromising attitude, however, had one important result. It induced de Grey to make what was, from a British point of view, a fatal concession. He had come to the conclusion that San Juan was the most difficult of the questions facing the commission, and he now decided that, if the Americans persisted in rejecting the offer of arbitration adumbrated in the Johnson-Clarendon convention, he would offer to adopt the Middle Channel as the boundary line, with the navigation of all channels between the mainland and Vancouver Island free to both countries; he would also agree that there should be an undertaking on both sides not to fortify any of the islands of the San Juan group, an idea which had originated with Fish. He decided to put the new proposition to Fish privately, "almost in the form of an ultimatum," and, if it was not acceptable, he would postpone the question of San Juan till everything else was settled "when they will be much disinclined to break off just in sight of Port."[13] Thus de Grey had resiled from the strong British line of a few weeks before. It is true that adoption of the Middle Channel would leave San Juan to Britain and make possession of the island the fundamental issue totally divorced from any question of interpretation of the terms of the treaty. But the very mention of compromise vitiated the whole British case on the water boundary. It is equally true that this was not the first occasion upon which such a concession had been made. The British government of 1856 had instructed its commissioner, Captain Prevost, to seek to induce his American colleague to accept the Middle Channel as boundary. It had also been suggested at Washington by Lord Napier as a compromise acceptable to the British. And it had been the line of "honourable compromise" suggested by Lord John Russell in August, 1859. So far as the current negotiations were concerned, the first bastion in the British position had been pierced. The secretary of state must have smiled when Thornton let him know privately about the same time that the British would accept the Middle Channel.[14] Fish's allusions to the non-fortification proposal in his subsequent discussion with de Grey assumed that all the islands, San Juan included, would be American, an adroit variation of what de Grey actually proposed. If the United States accepted the Middle Channel and left San Juan to Britain, the British would readily agree not to fortify it. But if the Americans got the island and also agreed not to fortify it, the position was different and unacceptable to Britain. Fish and Schenck both assured de Grey that their difficulty was finding a solution acceptable to the Senate, while Williams, spokesman of the West, refused to consider any concession whatsoever on San Juan.

The decision of the British to postpone further discussion on San Juan upset the Americans, and Bancroft Davis hinted that San Juan might be left out of the final treaty altogether. However, when approval of the de Grey offer came from London,[15] and de Grey formally offered the Middle Channel, Fish pressed strongly for San Juan. De Grey was adamant, telling him "if we did not settle San Juan we should settle nothing."[16] The secretary made it clear again that the United States could not run the risk of abandoning San Juan to Great Britain, and once more he talked of purchase, direct or indirect, of the island by his country. For the first time, however, the secretary hinted at a reduction in his demands when he suggested that if all the islands except San Juan were ceded to the United States he might agree to arbitrate San Juan alone. It was even suggested unofficially that the San Juan Archipelago might be exchanged for a piece of Alaska.[17] Of course, if all else failed, the parties might agree to continue the joint occupation of the island for an indefinite number of years.

Meanwhile, de Grey assured Lord Granville that on the water boundary he was still speaking "stiffly."[18] Tenterden and Bancroft Davis were also having their discussions on the matters in dispute. Tenterden reminded his American counterpart that the *Alabama* claims arrangement effected by the commission was contingent upon all other matters being satisfactorily settled, and he also reminded him that Britain would never surrender San Juan. Davis's answer was that British Columbia was about to join Confederation which would mean that San Juan would become a Canadian question, and he hinted that the United States might give up the island in return for territory "or some other equivalent" from England.[19]

The more or less even flow of negotiation was not interrupted. One concession begot another. When the British offered the Middle Channel Fish was magnanimous enough to assure de Grey, on April 15, that if all questions were settled the United States would consent to refer the water boundary to arbitration. A general settlement thus seemed to be within reach.[20] Fish and President Grant had been almost solely responsible for the presentation of American policy up to this point, but now that some of the difficulties were resolved the secretary deemed it prudent to consult members of the Senate.[21] On April 13 Fish got the President to agree to arbitrate San Juan as "a last resort," and Senator Chandler, when consulted, approved this "if nothing better can be had."[22] Fish was able to tell de Grey that if the fisheries and *Alabama* claims could be settled on "somewhat reasonable lines," he would be disposed to agree to arbitrate San Juan, though Macdonald's stubbornness on the fisheries made him think "there was no inducement to consider the possibility of" arbitration for San Juan.[23]

It was now the problem of the fisheries which was proving the greatest obstacle to the conclusion of a general settlement. The *Alabama* claims issue was no longer offering insuperable difficulty, and it was agreed that the claims should be submitted to an international arbitration tribunal at Geneva which should decide the degree and extent of British responsibility and the extent of damages, if any. On the fisheries the Canadians wanted an agreement which would resuscitate the arrangements of the Reciprocity Treaty of 1854, and they were determined to see that the fisheries were not to be a makeweight on an *Alabama* claims or water boundary agreement. But from the outset Fish made it clear that Congress would never agree to reciprocity, for any alteration of the tariff would have to pass both Houses of Congress. The duties which the

Canadians wanted to have repealed principally affected Pennsylvania and the western states whereas it was Maine and Massachusetts which sought fisheries concessions. Very naturally the industrial workers of Pennsylvania were unwilling to give up protective duties as a *quid pro quo* for fishing rights for New England.

Sir John A. Macdonald insisted that any final fisheries agreement must be acceptable to Canada in the same way that an *Alabama* claims settlement must be acceptable to Great Britain. The Canadian prime minister found himself in an unenviable position. "If a majority of my colleagues should at any time conclude to accept terms which I do not approve of, I must, of course, either protest and withdraw, or remain on the Commission and trust to the non-ratification of the treaty by Canada."[24] The fundamental issue between Macdonald on the one hand and his colleagues on the commission on the other was whether all the questions before the commission, including the fisheries, were to be considered as imperial problems and therefore more important than purely Canadian ones. Macdonald argued, emphatically and tenaciously, that only an arrangement on the fisheries acceptable to Canada should be considered, while de Grey and the others would have accepted what they considered an equitable adjustment viewed from the angle of the give and take necessary to achieve a settlement covering all the questions in dispute. In other words, Canada should not wreck the commission by insisting upon what the commissioners deemed impossible fisheries terms. De Grey got sympathy for his view from Granville who informed him on March 25 ". . . we cannot allow our friendly relations with foreign countries to be affected by unreasonable opposition from the Dominion."[25] The British leader was emphatic that failure to settle the fisheries would sink the whole negotiation, and if, for instance, the *Alabama* claims were not settled, war might easily ensue. To this Macdonald retorted that the British had been in error from the very start by commingling all matters for discussion.[26]

There was somewhat natural confusion regarding the status and role of Sir John. Was he a member of the Joint High Commission as a Canadian minister or as a British subject? It was a question that was never answered. Macdonald maintained that he was primarily an ambassador of Canada, "acting directly as an officer of the Imperial Government, over which commission, of course, the Canadian Government has no control."[27] De Grey and the other British members of the commission were in varying degrees proponents of the view that the paramount interest of the commission was to effect a means of arriving at a lasting peace between the two countries. Indeed in the early days of the Joint High Commission de Grey reported to Granville that he would make it clear to Macdonald that he was representing Great Britain rather than Canada.[28] De Grey said: "We of the English portion of the Commission are not separate members of a conference acting each by himself, but we are jointly the plenipotentiaries of our Sovereign, bound by the instructions which we receive from Her Majesty's Government. . . ."[29] There is something to be said for de Grey's point of view because Macdonald took little or no part in the discussions on matters other than the fisheries. Even on San Juan, which was a Canadian more than an instrinsically British problem, he had not made up his mind to adopt a purely Canadian attitude; yet the importance of San Juan had been officially stressed by his fellow Canadians of British Columbia which was then on the point of joining Confederation. It is true that he believed the American case on the water boundary to be superior to Great Britain's, "stronger in equity than ours which can only be maintained by the most technical construction of the actual words of the Treaty."[30] And in prophetic mood later he said: "I am inclined to think that in a quarter of a century the San Juan question will solve itself. If the Dominion is then a portion of the Empire or an independent state, it will be manifest to America that there is no chance of annexation. . . ."[31]

On the other hand, de Grey was inclined to be precipitate in making up his mind on the fisheries, a purely Canadian question, and he was impatient of protracted opposition to the American proposals on the subject lest it might jeopardize a comprehensive agreement. In the early stages of the negotiation he was kept in the dark about the real desires of the British government in the matter, and Fish seems to have perceived the dichotomy. Granville's early summary of the situation was neat: "We cannot press Canada to exchange proprietary rights for tariff concessions only."[32] The Canadians, mindful of the fact that the fisheries were Canada's "greatest commercial asset," opposed and the British favoured, sale of the fisheries in perpetuity. De Grey accepted at its face value Fish's emphatic assurance that Congress could never be induced to accept Macdonald's demand for renewal of reciprocity.

By the middle of April it was apparent that the Americans would settle the fisheries problem by agreeing to free fish and the purchase of the inshore fisheries at a price to be decided by an arbitrator. In the eyes of the British commissioners except Sir John this was "an equitable arrangement."[33] Macdonald refused sale in perpetuity; he wanted money plus the admission free into the United States of Canadian coal, salt, fish, and lumber. The other British commissioners were convinced that the Americans would never accept Macdonald's terms, and Macdonald for his part was sure that no less was acceptable to the Canadian Parliament. "I was resolved not to let any blame be attached to Canada . . . and thus strengthen the hands of the party in England who consider Canada a burden to be got rid of and an obstacle to friendly relations with the United States."[34]

In view of the impasse on the fisheries it was not surprising that de Grey now took the gloomy view that "if no arrangement can be come to about the Fisheries there seems to be little prospect of any result to our negotiations."[35] "If you do not back us up against Macdonald he will be quite unmanageable and I see no chance of our coming to an arrangement."[36] De Grey came to the conclusion that Macdonald opposed the views of his colleagues in order to be able to tell his Canadian government friends that his hand had been forced.[37] The British commissioners hoped that arbitration might now become the basic principle of a comprehensive agreement which would mean the triumph of a principle they had sought from the outset of the negotiations.[38] Thus if Macdonald would agree to it for determining the total sum to be paid for the fisheries, the way would be clear to adopt it also for the water boundary and thus evade the Senate's rooted objection to arbitration on the San Juan question.[39]

The dour Canadian's intransigence was irritating his colleagues as much as the Americans, and there were displays of temper among the British commissioners. Macdonald, however, was good-natured and took all the adverse criticism in good part.[40] Nevertheless he did not conceal his exasperation and frustration in his correspondence with his Canadian colleagues in Ottawa. Thus he told Cartier: "Canada must be either English or American, and if protection was denied by England, Canada might as well go while she had some property left with which she could make an arrangement with the United States."[41] Only extreme irritation could produce views like this, for Macdonald's whole political career was a manifestation of faith in Canadian nationhood. He realized that extension of British institutions and the British way of life, not to mention British capital and British markets, were all essential to a developing Canada. No Canadian who believed in Canadian nationhood could ever look with equanimity upon the intrigues and publicized schemes of American annexationists.

The British cabinet were at first unanimous in their opinion that the commissioners should "hold a little" with Macdonald, and Prime Minister Gladstone himself was the champion of a policy of tolerance. "I do not . . . feel at all more inclined to concuss (as the Scotch say) Canada into an arrangement about the Fisheries. On the contrary, I have fears lest our Commissioners in their anxiety to settle all disputes should virtually make the acceptance of some Fisheries arrangement a British claim upon Canada. We ought not to let our own credit, or even that of the Commission, weigh a single hair in the balance. If we place a burden or apparent burden upon Canada, we shall pay for it dearly, shall never hear the last of it, nay may perhaps tempt Canada to say "if gifts are to be made to the United States at our expense, surely we had better make them ourselves, and have the credit of them."[42] But even Gladstone's patience could be exhausted, and he feared that the whole settlement might be in jeopardy if Macdonald would not climb down. To him the latest American proposal was eminently reasonable. Accordingly, after allowing several days to elapse for diminution of Macdonald's claims, and beset by constant promptings from de Grey, the British government eventually sent word that negotiations should be concluded on the basis of the American offer. Macdonald had to give way, after threatening to resign from the commission, though he made it clear to de Grey "that the arrangements were decidedly injurious to Canada, whose interests had been sacrificed, and made altogether of secondary importance, for the sake of getting a settlement of the Alabama and San Juan matters."[43]

Developments on the water boundary negotiations contributed to this fisheries development. De Grey telegraphed home on April 18 that the Americans would consent to arbitrate San Juan if a fisheries agreement based on arbitration was also reached. Granville replied privately by cable at once, telling de Grey that Great Britain would accept the American fisheries offer of free fish and a sum of money determined by arbitration.[44] On April 19, therefore, the way was clear for the commission to return to consideration of San Juan. De Grey proposed to the Americans that the Middle Channel should be the boundary line with the navigation of all channels free and open to both sides. Fish said that he could not refuse to discuss the water boundary, but he and his colleagues had grave objections to the Middle Channel as boundary; it was intricate and tortuous, and they could not accept it as being meant by the treaty of 1846. If the British would accept Haro channel as boundary, the United States would be prepared to neutralize all channels; she would undertake to erect no fortifications on the islands and to respect the property and claims of British subjects on them. De Grey asserted that the British government could never let San Juan go to the

United States unless an arbitrator so stipulated. He urged the Americans to agree to reference of the disputed line to an arbitrator, and he indicated that no other proposal would be entertained by his government.[45]

Fish replied that if all the other questions could be satisfactorily adjusted, the United States would agree to put the water boundary to arbitration, that is, an arbiter would be asked to decide between Haro and Rosario channels as to which was the true line. De Grey expressed regret that only two lines were to be considered, to which Fish replied that the United States wanted a decision not a compromise. The Middle Channel was scarcely practicable for navigation; it was tortuous and it would leave the possessions of the two countries in such close proximity that smuggling would become rampant. Fish's case against the Middle Channel was thus by no means formidable, but de Grey found himself unable to answer it adequately. He did observe, however, that an alternative, compromise line had been contemplated in the Stanley-Johnson protocol and in the Johnson-Clarendon convention. Fish retorted that this was one of the reasons for the rejection of the convention, and he made it clear that no argument could be adduced to convert the Senate to accept an alternative line.[46]

Fish had been struck by the vehemence with which the British commissioners had denounced his reflections on the British negotiators of 1846 and so, for the dual purpose of vindicating his statement and mollifying the British, he proposed that both governments might submit to the arbitrator as evidence "the contemporary correspondence including the instructions to their Envoys, any communications of facts and declarations such as that of Lord Aberdeen and the testimony of the diplomatic Representatives of either side."[47] De Grey smelled a rat, but he was not familiar enough with the diplomatic correspondence of the controversy to appreciate that the United States rested their case on the water boundary primarily on the contemporaneous evidence. Thus it was that he accepted Fish's statement on evidence. "Either party may include in the evidence to be considered by the Arbitrator the official correspondence on the subject between the two Governments; the contemporaneous debate thereon in either the Houses of Congress or Parliament; the official statements heretofore made by its own agents of interviews with the agents of the other party with reference to the Treaty of June 18, 1846 and the statements of any person who was a Cabinet Minister of either Government at the time the said Treaty was concluded."[48]

The comment on this by Lord Granville, written at the side of the despatch, is striking: "I believe neither claim to be strictly tenable, but if this is the decision of the arbitrator some time hence, we shall be no worse than at present, and a compromise might then be negotiated." In other words, the British hoped the arbitrator would declare that the Middle Channel and neither Haro nor Rosario channels fulfilled the terms of the treaty, for they had accepted the American commissioners' refusal "to entertain the idea of a settlement on the basis of the Douglas [Middle] Channel."[49]

All that was now needed was to choose a suitable arbitrator. Fish proposed the emperor of Germany or of Russia or Brazil, contending that Austria was too much under English influence. De Grey referred the matter to London, though he knew there was no chance of the Russian emperor's being chosen. He gave Fish the choice of Brazil or Germany, and the secretary of state chose the latter.[50] On yet another point the British gave way. De Grey sought the introduction of a provision for the mutual free navigation of all the channels in the disputed area, but they did not press this in the face of very strong objection by the United States Commissioners. Approval for the San Juan articles came on April 27, and the way was clear for their formal conclusion.

In the meantime the British government's decision on the fisheries had reached Washington, for the "positive order" that de Grey had exhorted Granville to transmit was despatched on April 21. The commissioners were instructed to negotiate on the basis of free fish and payment of a sum fixed by arbitration; in other words, the Canadian objections were rejected and coercion was applied. The British government had been much influenced by de Grey's report that failure to coerce Macdonald would mean a patched up treaty which omitted the fisheries, and it was not even certain that the United States would accept such an arrangement.

Thus unceremoniously defeated on the fisheries matter, Sir John A. Macdonald had more hopes of the Fenian raids claims. They had long been in the Canadian eye, and Lord Lisgar, the governor-general, had reminded the Colonial Office of the Fenian raids claims as long before as January 26, 1871, when he forwarded a memorandum of the Canadian Privy Council on the subject. Macdonald soon discovered that Thornton and Rose, in the pre-Joint High Commission negotiations, had neglected to make it clear that Canada's claims arising from losses incurred by the Fenian raids were to be matter of negotiation at Washington, and the Americans refused to admit the subject. Thornton had indeed mentioned the losses to Fish in a letter of February 1, but the secretary of state maintained that this was the first mention of the subject made to him. Actually, as de Grey was aware, this was not the first mention made to the Americans, for Sir Frederick Bruce, on instructions from Lord Stanley, the foreign secretary, had raised the subject at the State Department.[51]

The British cabinet were well aware of the Canadian views on the Fenian raid claims, and on February 21 Gladstone had told Granville that the Joint High Commission ought to do something about them. While admitting that he was "most commonly" against the colony, the prime minister confessed that their claims on the Fenian raids were "equitable."[52] A month later, on March 25, when Macdonald protested to de Grey at neglect of the Fenian raids claims, the British leader was told by Granville that the British government would pay Canada for losses caused by the Fenian raids, though this was not be to regarded as a precedent but rather as a part of the final settlement between Great Britain and the United States.[53] This offer, however, was not implemented, and the British attitude was summed up in a despatch of as late date as May 1: "You should press Fenian claims but if the opposition is serious you may state that we agree not to include them in the present treaty, the more readily as a portion of the Claims are of a constructive and inferential character."[54]

Forced to accept the fisheries clauses of the 1871 Treaty of Washington against her wishes, and her Fenian raids claims repudiated by the United States, Canada could with justice claim to have come badly out of the treaty. Macdonald saw the dilemma: ". . . I must in some way manage to have my non-concurrence unmistakably and publicly affirmed. The simplest mode of doing it would be to refrain from signing the Treaty, and the only doubt I have as to the propriety of this course is the apprehension lest the absence of my signature might lead the Senate to believe that there was no chance of the fishery articles being confirmed by our Parliament, and thus render them less willing to ratify the articles relating to the Alabama and San Juan matters." [55]

And so, after weeks of courageous battle against hopeless odds, Macdonald had to accept the inevitable and sign the treaty. It was signed by all the commissioners on May 8, 1871. Articles 34 to 42 dealt with the water boundary, referring the controversy to the arbitration of the Emperor of Germany, who was to decide which of the two channels, Haro or Rosario, "is most in accordance with the true interpretation of the Treaty of June 18, 1846." [56]

The Treaty of Washington, a triumph for the principle of arbitration, undoubtedly represented a great step forward in Anglo-American relations, and besides closing an era of uncertainty and mistrust, it opened a new one of arbitration and closer relationship. In addition to laying down important new laws on neutrality, the treaty had the great merit of establishing means for the removal of all major grounds of dispute between the two countries. Especially important was the implicit acceptance by the United States that Canada was determined to remain British. As for the actual terms, neither side was completely satisfied, though it is probable that the best possible terms were secured by both. At any rate the press of both countries generally hailed the treaty with enthusiasm, and the only noteworthy adverse critic was Lord John Russell, who had less reason to criticize than almost anyone. It was he who had initiated the policy of proposing the Middle Channel and thus ruining the case for the Rosario line; then, later, by reserving the claim to the Rosario he liquidated the case for the Middle Channel. On the whole, it is true to say that the Americans had been more successful, but the British losses were deemed minor. Though the British had to apologize for the depredations of the *Alabama* they had come to agree that the Americans were due an apology, and only the most recalcitrant diehards persisted in denying that the Americans were right in complaining of negligence in allowing the famous ship to put to sea.

The adjustment of the fisheries was hardly a British success, but to have held on to them would have meant continual irritating disputes about encroachments. Canada rather than Britain was the immediate loser, and Canada was the loser too in the matter of the Fenian raids claims, for the failure to deal with them was heinous carelessness. The decision to put San Juan to arbitration was a wise one from the point of view of both the United States and Great Britain, but the agreement to restrict the arbitrator's choice to Haro and Rosario channels was a resounding victory for Fish and company. The latter took the correct line that a conclusion and not a compromise was required, and the decision to restrict the choice, in view of the earlier "We won't cede San Juan" protestation by both sides, would prove most advantageous to the United States.

The British could have argued, however, that the Grant administration, which had assumed office under the best possible auspices in respect of the annexation of Canada, had been decisively rebuffed. Secretary Fish had started off in the saddle resolved to get Canada, his views on the matter being coloured by a number of notable factors. "Manifest destiny" ambitions were by no means dormant, and Americans still loved to acquire territory. Moreover, an administration could always use territorial acquisition to cover up inadequacies and failures of policy. Further, the acquisition of Canada had been for so long an unfulfilled American ambition, that Fish saw himself gaining renown by securing the Dominion. At one stroke he would gratify Grant and mollify Sumner, pre-eminent apostle of the annexation of Canada and former personal friend of the secretary of state. He had held grimly on, therefore, to his Canadian ambitions right through the Red River and British Columbia disappointments until he was left with only San Juan to reward him. The British could be pardoned, therefore, for congratulating themselves that Fish's schemes for the "mountain" of Canada had had to be content with the "mouse" of San Juan.

The great difficulty affecting both sides was that the possession of San Juan had been in dispute for so long that the side giving it up would be sure to lose face. This was the "point of honour" so often referred to by negotiators of both countries. After its being held in joint occupation under disputed title for so long, it was unfortunately inevitable that one side would eventually be sharply disappointed. That is why Lord Granville telegraphed both Thornton and Rose in January, 1871, "we cannot cede San Juan." And that is why Hamilton Fish employed exactly the same forthright phrase in his early discussions with Thorn-ton and later with de Grey. The military importance of the island, which had so bedevilled the controversy in the 1850's, was still not lost sight of, but it now took a minor place in importance to the fear of the loss of face. The Americans attached more importance than the British to the military importance of San Juan largely because the British believed that, in an emergency, their naval pre-dominance would enable them to seize possession of the island. The Americans found themselves constantly beset by the importunities of the government of Washington Territory which believed that possession of San Juan was essential to offset the British control of Vancouver Island. The British felt that face could be saved if an arbiter awarded San Juan to the Americans, and this fact goes far to explain their enthusiasm for arbitration. Thus de Grey said: "If such a conces-sion [surrender of San Juan] is to be made, it can only be under the decision of an arbitrator and after full discussion of the respective claims of the two coun-tries." In other words, we do not care if you have the island, but you must get it only from an arbitrator. Thornton spoke to Fish in exactly similar terms.

CHAPTER ELEVEN

THE AWARD OF 1871

CAPTAIN PREVOST'S OFFER of his services to the British government for preparation of the case to be presented to the arbitrator was accepted with thanks,
promise of every facility being given him. In preparing the case Prevost left
nothing undone in making the best use of his arguments, and he examined
almost every source of information. His earlier experience as British member of
the Boundary Commission in 1856-7 proved invaluable. For instance, he prepared a series of questions for the consideration of Sir James Douglas; he had Sir
Edward Thornton ransack the embassy archives at Washington; he wrote to the
Admiralty for all obtainable material relating to the Meares voyage of 1789-91;
he opened communication with Lord Lisgar, governor-general of Canada, from
whom he secured first-hand information; he learned from Admiral Gordon, who
commanded the *Cormorant* at Vancouver Island in 1846, that the Rosario and
never the Haro Strait was used by him at that time; he enlisted the aid of Sir
Travers Twiss, formerly professor of International Law at King's College, London, and author of a work on the Oregon question, to prepare his case; he
consulted the log of the *Raccoon*, 1813-18; he secured, through the medium of the
Spanish ambassador, translations of much of the relevant data about all early
Spanish voyages from the Spanish archives; then he succeeded, through Lord
Lisgar, in having J. S. McCreight, attorney-general of British Columbia, obtain
the testimony of local master mariners as to the extent to which Rosario Strait
was used in 1846.[1]

It cannot be justly argued, therefore, that the British case was ill-prepared or
neglected consideration of any of the vital available evidence. Prevost had conducted the British process ever since attempts had been made to decide between
Rosario and Haro channel; he was familiar with every argument, both American
and British, and he had himself been on the scene of the dispute. We must then
subscribe to the view of Lord Tenterden of the Foreign Office that the case was
"very well drawn and presented a clear, concise and closely-sustained argument."[2] It met with Canadian approval too, which was certainly not its least
valuable virtue. Governor J. W. Trutch of British Columbia, after having
discussed it with his Executive Council, pronounced it "complete and conclusive
and admirably argued throughout."[3]

Before the preparation of the British counter-case Sir Travers Twiss became
personally involved in a *cause célèbre*, and had to retire from public life. Mr. F.
S. Reilly of the Foreign Office was chosen to succeed him, and he proved to be
as thorough in his work as his predecessors.[4] The Foreign Office records show
that he caused to be prepared for him an authoritative account of the early
history of the Hudson's Bay Company; he went over the reports of all Senate
debates on the Oregon treaty; he examined all the maps at the Foreign Office;

he consulted all Pakenham's and Aberdeen's correspondence of 1845-6; he asked the United States for copies of all McLane's correspondence with Secretary of State James Buchanan relating to the Oregon dispute in the same years. From all this he produced the British Second and Definitive Statement, presented to the arbitrator on June 11.

The United States' case was prepared by George Bancroft, American minister at Berlin, who had been a member of the Polk cabinet in 1846. He had therefore taken a responsible, active part in the most important and vital stages of the development of the controversy, and he had followed the case throughout its progress. Further, he had been particularly prominent in asserting the extreme American claims. He had strongly deprecated the trend of the negotiations after the Civil War and deplored particularly the arrangement of January, 1869, whereby the president of the Swiss Republic was to arbitrate the water boundary dispute with all three channels within his purview. When he heard of the terms of the protocol framed by Reverdy Johnson and Lord Stanley he immediately wrote his government urging them not to allow a compromise line to be considered, advising at the same time that the king of Prussia should be appointed arbitrator. The conduct of the question in 1871-2, the first presentation of the case as well as the reply to the British case were every word composed by Bancroft.[5]

On August 18, 1871, the German emperor agreed to act as arbitrator; on December 11 the American statement was presented; Prevost arrived in Berlin two days after this and presented the British case.[6]

Generally speaking, it is correct to say that the British based their case for Rosario Strait as line of boundary on the words of the treaty of 1846, while the Americans inclined more to the evidence of contemporary statesmen. The British, if they wanted to use contemporary evidence would have relied more on that of contemporary mariners. The Americans maintained that Haro Strait must be the channel meant in 1846 because it was the widest, deepest, shortest, most suitable, and most conspicuous channel; the British, for their part, insisted that Rosario was more navigable and its flow was less impeded by currents. Both adduced a number of charts and maps to substantiate their opinions, though both were able to deduce different opinions from the same map. The Americans said the chief purpose of the treaty was to give Vancouver Island to Great Britain; the British replied that the main purpose was, as the preamble states, to end a state of doubt respecting the sovereignty of the area.

The German emperor submitted the whole dispute to three experts and jurists, Professor Heinrich Kiepert, professor of Geography in the University of Berlin, Councillor Levin Goldschmidt of the Imperial High Court of Commerce, and Dr. Ferdinand Grimm, vice-president of the High Court, who delivered their opinions in September, 1872. There was a majority report signed by Professor Kiepert and Dr. Grimm, and a minority one prepared by Dr. Goldschmidt. All three conferred in an unsuccessful attempt to produce a unanimous report. The German emperor adopted the arguments of the majority and gave his decision accordingly: "We, William, by the grace of God, German Emperor, etc. . . . find after examination of the Treaty between the Government of Her Britannic Majesty and that of the United States of America dated at Washington, May 6 [8], 1871, by virtue of which the above-named Governments have, after taking into consideration the statement of the experts and jurists appointed by us to report upon the contents of the respective cases and counter-cases with their enclosures, given the following decision: The claim of the Government of the United States . . . is most in accordance with the true interpretation of the Treaty concluded. . . ."

The British statement contends that two important rules of international law for the interpretation of treaties govern the case under review: first, that the interpretation of the treaty should be drawn from the connection and relation of the different parts, and secondly, regard must be had to the context and spirit of the whole treaty. The only part of the Oregon treaty of 1846, submits Great Britain, which causes disagreement is the second sentence of the first article, namely, "and thence southerly through the middle of the said channel and of Fuca's Straits to the Pacific Ocean." Regard must be had, therefore, to the context of the sentence and of the preceding sentence, in order to secure the meaning of the words, "the said channel." There are three phrases in this sentence to be considered: "thence southerly through the middle of the channel;" "the middle of the channel;" "provided the navigation of the whole be free." The British position is that the second sentence may be read as if written *in extenso* thus: "and thence southerly through the middle of the channel which separates the continent from Vancouver's Island, and through the middle of Fuca's Straits to the Pacific Ocean." The treaty of 1846 used the term "Fuca's Straits" to denote the lower portion only of the larger channel, that is, the inlet of the sea extending eastward from the Pacific to the entrance of the narrow waters through which Captain Vancouver continued his voyage. The term "Fuca's Straits," therefore, must be taken to have been inserted in the second sentence of the first article of the Treaty for the sake of describing with greater precision the course of the boundary line, and it is one of the necessary conditions of the line that it should be drawn through the middle of the inlet of the sea which had Cape Flattery as southwestern and Deception Bay as northeastern extremities.

In order that the navigation of the whole of Fuca's Strait may be secured to both Great Britain and the United States the second phrase must be interpreted as requiring the line to be drawn southerly through the middle of the "channel" which will enable it to enter the headwaters of the Straits of Juan de Fuca and proceed thence to the Pacific; in other words, the boundary line, after it has entered the straits, must divide some parts of them in such a manner as to render necessary the phrase which secures free navigation of the whole straits to both countries. This is substantiated, claim the British, by the fact that the straits are eight miles in minimum breadth (between Race Island and the south shore). To maintain that this provision would allow an interpretation of the treaty which would continue the boundary line through Haro channel is to deprive the proviso of any rational meaning; since American vessels would possess the right of navigating the straits to the eastward of Haro without any such proviso, because they would be within their own territory; at the same time, British vessels would not require any such liberty to enable them to enter or leave the "channel" through which the boundary line is to pass from Fuca's straits into the upper waters of the Gulf of Georgia because the west side of the channel would wash British territory.

The American argument on the wording of the treaty of 1846 is simple and succinct. "Channel" can only mean navigable channel, and there is no need for circumlocution. Haro is the broadest, deepest, safest, and best channel. It separates the continent from Vancouver Island, whereas Rosario Strait touches neither the mainland nor the island. As a matter of fact, states the memorial, Rosario is not a strait at all but is merely the track of Captain Vancouver's vessel in 1792 in his voyage from Admiralty Inlet to the north.[7]

Dr. Grimm comes down on the American side in this part of the argument and he says that the statement that the channel is to separate the continent from Vancouver Island points to Haro Strait,[8] because the latter touches Vancouver Island. If Rosario had been intended, the phrase "the channel which divides the continent from Vancouver's Island" would be meaningless because it would divide the whole archipelago from the continent.

Grimm also concludes that the phrase "thence southerly through the middle of the said channel and of Fuca's Straits to the Pacific Ocean" favours Haro Strait. It is impossible to draw the line due south from the forty-ninth parallel because it has to follow "the middle of the channel." "Southerly" therefore means deviation towards the south. Obviously, argues Grimm, the line must be drawn southerly with the least possible deviation to connect the starting-point at the forty-ninth parallel in the north and the other treaty point, Juan de Fuca's strait. A glance at any map of the region especially Vancouver's shows that Haro and not Rosario Strait best meets this condition.[9]

Grimm also rejects the British contention that the line can only be drawn in a southern direction if it goes through Rosario and not Haro, and he points out that the eastern end of Fuca's straits belongs, as Vancouver's map demonstrates clearly, not to the strait but to the Gulf of Georgia.[10] Nor can he accept, arising from this fact that Rosario does not lead into the Strait of Juan de Fuca, the British contention from the words of the treaty "that the navigation of the whole of the said channel and Straits south of the forty-ninth parallel of North latitude remain free and open to both Parties" is only feasible for Rosario and not for Haro.

The British assumption that the treaty means Rosario which they say had no name in 1846 while Haro had one is also thrown out by Grimm because Rosario had had a name ever since 1791 when it was called "Canal de Fidalgo." "It is very natural that in boundary delimitations particularly in little-known regions, little importance is attached to names, since these too often admit of change."[11]

On this matter of interpretation of the words of the treaty, Dr. Goldschmidt, writer of the minority report, has several interesting things to say. He says that there is only one waterway which crosses the forty-ninth parallel and then divides the continent from Vancouver Island. This is "the totality of the waters" of the Gulf of Georgia, and the early Spanish maps refer to it as a "channel." The "totality" of waters branches into several channels, and "middle" of the "said channel" can only mean the middle line of the "totality of the waters."[12] The treaty speaks of the "same channel" and the words do not accord with the assumption that any particular water other than the middle water line could be meant.

Goldschmidt cannot agree that the words of the treaty fit either Haro or Rosario. "A line drawn southerly through the middle of the 'Gulf of Georgia,' a line which therefore keeps throughout to the middle between Vancouver Island

and the American continent is distant almost equally from Haro Strait and Rosario Strait; only in its upper part would it coincide with the line of Haro Strait; in its further course, on the contrary, it would not, as does Haro Strait, turn westward, but in an almost due southerly direction would meet with the Strait of Fuca. . . ."[13]

It is clear, thus, that the arbitrators are in conflict in their interpretation of the words of the treaty, and the vehemence of Dr. Goldschmidt rather cancels out the confident assurance of Dr. Grimm. Neither, however, is prepared to accept the British interpretation of the treaty phraseology, and Grimm decidedly, and Goldschmidt partially, shows inclination to the American contention for Haro. One inclines to the view that the words of the treaty, "thence southerly through the middle of the said channel and Fuca's Straits," as between Haro and Rosario point to Haro Strait as the boundary line. "Southerly" can only mean deviation to the south from a line running west along the forty-ninth parallel; in other words, the line is to take the middle of the Gulf of Georgia and, once it has reached the archipelago of which Orcas Island forms the apex, if it is to retain the notion of "southerly," it is logical to maintain that it must follow the shortest connecting line between the fixed point of departure in the north (the apex just referred to) and the fixed terminus in the south (the centre of Juan de Fuca Strait). A glance at any map of the region shows that Haro Strait rather than Rosario satisfied this proviso. The same glance will show also that the waters of the Gulf of Georgia must flow into Haro rather than Rosario Strait.

Both sides enclosed with their statements a variety of maps in support of their case. The Americans maintained that Haro Strait was the only channel indicated on all maps surveyed by Spaniards as early as 1791, on the map of Vancouver and on that of Wilkes, who had led a United States' exploring expedition to the area in 1841 and had published an account of his voyage four years later. Similarly it was the only channel mentioned by the "impartial and authoritative" French geographer, Duflot de Mofras, who had also visited and explored the area, in his published work of 1844. Bancroft asserts that in the collection of maps of the disputed territory in the Royal Library at Berlin, not a single one anterior to 1846 mentions more than Haro Strait. Rosario, he explained, had been known ever since the Spaniard, Eliza, visited the area in 1791 and named the strait the Canal de Fidalgo. The United States had obtained from Madrid a certified copy of two reports to show how the channels of the area were named in 1791.

Bancroft goes on to attack the validity of Vancouver's chart, which was the chief British cartographical authority for the region. Vancouver used Rosario Strait because he had been instructed to keep close to the mainland; he did not even give Rosario a name, though he did name Haro; his chart was in a voluminous and very expensive work not available to fur-trading mariners; he shows two soundings for Rosario and six for Haro.

The British contention was that in 1846 they possessed only the chart prepared by Captain Vancouver. Is it likely that they would agree to accept a channel which they knew as unsafe and unsurveyed while there existed Rosario Channel which both parties knew to be navigable? Haro was known by name in 1846; why then did the negotiators not name it, if they meant it to be the channel, and thus end all the uncertainty?

The arbitrators review the cartographical evidence of both sides. Goldschmidt points out that Lord Aberdeen, Sir Richard Pakenham, James Buchanan, and the Senate did not use the same map, and the small map of Charles Wilkes, published in 1845, was not in the hands of the British government in 1846. Goldschmidt also makes the point that the British, if they had Rosario in mind in 1846, were under obligation to make the terms of the treaty, which they drew up, so clear that there would be no dubiety about the channel meant.[14]

The cartographical side of the problem would appear to be inconclusive in result. The Spaniards, the pioneer adventurers in the disputed region, clearly show Haro Strait on their charts. Wilkes, the official American geographer, who was in the waters adjacent to the disputed area during the years 1841-2, shows two channels, but only one, Haro, is named, and a glance at his map would lead one to infer that only one existed. Haro Strait is to be found clearly marked on Haro's and Eliza's unpublished maps of 1790 and 1791; on the map of Galiano and Valdes of 1792, which was published in 1802; on Vancouver's chart of 1798; on the map of de Mofras of 1844, though he gave no name to Rosario; on Wilkes's map of 1845, though he calls Rosario "Ringgold's." The contention that Wilkes considered Haro Strait much superior to Rosario and the inference that even Vancouver, who sailed via Rosario because he was instructed to keep close to the mainland, favoured Haro Strait which he named while giving Rosario no name, must carry considerable weight.

The British statement made much of the inference to be derived from their contention that the mariners in the disputed waters in 1846 favoured Rosario in sailing the area. They contended that the words of the treaty must be taken in the sense they had at the time of signing. Their argument here was that in 1846 Rosario Strait was the only known and commonly used channel. It was used by Vancouver in 1792; by the exploring vessels, *Sutil* and *Mexicana,* in the same year; by the *Beaver,* first steam vessel to sail from Fuca's straits to Fort Langley on the Fraser River; by the American exploring vessel, *Porpoise,* in 1841; by H.M.S. *Cormorant,* in 1846; and by all Hudson's Bay Company vessels without exception between 1837 and 1846, as their log-books prove. Appended statements from sea-captains certifying that Rosario was the only channel used in 1846 are supplied. The British argue that Rosario was the only channel known to the British government in 1846 as being navigable and safe. Further, a line through Rosario conferred equal advantages on both sides, whereas one through Haro would deprive Great Britain of the right to pass to her own territory along the channel she had always known and used. Also since no name is given, Haro, which had one, could not be meant.

The American answer to this part of the argument is that the British had to choose obscure men, not well-known ones like Governor Douglas, to testify that mariners neglected Haro Strait in 1846. De Mofras, French geographer, gives "clear and unequivocal" evidence in favour of Haro, and one must conclude that "if between a channel that had a name and one that had none, the British Government intended to take the channel without a name, it should have described it with distinctness and care...."[15] The United States' memorial points out that Haro Strait was the first discovered, by the Spaniard, Eliza, in June, 1791, and United States navigators like Captain Kendrick were in the disputed waters before Captain Vancouver.[16] The Americans maintain that the British cannot produce a map older than 1848 in which Rosario is named. Not a single American ship had used it between 1810 and 1841 when Wilkes arrived. The reason the Hudson's Bay Company had used Rosario was because their ships ran between Fort Nisqually and Fort Langley, and for that route Rosario was the natural channel.

Bancroft argues also from contemporaneous evidence and points out that Governor Pelly of the Hudson's Bay Company had drawn the attention of Lord Aberdeen to the islands of the disputed archipelago two days before the despatch to Washington of the draft of the Oregon treaty.[17] It was, moreover, affirms Bancroft, the contemporary view that the treaty meant to allot only Vancouver Island to Great Britain and not the islands of the archipelago lying between the mainland and Vancouver Island. The United States contends that the British attachment to Rosario channel had not been consistently maintained; indeed, Lord John Russell had deserted their claim to it and argued for the Middle Channel; "in other words, he interpreted the Treaty simply as giving the Island of San Juan to the British by which they could gain the conclusive possession of the Haro Channel."[18]

Later, in his counter-statement, Bancroft asserts that Haro was used by British mail-steamers, and it was the only one used by the inhabitants of British Columbia as well as by the gold-diggers during the gold rush of 1857-8. "The Treaty does not designate the channel which was or was not most in use, but the channel which separates the continent from Vancouver Island." No waters anywhere on the globe had been better examined before 1848 than the area in dispute. Bancroft refuses to accept the British statement that Hudson's Bay Company mariners used only Rosario before 1846. They would hardly use it all those years and still affirm themselves to be unaware of the evidence for the existence of the broadest, deepest, shortest, nearest, and best channel to the Fraser River. Moreover, when the Hudson's Bay Company established their new fort at Victoria in 1843, they used Haro.

Dr. Grimm, whose view was shared by Professor Kiepert, has much to say on this in his report. He rejects the British contention that Great Britain did not know Haro to be navigable in 1846 as worthless; only what was actually the case, not what one side thought the position to be, can be considered. In actual fact Haro is the broadest and deepest of the various arms of the sea in the area, as the Americans contend, and it forms the natural connection between the Gulf of Georgia and Fuca's Strait so that "if the question is of the gulf and the waters leading southward to the Strait of Fuca as of one and the same channel, the designation, "the said channel," best fits Haro Strait.[19]

Goldschmidt is devastating on this angle of the argument: "Detailed examination sustains none of the arguments" on either side in this respect. "Priority of discovery is not decisive, and it is equally indecisive that the Treaty names no channel. Rosario is called Canal de Fidalgo on early maps and therefore had a name, a point which advances the British argument." The early Spanish maps, he goes on, have as many soundings for Haro as Vancouver has for Rosario. Goldschmidt proceeds to demolish the British argument on this by saying that after the establishment of Fort Victoria on Vancouver Island, trade flowed thither and it must have become known that Haro Strait was a good channel. He accepts the American statement that the Hudson's Bay Company's ships had to use Haro because much of their trade was from Fort Nisqually, at the southeast corner of the Gulf of Georgia, with Fort Langley on the Fraser River and with Fort Victoria on Vancouver Island.

One must conclude, therefore, that the geographical argument weighed heavily on the American side. Haro Channel—Richards's chart and report of 1858 had proved this conclusively to the British government—was by far the broadest, shortest, most direct, and deepest channel. The evidence adduced by Great Britain that its excellences were not commonly known to mariners in 1846 is negative and inconclusive. Moreover, and this is a point of paramount importance, Haro is the natural connecting passage between the Gulf of Georgia in the north and Fuca Strait in the south. The treaty seems to define not the channel most in use in 1846 (the British contention), but the *main* channel, that is, the most conspicuous and open one, most adapted to navigation, that separates the mainland from Vancouver Island (the American argument). In treaties the term "channel" is taken to comprehend the deep water or navigable channel. If Rosario was more used by British ships before 1846 it was not because it was the main channel, but because it was the shortest route connecting Hudson's Bay Company forts.

Finally, the British argument that in 1846 they could not have intended Haro Strait to be the treaty channel because they had not known it to be navigable and safe for shipping is untenable when one recalls that the Company had settlements on the shores of Haro Strait at least twenty years before the treaty, and that Vancouver's chart shows several soundings for the channel. On the other hand, the United States statement that never at any time did they accept Rosario as comparable to Haro is supported by the fact that soon after, if not actually before, 1846, the pre-eminence of Haro as the regularly used channel through which all steamships passed, and as the passage used almost solely by the inhabitants and traders of British Columbia, was accepted.

In his statement Bancroft argues from contemporaneous evidence, in which he put so much trust to establish his case, and points out that Governor Pelly of the Hudson's Bay Company had drawn the attention of Lord Aberdeen two days before the despatch of the draft treaty to the fact that there were islands in the disputed water region. He makes reference to, and quotes from, the correspondence and speeches of Lord Aberdeen, Sir Robert Peel, Senator Benton, Edward Everett, and Louis McLane to show that the treaty intended to establish the Haro Strait as boundary channel. McLane, the United States minister in London in 1846, wrote to Secretary of State Buchanan on May 18, 1846, that he had discussed the Oregon treaty negotiations with Aberdeen during which he had learned that Richard Pakenham, British minister at Washington, would probably be instructed to offer the forty-ninth parallel and the "Canal de Arro" and Strait of Juan de Fuca as the boundary line.[20] McLane also told Buchanan there was no chance of the United States' being allowed to keep the southern tip of Vancouver Island.

Lord Aberdeen, in his instructions of May 18, 1846, to Pakenham had told him to offer the forty-ninth parallel beyond the mainland with a line going in a southerly direction through King George's Sound [Gulf of Georgia] so as to leave "the whole of Vancouver Island with its harbours and roadsteads in possession of Great Britain." Senator Benton made a speech in the Senate debate on the ratification of the treaty of June 15, in which he said the line would run through "the channel de Haro (wrongly written Arro on the maps) to the Straits of Fuca."[21] Prime Minister Sir Robert Peel, in a speech in the House of Commons on June 29, 1846, said that the line would follow the forty-ninth parallel "till it strikes the Straits of Fuca; that that parallel should not be continued as a boundary across Vancouver's Island, thus depriving us of a part of Vancouver's Island. . . ."[22] Bancroft also mentioned the evidence of Edward Everett, predecessor of McLane as minister in London, who had proposed a line running through Haro Strait in earlier negotiations with Lord Aberdeen.

In his second statement Bancroft takes his case a little farther. He asserts that, when minister to Great Britain after 1846, he had three times reminded Lord Palmerston that Haro Strait was the treaty channel and Palmerston had offered no comment. He points out also that Lord Aberdeen, who became prime minister in 1852, did nothing the following year when the Oregon legislature included the Haro archipelago in Oregon. And during his three years in London never once did Lord Aberdeen or Sir Robert Peel speak in contradiction of Louis McLane's views on the Oregon boundary.

The second British statement attempted to answer this formidable part of the American argument. It is asserted that McLane's statement can in no way bind Great Britain, for McLane was not negotiating with Aberdeen, and the latter never mentioned Haro to McLane. And it is probable, say the British, that Senator Benton founded his words on McLane's despatch. Further, we must take into consideration Secretary Buchanan's words to Mr. Crampton in 1848. McLane's geographical mistake, in which he spoke as though Birch Bay lay below the forty-ninth parallel, is mentioned by the British to vitiate the quality of his evidence. The Americans are reminded that Aberdeen in 1859 denied that he had ever discussed the boundary line with McLane. The "fair inference" from Mr. Everett's statement is that he did not speak of the water boundary at all, but only pointed out on a map "how much of Vancouver's Island would be cut off." In 1858 Mr. (now Sir) Richard Pakenham had also asserted that Buchanan had never mentioned Haro Strait to him.

The Americans also used the evidence of contemporaries to establish their argument that the purpose of the treaty of 1846 was to give all Vancouver Island to Great Britain with the obvious corollary that Haro Strait, which touches Vancouver Island, more accurately satisfies the stipulation that it "separates the continent from Vancouver's Island." The British denied this, declaring that the intention in 1846 was not merely not to cut off the end of the island. If the object had been this, they say, it would have sufficed to say that all Vancouver Island should belong to Great Britain, and in this connection Aberdeen's instructions to Pakenham in Washington cannot be read to contract the effect of the treaty. We have noted how McLane, Peel, Aberdeen, and Benton were all quoted by the Americans to support this contention.

The majority report of the arbitrators, that of Grimm and Kiepert, devotes a considerable part of its material to this part of the argument. They conclude from the testimony of the British and American statesmen quoted that it is "clear that on both sides the deviation from the generally governing rule of the 49th parallel was regarded as for the purpose, indeed the sole purpose, of keeping the whole of Vancouver Island for Great Britain." This is "not inconsiderable support for the hypothesis that that channel was meant which lies nearest Vancouver Island."[23]

The minority report of Dr. Goldschmidt is more forthright. He divines from the quotations from Aberdeen's and McLane's correspondence that it "cannot be doubted that the designated channel of the beginning of Article I of the Treaty can be understood only as the *totality* of the waters called Gulf of Georgia. The statement of Louis McLane that the line would "most probably" be proposed was mere surmise; the speech of Senator Benton was only an individual opinion; these and the proposal of Edward Everett were all "wholly without significance."[24] Neither Aberdeen nor Pakenham saw McLane's despatch and Benton's speech was not reported in England until after the treaty was signed. And Secretary Buchanan signed the treaty with McLane's despatch in front of him; yet he made no mention of Haro Strait; moreover, Buchanan "in no way maintains that he himself so understood or had understood the Treaty" as making Haro the boundary channel. Finally, "none of the statesmen of the two countries who took part in the negotiation and conclusion of the Treaty maintains that he upheld the one or the other line or even that he had one definitely in mind."[25] Dr. Goldschmidt quotes with approval Great Britain's quotation from a speech in the Senate by Daniel Webster on March 30, 1846: "The boundary of the 49th parallel is plainly to be adhered to as a basis; on the other hand, as regards all straits and sounds and islands in the neighbouring sea, these are appropriate subjects for settlement by stipulation. . . . Thus the 49th parallel is to form the continental boundary; all else is a subject of free negotiation. The British analysis of Webster's speech is therefore entirely correct."[26]

Dr. Goldschmidt finds untenable the American argument that the sole purpose of deviation of the line from the forty-ninth parallel was to leave southern Vancouver Island to Great Britain, because the Americans were not thereby giving up "an incontestable and indubitable right." On the contrary, the whole treaty was based on compromise, Great Britain giving up the area between the Columbia River and the forty-ninth parallel, and the United States giving up the southern tip of Vancouver Island, as she had agreed to do as long before as 1826. Moreover, neither side had ever accepted the other's title. The Americans gave up the right of free navigation of the Columbia River to the British, and the British gave up only what they had to; Britain had throughout made it clear that she must have unhindered access to her northern possessions.

Goldschmidt discounts the American reliance on the testimony of Aberdeen and Peel on the matter, for "both emphasize the remaining of the whole island in British possession only as *result* of the boundary line drawn; this consequence is stressed, but it is in no way said that only that island came to Great Britain." And even a line through Haro Strait would still leave a number of islands to Britain. "On the continent certainly there was unwillingness to give way below the 49th parallel, and consequently that was steadfastly adhered to; even the permission of free navigation of the Columbia was conceded only with reluctance. That result, however, "in no way extended to the water boundary and the islands. The numerous small islands were at the time of the conclusion of the Treaty as yet unexplored and in part were wholly unknown."[27] And he cites Bancroft to show that even as late as November, 1846, the United States cabinet knew nothing of the value of the islands.

"The true purport of the Treaty is perfectly in accord with the statement of
Lord Aberdeen that 'his intention was to adopt the mid-channel of the Straits as
the boundary line, without any reference to islands, the position and indeed the
existence of which had hardly, at that time, been accurately ascertained.' The
argument taken from the supposed purpose of the Treaty does not, therefore, at
all support the Government of the United States. It is not correct that the Government of the United States anywhere declared its desire that the dividing line
was to be so drawn that only Vancouver Island should fall to Great Britain; it is
not correct that the British Government ever declared itself in that sense."[28]
The omission to define the possession of the small islands was on both sides
deliberate and intentional. "The boundary line corresponding to the wording of
the Treaty in fact leaves all Vancouver Island to Great Britain, but it is nowhere
provided that it is to be drawn in a direction corresponding only to that
outcome."[29]

On the matter of the purpose of the treaty, which was fundamental in
evaluating the rival claims, the experts are therefore in direct conflict, Grimm
emphatic in the view that deviation of the boundary line from the forty-ninth
parallel was effected for the purpose of securing all Vancouver Island to Great
Britain. Goldschmidt, on the other hand, takes the diametrically opposite view
that it is not demonstrable that the only purpose of the deviation from the forty-
ninth parallel was to give all Vancouver Island to Britain. Grimm therefore
favours the opinion that the boundary line was meant to follow the channel
nearest the island, while Goldschmidt, in spite of the precise nature of the terms
of his remit, pronounces for the Middle Channel as most in accordance with the
terms of the treaty.

What could be more plausible and reasonable than the United States' contention that the treaty meant the boundary line to follow the channel, Haro,
whose waters actually wash the island? The obvious answer to this, that what
was necessary for the usufruct of Vancouver Island was also intended to be
ceded, the line of the Haro channel impeding the usufruct, is not highly
convincing. It is most difficult to maintain that the surrender of Vancouver
Island meant giving up such a large area—170 miles—as that contained in the
archipelago, and it is logical to assume that, had five-sixths or more of Vancouver Island been south of 49°, the island would have gone to the United
States without the slightest British demur. In that case there would have been
no water boundary dispute. But we must remember in this connection that from
the earliest days of the Oregon controversy both sides had strenuously sought to
secure the harbours of Puget Sound. Thus Lord Aberdeen, in September, 1844,
had reminded Peel that Britain must have all Vancouver Island so as not to be
excluded from the entrance to Puget Sound and all the harbours within it,
"which are the really valuable part of the territory."

The main argument of the United States that the Haro channel was the
boundary channel adopted by Mr. McLane and Lord Aberdeen in 1846 is supported by so much contemporaneous positive evidence that, in the absence of
any corresponding positive data for Rosario Strait, it is very difficult to ignore.
McLane's despatch of May 18, 1846, said that the British proposition would
divide the territory by the forty-ninth parallel to the sea: "that is to say, to the
arm of the sea called Birch's Bay, thence by the Canal de Arro and Straits of

Fuca to the Ocean. . . ." This letter, placed before the Senate by President Polk on June 10, and the speeches of Senator Benton and General Cass during the subsequent Senate debate, delivered so soon after the signing of the treaty and made public in the absence of any parallel statements on the British side, or without any denial by the British government, which followed the Senate debates meticulously, must constitute powerful evidence. In this connection also it is to be remembered that Cass, who led the opposition in the Senate to ratification of the treaty of 1846, was keen to show up the agreement in the most unfavourable light; yet he seems never to have doubted that Haro Strait was intended to be the line of demarcation.

On the other hand, however, it should be noted that Benton and Cass would naturally adopt the view of the accredited American representative in London, Mr. McLane. We know from Lord Aberdeen's papers that McLane was shown a copy of the British project of May 18 before it crossed the Atlantic, and it does not appear to have occurred to him, if he knew more than one channel existed, to suggest to Aberdeen that he should indicate exactly how the boundary line should run west of the mainland. Moreover, McLane speaks of Birch Bay as though it lay south of the forty-ninth parallel. He further demonstrated the hazy nature of his impressions when he told Secretary of State Buchanan a fortnight after the treaty was signed that the right of free navigation of the Columbia River, strenuously insisted upon by the British for inclusion in the treaty, was due to end in 1859 when the Hudson's Bay Company's licence to trade in the area was due to expire. Yet all the evidence makes it clear that the foreign secretary had been most careful to impress upon Pakenham, in his instructions to him, that there was to be absolutely no limit on the duration of the right of free navigation of the Columbia River. In that sense Aberdeen had meant his project to be an ultimatum, and Pakenham had power and direct instructions to withdraw the draft if an indefinitely free Columbia were not acceptable to the Americans. We know also that, as early as June 6, Buchanan was aware that Haro Strait was not specifically mentioned in Aberdeen's draft of the treaty of 1846.

One remembers that, in spite of McLane's assertion in his despatch of May 18, it is almost certain that he and Aberdeen never at any time discussed a specific channel or the very existence of islands between the mainland and Vancouver Island, and it may therefore be straining things to suggest that the intention of the treaty of 1846 was merely to secure Vancouver Island to Great Britain. The knowledge of the geography and topography and the disputed area possessed by both was, to put it mildly, imperfect. They used different maps, Aberdeen depending on Vancouver's and McLane probably on Wilkes's. McLane's calling Haro as Wilkes had it, "Arro," rather indicates that he had seen the map of Wilkes. How recently before May 18 the two negotiators had consulted their authorities, it is difficult to say; probably it had been some time previously. In short, McLane thought that only one channel, Haro, existed,[30] and Aberdeen thought only the channel represented by the route taken by Vancouver in 1792, Rosario Strait, existed. Aberdeen chose to ignore the "explicit views" of Sir J. H. Pelly, who had told him on May 16: "The next question on which the Governments of the two Countries will have to decide, will be as to the Islands abutting on and in the Gulf of Georgia, vizt. one Vancouver Island intersected by the parallel of 49° and others which are wholly on the South of that parallel."[31]

It should in this connection be stressed that Pelly had told Sir George Simpson of the company on June 3: "I think we shall consent to continue the Line of the 49° from its present Terminus at Rocky Mountains to the Middle of the Gulf of Georgia where it divides the Continent from Vancouver's Island and from that point keeping the Center till it strikes a line drawn through the Center of the Straits of Juan de Fuca if this is agreed to."[32] If Lord Aberdeen had had the prescience to insert this clause of Pelly's in the treaty draft, there would have been no water boundary question, especially if he had added Pelly's more definite opinion also conveyed to the foreign secretary on May 16 that "... the water demarcation line should be from the center of the water in the Gulf of Georgia in the 49° along the Line coloured red as navigable on the chart made by Vancouver (a tracing of which I enclose) till it reaches a line drawn through the center of the Straits of Juan de Fuca."[33] The fact that Pelly held such views and gave expression to them must be taken to vitiate any American argument based on contemporary statesmen's views of what the negotiators meant in 1846.

We can conclude with confidence that the negotiators at London, Lord Aberdeen and Mr. McLane, were not influenced in their discussions by the geography of the area in dispute. It is almost equally certain that the negotiators at Washington, Secretary of State Buchanan and British Minister Pakenham, did not allow themselves to be affected unduly by cartographical or topographical references. Buchanan seems never to have held very definite views on the subject of the channel meant by the treaty. In January, 1848, he told J. F. Crampton, the British minister of the day, that in 1846 he had meant the boundary to follow the "main, navigable channel." This narrows the issue to Rosario and Haro, and it also helps to explain Britain's adherence to Vancouver's chart upon which Rosario Strait was shown to be the main navigable channel, and Haro is ignored. The possibility of the existence of more than one channel seems never to have entered into the discussions between Pakenham and Buchanan. We have Pakenham's word for this in addition to the testimony of the Aberdeen MSS. that, had Buchanan demanded a minor change in the projected terms such as the addition of phraseology accurately defining the channel, Pakenham had power so to emend the Aberdeen draft.

On Vancouver's chart the Gulf of Georgia extends as far south as the eastern extremity of the Strait of Juan de Fuca and the name as printed appears to embrace the whole space between the mainland and Vancouver Island. This goes some way to explain Aberdeen's mistake and justifies the British position for the Middle Channel, though hardly for Rosario because the centre of the area between the mainland and Vancouver Island never at any point touches the Rosario channel. Aberdeen apparently confused "King George's Sound" with the Gulf of Georgia in spite of the fact that he was guided by the knowledgeable governor of the Hudson's Bay Company who, as we have noted, distinctly advised that the line of boundary should follow "the line coloured red as navigable on the chart made by Vancouver." It may be a mistake to put any great stress on this part of the argument because it appears clear that, if the negotiators of 1846 had had one channel distinctly in mind, they would have indicated their preference by naming it in the treaty. We know that Aberdeen deliberately refrained from inserting a clause defining a channel in case that by doing so he might complicate matters and delay a settlement. His draft treaty of May 18, 1846, arrived in the United States on June 3. That left plenty of time for the Americans to insert the name of the channel before the treaty was accepted or ratified. It is apparant that the British negotiators of 1846 had no knowledge of the existence of Haro Strait; they could not have meant Haro as a boundary because, reprehensible though it was, they did not even know it existed.

It is very difficult to exonerate the negotiators of 1846 from almost culpable negligence. How is it possible to explain the failure of those responsible states-men, during negotiations and deliberations almost continuous over a period of years regarding the possession of a large tract of land, to use a modern map at all and to consult frequently and know accurately the ancient ones at their disposal? How was it possible for eminent diplomatists, who decided upon the line of boundary they would demand as early as 1844, to proceed with intensive discussions during the succeeding two years apparently without once realizing that the line they had chosen was very imperfectly marked beyond the main-land? It is amazing to find that Aberdeen, Peel, Pakenham, and their assistants seem to have troubled little about the complex nature of the important area between the mainland and Vancouver Island.

It is difficult to believe that Lord Aberdeen, who did not even know the correct name of the waterway between the mainland and Vancouver Island on the forty-ninth parallel,[34] and the prime minister, Sir Robert Peel, who, according to the terms of his prepared speech of June 29, 1846, in the House of Commons, was under the impression that the forty-ninth parallel actually touched the Strait of Juan de Fuca, had adequate knowledge of the topography of the disputed area. Yet, that they knew of the existence of the network of islands between the mainland and Vancouver Island seems certain from the evidence of Sir J. H. Pelly and of H. U. Addington, permanent under-secretary at the For-eign Office.[35] When the news of the Senate's decision to abrogate the convention of 1827, the first essential move in the direction of settlement of the Oregon question, reached London in May, 1846, Lord Aberdeen immediately got in touch with Pelly to discuss the boundary question, the celebrated despatch of May 18 being the sequel to their discussions. Four days later Pelly wrote to Aberdeen giving explicitly the views he had conveyed verbally a few days before, and this statement of his contains clear mention of the complex nature of the area directly west of the mainland at the forty-ninth parallel.[36] But there is no mention of any channel other than that used by Vancouver in 1792. This would indicate conclusively that the foreign secretary knew of the existence of the San Juan Archipelago, though not of the existence of more than one navi-gable channel, and deliberately ignored it in case admission of the presence of islands in that region would complicate or delay settlement of the larger issue. The clue to this amazing negligence is to be found in the Foreign Office records. Trouble over the line of demarcation had been foreseen in 1846, "but this con-sideration being of less importance than the conclusion of the Treaty, the Treaty was concluded and signed."[37]

In the light of this positive evidence it is clear that the British negotiators of 1846 could easily have inserted in their draft of the Oregon treaty a clause which would have obviated the controversy over San Juan of the subsequent quarter-century. We can only say in extenuation of this neglect that the American negotiators entered the discussion with equally befogged minds. The American minister, Louis McLane, as we saw, had made no effort to have inserted in the treaty a clause defining the line west of the mainland and Secretary of State Buchanan, when he heard Benton, Cass, and others speak of Haro, blandly asserted that he assumed it to be the "main, navigable channel." Buchanan noticed that Aberdeen's projet, which became the final Oregon treaty of 1846, did not provide for the line passing through Haro Strait but, casual as ever, he thought "this would probably be the fair construction."[38] The possibility of the existence of more than one channel seems never to have been understood in Buchanan's discussions with Pakenham, or in McLane's with Aberdeen. The British negotiators could with fairness argue that the Americans were as culpable as they in failing to delineate carefully the boundary channel. Had the United States demanded a minor change in the projected terms of 1846, such as a phrase accurately defining the channel to be observed as boundary, we know from his instructions that Pakenham had power so to emend the draft sent to him by Lord Aberdeen. The embarrassment of the Mexican War goes far to explain the Americans' omission, for it is probable that, at this vital moment in their history, they would not risk alienating Great Britain by insisting upon a change in the draft. Pakenham expressed to the foreign secretary his amazement at the anxiety of the United States government to hasten an Oregon settlement in June, 1846, and the Mexican War was the cause.[39]

CHAPTER TWELVE

THE MIDDLE CHANNEL

THE DECISION by Great Britain to agree to exclusion of the Middle Channel is inexplicable; it was hardly prompted by a desire or readiness to pursue her claims to the limit. Gladstone and Granville both believed "neither claim to be strictly tenable,"[1] and Macdonald and others concurred. This was surely a valid reason for *not* excluding the Middle Channel, because it was the only alternative left if the lines of Haro and Rosario were found to be faulty. It was the British who had first introduced the claim for the Middle Channel, a tacit admission that their claim to Rosario was intrinsically weak. It had been proposed as an alternative, for the first time, as early as December, 1856, when Lord Clarendon, at that time at the Foreign Office, had advised Captain Prevost to accept it as boundary if his efforts to induce Archibald Campbell to accept the line of Rosario were not successful. Lord Napier, too, while ambassador at Washington, had mentioned it as a compromise line in 1858 when he had private conversations with Mr. Campbell. E. H. Hammond, permanent under-secretary for foreign affairs, as we saw, had advised that "we might first propose to adopt the Middle Channel ... and if that failed, "we should act upon our interpretation of what is right and continue to hold the Island of San Juan as an undoubted possession of the British Crown."[2] A policy of concession is always difficult to initiate and carry out, for the other side invariably considers concession a sign of weakness and lack of faith in a cause. Concession had come too early in the San Juan dispute and its direct object (to win San Juan) was too obvious to delude anyone. When it could not be proved to demonstration that the channel intended by the treaty was Haro or Rosario, it was always plausible to suggest that the Middle Channel was in consonance with the words of the treaty.[3] The Derby ministry of 1858-9, which had the Earl of Malmesbury at the Foreign Office, would also have been well satisfied to secure the Middle Channel as boundary. Moreover, it was the line of Lord Aberdeen, Sir Richard Pakenham, the Hudson's Bay Company, and the permanent officials of the Admiralty, the Foreign and Colonial Offices, all of whom insisted that the middle of the whole area west of the mainland had been meant in 1846.

From a British point of view the decision to suggest the Middle Channel as the boundary line had been proved to be a blunder, but the later decision to allow the arbitrator in 1871 to exclude the middle strait from his purview and restrict his judgment to Rosario and Haro channels only was flagrantly mischievous. Since a direct line, as obviously desired by the treaty of 1846, could not be conveniently adopted because it would run partly overland, the next and fairest course would surely have been to lay down a line involving least deviation from the terms of the treaty. It is quite obvious that neither a line of demarcation which ran close to Vancouver Island (that is, via Haro), nor one which ran close to the mainland (that is, via Rosario), could exactly fulfil the terms of the treaty. Further, if one side had in mind a certain channel, and the other had in mind another one, and both sides failed to define adequately their positions when the treaty was drawn up, the case for subsequently adopting a compromise line seems very strong. Unfortunately, however, when the issue was reopened ten years later after the signing of the treaty, both sides found their views coloured by their estimate of the strategic importance of the Island of San Juan. This was the factor that complicated the whole problem and made it difficult of solution. This was the factor, also which was responsible almost solely for any acrimony that was allowed to creep into the negotiations and discussions.

It is almost certain that the negotiators of 1846, Pakenham, Aberdeen, and McLane in particular, meant the boundary line west of the mainland to follow the middle of the whole water area between the mainland and Vancouver Island. But Lord Aberdeen thought the middle was the line appearing on Vancouver's chart, and McLane thought Haro was the channel near the middle of the whole water area. The use of the words in the treaty "whole of the said channel" rather confirms this and, in the absence of a precise name, the impression is that "said channel" means the whole sea area. It is true that the Middle Channel does not run exactly through the middle of the whole area in question, but its course is quite close enough to the centre of the area to justify the argument that the negotiators meant it to form the line of demarcation. The Strait of Georgia and the Strait of Juan de Fuca evidently with much reason were deemed to be one channel which could be connected by a centre line of demarcation which would have no regard to tortuous passages or minute islands. Nor must the "channel" necessarily mean a single, unbroken water passage. Vancouver's chart has the Strait of Georgia extending as far south as the eastern extremity of Juan de Fuca strait with the result that it could be, and actually was, contended from the start, therefore, that the whole area was to be divided by the Middle Channel.

The words of the treaty of 1846 could be interpreted, too, to sanction the adoption of the Middle Channel as boundary. It could be maintained that the third phrase of Article 1 of the treaty provided for free navigation of the "said channel and straits" because it was realized that the line drawn midway through the whole area between the mainland and Vancouver Island ran overland part of the way. Article 1 draws the boundary line to the *middle* of the straits to the Pacific. Does not this repetition of the word "middle" furnish a certain, positive clue to the intentions of the negotiators of 1846? Surely, it ought to have been contended, the negotiators could never have intended their line to be deflected either to the east or west to the extent implied in the adoption of Haro or Rosario channels. Repeatedly it had been asserted by British negotiators that the words of the treaty were the backbone of the British case. It had therefore been virtual surrender of the whole position to depart from the words of the treaty of 1846. The government of 1871, by agreeing to ignore the claims of the Middle Channel, were throwing away the whole British case. As early as 1856 Great Britain had, perhaps negatively, given up hope of securing the adherence of the United States to an agreement establishing a line along Rosario Strait, and the efforts of her diplomatic representatives after that date had been mainly directed towards obtaining the Middle Channel. Yet, most magnanimously, the negotiators of 1871 agreed to waive the claim to the Middle Channel and put their faith in a line for which no British government had ever shown any real enthusiasm and for which, as the Foreign Office records demonstrate, the British title was known to be, to put the position at its lowest, inconclusive.

The failure by Thornton and Rose to deliver the ultimatum that Britain would never cede San Juan gave Fish a false impression of the British attitude to the island, and he cannot be blamed for assuming that an accommodation acceptable to the United States would be as easy to achieve as that on the *Alabama* claims. It should have been pointed out to him that, if arbitration were to be resorted to, the arbiter ought to have a completely free hand to decide among the three possible channels. But the Americans feared that an arbiter, with the disposition often displayed by such individuals, unable to declare positively between Rosario and Haro channels, would be tempted to decide for the Middle Channel as the boundary line. It was an admirable line for compromise, but its adoption would have meant for them the loss of the Island of San Juan, a disaster which they could never risk. The Americans had often made it clear that they would never consider the adoption of arbitration to settle a territorial dispute. During the Oregon treaty discussions Great Britain had repeatedly proposed arbitration, and just as repeatedly the United States had vehemently rejected the device. The American argument was that, where the importance of the territory in dispute was considerable, they would not risk losing it; the territorial rights of the United States were not proper subject for arbitration, maintained President Polk.[4]

Remarkable confirmation of the potent nature of the case for adopting the Middle Channel is to be found in the reports of the experts appointed by the German emperor. In both reports there is abundant manifestation of the surprise of the experts that the Middle Channel was not to be within their purview. Thus, in several parts of the majority report of Messrs. Grimm and Kiepert surprise is expressed that the Middle Channel is not to be considered by them, "however much the wording of the Treaty in itself might support this supposition."[5]

The minority report of Dr. Goldschmidt, however, goes considerably farther. In his discussion of the wording of the treaty of 1846, he quotes Lord Aberdeen, "the author of the draft treaty which was accepted without alteration," in his instruction to Richard Pakenham that the boundary is to follow the forty-ninth parallel to the sea and thence in a southerly direction through the *centre* of King George's Sound (the modern Strait of Georgia) and the Strait of Juan de Fuca to the Pacific Ocean, and Goldschmidt finds "the true purport of the Treaty to be perfectly in accord" with Aberdeen's intention "to adopt the mid-channel of the straits as the boundary line, without any reference to islands. . . ."[6] He concludes that the "totality" of the waters is meant, and he goes on to say that "nothing else can be said by the words that the boundary line is to go on through the middle of the 'said' channel than that the middle line of the totality of the waters is to form the boundary line. . . ." The clear wording of the treaty is wholly irreconcilable with the assumption that the words "and thence southerly through the middle of the said channel" were to have denoted any particular channel which does not appear as the middle water line of the whole channel, that is to say, of the Gulf of Georgia." ". . . that each of the two parties was thinking of a particular channel may perhaps be so, but they have declared unequivocally only for that particular channel as boundary line which appears as the middle continuation of the Gulf of Georgia."[7]

He concludes that the fact that the treaty named no specific channel argues in favour of the Middle Channel. "It is most simply to be explained, if the parties had not particularly thought of a clearly defined specific channel, but wished to draw the boundary line through the middle of the entire body of boundary waters whether the boundary line went or not, through an already known and named channel."[8]

If that is not enough, Goldschmidt goes to the extreme of asserting that "it appears highly probable that the parties would have chosen the true middle line, if they had had before them even the present exact maps."[9] And he goes on to adduce several reasons for his choice of the Middle Channel as treaty line: (1) "It is the exact mathematical dividing line of the disputed territory, that is to say, of that which alone was still in question after the British Government had renounced her continental possession to the south of 49° North Latitude."[10] (2) "It could and can even at this time hardly be known whether this line is more advantageous" to either side for, "it divides the islands into two nearly equal groups." (3) "As exact dividing line it corresponds most with the presumable intention of the parties who did not possess exact knowledge of the Gulf of Georgia, its islands and channels.... It was much more important for them to avoid threatened war by a friendly, reasonable agreement...." (4) "Regarding free navigation," it is asserted that "the middle line is as little decisive as one of the side lines. This remains to both parties in the whole gulf." He quotes Vattel to show that this accords with the accepted principle that "in doubt, the interpretation must be in favour of equal treatment of the two parties." (5) "It conforms also to the principle of international law that boundary lines of straits, the coasts of which belong to different states, are drawn through the middle of the strait." He quotes Phillimore and Heffter in support. (6) The parties decided that "wherever the boundary line lies, whether in a broader or a narrower water, nevertheless, no right of sovereignty of any sort of one or the other party shall be opposed to the free navigation of both parties."

From all this argument for the Middle Channel Goldschmidt concludes: "that if the parties intended the middle line, they must have chosen the wording of the Treaty of June 15, 1846; had the parties intended another line they could not have chosen this wording. If the middle line is intended, the result is reasonable and equally satisfactory for both parties; if another line was intended, a sacrifice would be exacted from one or the other party...."[11] And in view of his thus finding for the Middle Channel so confidently, Dr. Goldschmidt concluded his report thus: "Neither of the two claims is in accordance with the true interpretation of the Treaty of June 15, 1846; preponderating reasons support neither of the two claims."

Conferences were held of the three professional arbitrators in an effort to resolve their differences. It was finally agreed, at the suggestion of Dr. Goldschmidt, to issue an interlocutory award asking the two parties: "Whether by conclusion of the Treaty of June 15, 1846, according to the interest of both parties, every other boundary line than that running through Haro Strait or that running through Rosario Strait was to be excluded."

Dr. Grimm, however, in further "Observations on the Opinion of Dr. Gold-schmidt," declares that even if the Middle Channel is the boundary channel proposed by the parties, neither wanted it at the conclusion of the treaty; and the declaration asked from the two sides by the proposal of Dr. Goldschmidt is "already before us." It was not feasible to inform the two powers that the lines they contend for do not fit the treaty, and that another line is indubitably pointed to by the treaty. Obviously they will be told that "only the parties can know what they have stipulated." To act on Goldschmidt's declaration would mean loss of time and it would also necessitate a new treaty of arbitration. Grimm and Kiepert reject the view of Goldschmidt that the Middle Channel is the boundary one, asserting that the reasons they have given in favour of Haro Strait as against Rosario also hold good against the Middle Channel. In any case, they reiterate, "neither of the parties claims it to be the boundary channel meant by the Treaty."[12] This last sentence allied to the finding for the Middle Channel by Goldschmidt must surely constitute implicit indictment of the British government's surrender of a claim to the Middle Channel as the boundary line of the treaty of 1846.

Possession of San Juan would have been secured by a decision to adopt the Middle Channel as the boundary line, and thus the British might have secured all they contended for, or at least all they had considered important to them since 1856. It had since that date been realized that occupation of San Juan meant virtual control of the very important Vancouver Island, "the window on the Pacific," and control of Vancouver Island comprehended control of the coast of British Columbia. It is true that the Admiralty inclined to minimize the importance of San Juan because of their overwhelming naval predominance, particularly in the Pacific, but they did not foresee the aerial warfare of to-day or the day of Anglo-American naval disparity. It was fortunate for Britain that the Colonial and Foreign Offices were inclined, if anything, to magnify the strategic value of the island.

San Juan lay at the western outlet of Canada, and the island would assume an entirely new significance now that there existed the possibility of the develop-ment of the vast prairie lands of the Northwest Territories. In those days the danger was seen by some that the Americans might establish San Juan as a powerful fort which would threaten the safety of the western terminus of a new transcontinental railway. Sir George Cartier, one of the "Fathers of Confedera-tion," had thought fit to see Lord Granville, the colonial secretary at that time, and to write to the British government in 1868, putting before them the Canadi-an attitude towards San Juan. He stressed the vital importance of the island to British Columbia, and reminded Great Britain that Canada's experience of past diplomacy in the settlement of boundaries in North America, where the disposi-tion on the one side to concede, and on the other to encroach, was always present and always resulted disastrously for Canada, suggested that a similar disposition and parallel results might be feared in the future, and he urged that "... every resource of diplomacy, and every argument derived from the practice and policy of coterminous nations, from the geographical position and maritime requirements of the respective countries in the gulf, as well as from the language of the Treaty should be exhausted before a strategic position be given up, which future generations of loyal subjects may have occasion to regret...."[13]

Sir John A. Macdonald had expressed his conviction at Washington in 1871 that, no matter what line of boundary the arbitrator decided upon, all three channels should be free to both sides and no fortifications should be erected on the islands of the San Juan Archipelago. Yet when the terms of the Treaty of Washington, submitting the subject to a restricted form of arbitration were made public, there was no complaint from the Canadian public or from the Canadian government, either that a mistake was being made in referring the whole question to arbitration or that an error was being committed in ruling out the possibility that the Middle Channel might be adopted. Had they offered criticism then, that is, in 1871, they would have been justified later in denouncing the award of October, 1872. They accepted the decision without demur and, indeed, were able to predict the arbitrator's terms some time before their publication. The *British Colonist,* published in British Columbia, for instance, the best informed newspaper on the subject of San Juan, was able on September 20, 1872, to anticipate the adverse decision. Yet *The Times* reminded its readers after the award that "the lost channels lead to Canadian waters, Canadian shores, and Canadian rivers." In the division that took place on the matter of the treaty in the Canadian House of Commons all six British Columbia members voted for the treaty.[14]

Indeed, the British government appear to have been more concerned about Canadian reaction than the Canadian government. A "Very Pressing" minute by Lord Tenterden of November 3, 1872, to the following effect is in illustration: "Lord Granville [now Foreign Secretary] wants to know whether there was any criticism from Canada or from Sir John Macdonald as to the terms of the submission of the San Juan question before the award was made." The answer that "the Colonial Office are not aware of any such criticisms having been made" proves that the Canadian government made no complaint in 1871.[15] If the San Juan articles of the treaty of 1871 were unfortunate from a Canadian point of view, the treaty was, nevertheless, a landmark in Canadian history because it "liquidated a decade of the worst relations since the War of 1812," and it was a double achievement, "a place in British policy for the newly-federated dominion which supplied one of the British plenipotentiaries and ratified the Treaty, and a recognition (it was hoped) on the part of the United States of another 'Manifest Destiny' in North America."[16] If San Juan had been used by the negotiators merely as a bargaining weight, its loss, in Canadian eyes, was not catastrophic. Excluding the Middle Channel and surrendering San Juan were a small price for Canadians to pay for initiating an era of better understanding on the North American continent.

There was great disappointment in England at the nature of the award, for no matter how lightly the British people may have estimated the worth of San Juan, it was a blow to their national pride to be told that during the negotiations of half a century they had been totally in the wrong, and that the cause which had been sustained and prosecuted with so much vigour by some of their most prominent statesmen was worthless. Their immediate feeling was one of extreme irritation at the German emperor, or rather at his agent, Chancellor Bismarck, and Bancroft. They seemed to think that there had been a German-American conspiracy to overreach them, and even the staid and usually discreetly careful veteran Hammond, later Lord Hammond, under-secretary of state for Foreign

Affairs for so long, inferred that Bancoft had done "his best to hugger-mugger the lawyers while employed in framing their reports."[17] The *Daily Telegraph* expressed what Englishmen were thinking when it wrote: "The Emperor, it is said, is a soldier, not a jurist, and he decided, not on the merits of the case, but, as some say, with a wish to conciliate America, or, as others allege, from a desire to gratify England's real, though not avowed, desire to cede away territory in every quarter of the globe."[18]

Some excuse for this suspicion of Bismarck undoubtedly existed. Mr. J. L. Motley, American minister at the Hague in 1872, was a lifelong friend of the Chancellor.[19] It may have been mere coincidence that in July, 1872, Motley offered to visit the friend whom, although he had many times been in close proximity to him, he had not seen for fully eight years. Bancroft was a slavish admirer of Bismarck, and he was convinced that "our foreign political interests almost always run parallel with those of Germany. . . . And Bismarck loves to give the United States prominence in the eyes of Europe as a balance to Great Britain."[20]

Anglo-German relations were not good, and Germans could not forget that Britain had never shown much enthusiasm for German unity during the period of its evolution, 1848 to 1870, although she had shown enthusiasm for the synchronous movement towards unity in Italy. The British attitude to Schleswig-Holstein and Luxemburg had delayed the establishment of German unity, believed the Germans. They thought, rightly so, that English public opinion was extremely antipathetic to the Prussian cause and resented the manner in which the English press delighted in ridiculing, among other features of the German political system, the "barbarous" administrative system and the German legal organization. The Germans believed that the struggle with France had been prolonged, and many German lives lost, after Sedan by the arms which the French were able to buy in Britain. France had now been crushed, and Bismarck was preparing for the inevitable war of revenge. He had neutralized Russian influence by alliance and had acquired the power to crush Austria between Slav and German. There was much truth in Odo Russell's estimate of the position: "England alone remains unconquered and unconquerable with her neutrality, her fleet and her freedom—three black spots on his [Bismarck's] political horizon."[21]

The British press, in general, reflected the political affiliations of their respective proprietors when they discussed the arbitration award. The Conservatives blamed the Liberal government of the day; the Liberals blamed the Tories of 1846; those who had not troubled to study the history of the problem tended to blame the German emperor. The truth is, of course, that neither Conservatives nor Liberals were wholly right; nor were they wholly wrong.

The Times said bitterly: "It is not easy to look back upon the history of the San Juan controversy with any feelings of pride."[22] But the Liberal *Daily Telegraph*, after condemning the Conservative government of 1846 came to the conclusion that ". . . it is a great thing that we have bound over to keep the peace the only Power whose subjects, if not restrained by due diligence, could seriously vex our mercantile marine."[23] *The Standard,* while deploring the "substantial injustice" committed by the judges, felt that the United States "in this unhappy matter," had triumphed "all along the line."[24] *The Morning Post* pompously expressed its disappointment thus: "Had Lord Palmerston, Lord Russell or Lord

Clarendon been at the head of affairs, the San Juan question, like other questions, would have been settled after a very different fashion."[25] The Palmerstonian *Pall Mall Gazette* bitterly declaimed that "humiliation of this kind is a weakness we have outgrown in our later days."[26]

Conservatives were beginning to argue that to leave the right to possession of San Juan unsettled might be a not unmixed blessing. It is true that it might invite trouble and a possible war, but it was becoming apparent that, in spite of the Ebeys and Harneys, to have left the question unsettled might have proved profitable to Great Britain. The weakness in the British position when negotiating on colonial matters was the lukewarmness and apathy of the British negotiators. Throughout the earlier part of the century the fashionable attitude towards the colonies was, as has been seen, one of contempt, or at least of indifference and neglect. After the middle of the century that attitude tended to change, and even the Liberals, who were consistently strong in their attacks on the policy of maintaining colonies, were beginning to modify their views. Moderate Liberal opinion, at least, was beginning to perceive that it was inconsistent with British tradition continually to remind the colonies that they were retained on sufferance and that they could detach themselves at will. As the *Daily News,* which was inclined to be radical in tone, reminded the government: "The guest who is being repeatedly reminded that the door is open will very soon ask for his hat."[27]

Had it been decided to refuse to accede to the American demands on San Juan in 1871, and had Great Britain insisted that three, and not two, channels should have been within the scope of the arbitrator's consideration, it is quite safe to say that, in view of the changing attitude towards the colonies and their interests, no succeeding government would have agreed to abandon the claim to the Middle Channel and the Island of San Juan. Certainly, the Conservative party, which was beginning to favour a policy of imperial expansion, would have exerted itself to maintain the British position in the San Juan dispute to the full. By the early seventies there had grown up in England a considerable imperialist movement. The market uses of the colonies for British goods, the gradual withdrawal of imperial troops and the consequent reduction of expenditure, the growth of telegraphic communication, the vision of a new, powerful Canada after Confederation, the evident desire of other powers to acquire colonies, the decline of the influence of the Manchester School, the reaction against the Gladstone government which was accused of being anxious to cut the colonies adrift at a time when Italy and Germany were achieving national unity and consolidation and the United States was emerging from a long civil war to vigorous nationhood—all these were factors conspiring to create a new climate of imperial opinion in Great Britain. A powerful Canada would be the best British bulwark against possible American aggression, and would be instrumental in establishing a very desirable political equilibrium on the North American continent. The arrogance of Sumner and his allies was bearing the wrong kind of fruit.

When Disraeli, a recent convert to the new imperialism, came into office in 1874 the new movement was assured of success, for the new prime minister when putting his policy before the country had announced that the future of Britain lay in the growth and splendour of her overseas possessions, and in the terms of rhetoric peculiar to politicians he had two years before proclaimed himself the enemy of the "Little Englanders." "There had been no effort," he affirmed, "so continuous, so subtle, supported by so much energy, and carried on with so much ability and acumen, as the attempt of Liberalism to effect the disintegration of the British Empire."[28]

In view of all the misunderstanding of the British position on the water boundary, one would want to attempt to fix responsibility. Everything seemed to stem from the failure to attach a map to the Oregon treaty of 1846, but the situation had not been improved when, in the following year, the subject had been raised with Lord Palmerston and the great man, instead of affirming with his normal emphasis that Rosario was the channel meant by the treaty, lamely admitted that "some difficulty might arise in deciding which of the channels" ought to be the boundary. This casual approach was in marked contrast to the efforts of the American government to secure an official admission at that time from the British that Haro had been the channel meant by the treaty.

The Foreign Office must bear responsibility for mismanagement, but it is impossible accurately to apportion blame between the foreign secretary and the permanent under-secretary. It can be argued with some measure of reason and justification that the permanent officials at the Foreign Office in 1846 were deserving of censure for their failure to be completely *au fait* with their subject and to keep their superiors informed of all possible contingencies in the situation. We know that the Foreign Office librarian, G. M. Featherstonhaugh, who was a geographical expert, and the permanent under-secretary of state, H. U. Addington, were consulted before the treaty was drafted. Addington's explanation of the failure properly to define the boundary, given eight years later, was that trouble had been foreseen "but this consideration being of less importance than the conclusion of the Treaty, the Treaty was concluded and signed."[29] But this extraordinary statement, a positive indictment of the Peel-Aberdeen government, loses some of its pungency when we examine the character and career of the man who made it. Can we accept it as an accurate picture of the situation? Nephew of the prime minister at the turn of the century, Addington was permanent under-secretary at the Foreign Office from 1842 until 1854, and he had been selected by the foreign secretary, Lord Aberdeen, because of his vast diplomatic experience. In the Foreign Office service since 1807, he had served on missions at Madrid, Stockholm, Berne, Copenhagen, and Washington, and he had been, along with William Huskisson, a plenipotentiary in the negotiations with the United States in 1826. Reports on his character and capacity are by no means flattering to him. He "had no talent as a political adviser and showed incompetence as a minister in Spain," says one critic. Sir Charles Webster in *The Foreign Policy of Palmerston, 1833-41*, pronounces him stupid and prolix, while Algernon Cecil describes him as "a man of no great mark, bearing indeed the name of 'Pumpy' in the office."[30] The famous Mellish of the Schleswig-Holstein controversy goes much farther and finds Addington's actions as "so underhand and so unlike a gentleman that I must confess I feel that we are called upon to express our sentiment with respect to it." Professor Frederick Merk castigates Addington for what seemed gross duplicity in 1842 in the initiation of the Webster-Ashburton negotiations. Though he had been a plenipotentiary in negotiations over Oregon in 1826, he had become "infected with the virus of British fur trade imperialism."[31] and he omitted to remind Lord Aberdeen of the "Olympic Peninsula" offer made by Britain in 1826 to solve the Oregon boundary dispute; moreover, when taxed with this omission he deliberately lied to Aberdeen, according to Merk. Still, Aberdeen retained him as under-secretary throughout his period of office.

In the face of all this evidence of the erratic nature of Addington's character, one might question the accuracy of his statement about the 1846 negotiations. On the other hand, however, it must be remembered that Lord Aberdeen was a member of the government in 1854 (actually he was prime minister) when Addington prepared his memorandum of February 27, 1854, a document which was almost certainly seen by the cabinet. Addington would hardly incorporate a deliberate falsehood in a document to be perused by a superior who was fully informed of the truth of the matter. Further, there was no lack of advisers for Lord Aberdeen in 1846, for, in addition to Featherstonhaugh and Addington, he was advised on the boundary by Sir John Pelly of the Hudson's Bay Company two days before the despatch of the draft treaty which Aberdeen boasted was his handiwork. Pelly did indeed discuss with him "as to Islands, abutting on and in the Gulf of Georgia, vizt., one Vancouver Island ... and others which are wholly on the South of the 49th parallel...." "... the water demarcation line should be from the centre of the water in the Gulf of Georgia on the 49° along the Line coloured red as navigable on the chart made by Vancouver till it reaches a line drawn through the centre of the Straits of Juan de Fuca."[32] At best, therefore, it might be asserted that all the British negotiators assumed that *the* channel must mean the *navigable* one which could only be, in their view, the channel nearer the mainland, that used by Vancouver.

What was the function of the permanent under-secretary in the middle of the century? We understand, of course, that the foreign secretary was responsible, ultimately and often immediately, for policy and official decisions affecting foreign affairs, but the politician was dependent upon the permanent officials for knowledge of the minutiae of everyday problems facing them. One of the three outstanding permanent under-secretaries at the Foreign Office during the nineteenth century, E. H. (later Lord) Hammond, helps to answer the question. "I reckon that the Under-Secretary of State has no business to give a decision upon any point; he is merely the channel and ministerial officer, who is bound to advise and to recommend to the Secretary of State what he thinks should be done, but he has no independent action at all."[33] Hammond, son of Canning's under-secretary, was in the foreign diplomatic service for most of his life from 1824 to 1874; actually, he was chief clerk in the Foreign Office in 1846 and succeeded Addington as permanent under-secretary in 1854. His view is confirmed by that of Sir Thomas Sanderson, famous under-secretary at the turn of the century, who "thought of himself as the chief of a department whose job was to carry out the instructions of his minister. He concerned himself with the machinery of his bureaucracy.... This last great Super-Clerk did not consider it his function to give advice ..."[34]

There was perhaps something like poetic justice in the fact that Aberdeen was suffering, unfortunately posthumously, for the inadequacies of his draft Oregon treaty of 1846. After all, he had had some months, at the very least the weeks of Senate discussion on giving the year of notice provided for by the agreement of 1827, to bring up to date his geographical knowledge of the island archipelago at the forty-ninth parallel. Though one does not for a moment believe that he knew of the existence of more than one channel in 1846, one must admit that the American accusation of deceit was not totally unreasonable in the circumstances. Wilkes's map had been published the previous year, and to a certain type of parochially minded American it was inconceivable that the foreign secretary could not have consulted it. The activities of the official American exploring expedition were not unknown to the Foreign Office, and Sir George Simpson of the Hudson's Bay Company, whom Aberdeen had sent to Oregon to report from there in 1845, mentioned the Wilkes expedition in his report. Aberdeen, a scholar of the highest integrity, whom Greville called the "most lady-like" member of the Peel cabinet, was the last man to practise deception, but this does not exempt him from the charge of negligence. Nor is *tu quoque* a valid defence among diplomatists.[35]

The water boundary negotiations illustrated the rival diplomatic methods of the two countries, Great Britain and the United States. The positive, brash, confident, uninhibited approaches of the Americans were usually in sharp contrast to the slower, hesitating, tentative measures of the British. The opinion prevailing in the United States during the greater part of the century was that Britain would yield in the end to American demands, however impossible, rather than go to war. All British ministers to the United States note this phenomenon, Pakenham and Lyons making frequent reference to it. Even Odo Russell, British ambassador at Berlin, marvelled at Britain's "most decided terror of the Americans, to whom five milliards would willingly be paid for the sake of a quiet life."[36] Indeed, it was more or less openly asserted in 1872, both in England and Canada, that the express exclusion of a centre line of demarcation from the consideration of the arbitrator was conceived purposely as a device to conciliate the United States by ceding San Juan to them.

Experience should have taught the British the futility and folly of leaving lacunae in treaties, especially in treaties with the United States. The American diplomatists were always shrewd and quite properly alert to interpret treaties in the sense most beneficial to the United States. As in the Oregon negotiations, credit for initiating discussions over the water boundary is clearly due to Great Britain, although, since her representatives composed the terms of 1846 and were therefore responsible for the difficulties of interpretation, it was meet that she should take the first steps towards securing clarification of those terms. This put Britain at a disadvantage because when the United States saw her eagerness for adjustment its own attitude was disguised under an appearance of indifference and apathy.

The offer by Britain of the Middle Channel as a compromise line was interpreted by the Americans not as a gesture of goodwill but rather as demonstration of lack of faith in the validity of the British claim to the line of the Rosario; it was a sign of weakness prompted by a desire to gain a part of the disputed territory, and they consistently believed that Great Britain would not risk war to gain the whole area. In negotiations with England it was the settled American policy to refuse every initial offer made by Britain with the expectation that the next one would be more favourable. The Americans always knew what they wanted, and they are to be commended for the tenacity with which they held their views and the determination they always displayed in the presentation of their case. They succeeded in convincing themselves that Britain had over-reached them in 1842 and in 1846, and they were resolved not to suffer "humiliation" over the water boundary. They firmly believed that Great Britain had surrendered the harbours of Puget Sound in 1846 only after great pressure and a display of great determination on the part of the United States. They never doubted that the British attempt to gain San Juan was inspired by their desire to control egress from the harbours of Puget Sound and cut the United States off from the North Pacific. This was a typical American over-simplification of the issue, though it was nevertheless based on fact.

APPENDIXES, BIBLIOGRAPHY
AND NOTES

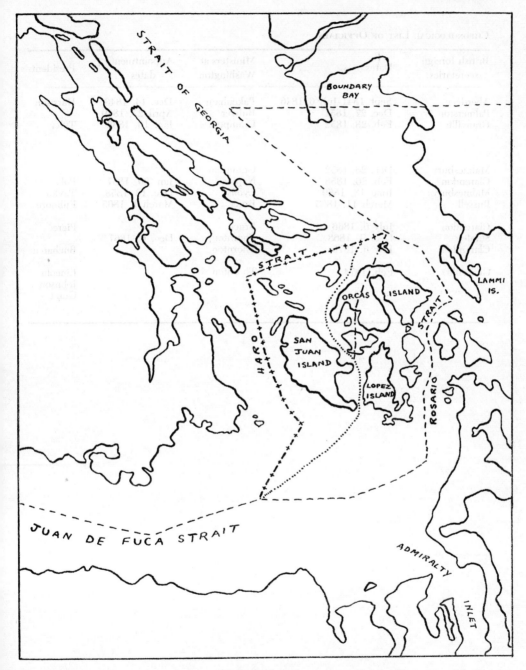

The respective claims of Great Britain and the United States as marked on the map enclosed in Prevost's letter to Campbell, Dec. 1, 1857 (F.O. 5/809)

Chronological List of Officials

British foreign secretaries	Dates	Ministers at Washington	Appointment dates	Presidents
Aberdeen	Sept. 1841-July 6, 1846	Pakenham	Dec. 14, 1843	Harrison
Palmerston	Dec. 27, 1851	Bulwer	April 27, 1849	
Granville	Feb. 28, 1852	Crampton	Jan. 19, 1852	Tyler
Malmesbury	Dec. 28, 1852	Crampton		
Clarendon	Feb. 26, 1858	Napier	Jan. 20, 1857	Polk
Malmesbury	June 18, 1859	Lyons	Dec. 13, 1858	Taylor
Russell	March 11, 1865	Bruce	March 1, 1865	Fillmore
Clarendon	July 6, 1866	Bruce		Pierce
Stanley	Dec. 9, 1868	Thornton	Dec. 6, 1867	
Clarendon	July 6, 1870	Thornton		Buchanan
Granville	Feb. 1874	Thornton		Lincoln
				Johnson
				Grant

Dates of office	Secretaries of state	Dates of office	Ministers at London	Dates of office
March/April 1841	D. Webster	March 1841-1843	Stevenson	
	D. Webster			
1841-5	Legare			
	Upshur	June 1843-Feb. 1844	Everett	
	Nelson	Acting		
	Calhoun	March '44-March '45		
			McLane	1845-Nov. 1846
1845-9	Buchanan	1845-9	Bancroft	to Aug. 1849
1849-July, 1850	Clayton	March 1849-July '50		
1850-53	Webster	July 1850-1852	Lawrence	
	Everett	1852-3	Ingersoll	
1853-7	Marcy	1853-7	Buchanan	Aug. 1853-March '56
1857-61	Cass	March 1857-Dec. '60	Dallas	May 1856-May 1861
	Black	Dec. 1860-March '61		
1861-5	Seward	March '61-March '69	Adams	May 1861-May 1868
1865-9	Seward		R. Johnson	Aug. 1868-May 1869
1869	Fish	1869-77	Motley	May 1869-June 1871
			Schenck	

BIBLIOGRAPHY

A. Manuscript Sources

British Museum
Aberdeen MSS (Additional MSS).
Peel MSS (Additional MSS).

Public Record Office
C.O. 305 [Vancouver Island, original correspondence], vols. 11, 15.
F.O. 5 [U.S.A., series II, 1793-1905], vols. 418-61, 715, 730, 809-16, 1296-1310, 1466-74.
30 G.D. [Granville Drafts], 29, vols. 55, 58, 63, 80, 106.
F.O. 361 [Clarendon Papers].
F.O. 362 [Granville Papers], vol. 1.

Printed United States Documents
Papers Relating to the Treaty of Washington (6 vols., Washington, 1872-4). V: *Berlin Arbitration.*
Papers Relating to the Foreign Relations of the United States, annually from 1866 to 1873 (pt. 2, vol. 3).
Serial 837: Report no. 251, 34th Cong., 1st Sess.
Serial 984: 35th Cong., 2nd Sess., Doc. no. 29; 1858-9 Report of Nugent.
Serial 1024: Sen. Ex. Doc., no. 2, 36th Cong., 1st Sess., 1859-60 Annual Report of Secretary of War.
Serial 1027: Sen. Ex. Doc. no. 10, 36th Cong., 1st Sess., 1859-60 Correspondence of Harney and Scott.
Serial 1031: Sen. Ex. Doc. no. 16, 36th Cong., 1st Sess., 1859-60 Campbell's Report.
Serial 1051: House Ex. Doc. no. 65, 36th Cong., 1st Sess., 1859-60 Harney's Correspondence.
Serial 1056: House Ex. Doc. no. 77, 36th Cong., 1st Sess., 1859-60 H. R. Crosbie.
Serial 1057: House Ex. Doc. no. 98, 36th Cong., 1st Sess., 1859-60 Harney's Correspondence.
Serial 1316: Sen. Ex. Doc. no. 29, 40th Cong., 2nd Sess., 1867-8 Report of Secretary of State, February 20, 1868.
Serial 1341: House Ex. Doc. no. 226, 40th Cong., 2nd Sess., 1867-8 Report of General Halleck.
Serial 1393: Sen. Ex. Doc. no. 8, 41st Cong., 1869 Vol. 1, Engineer's Report.

B. Secondary Sources

E. D. Adams: *The Power of Ideals in American History* (London, 1913).
—— *Great Britain and the American Civil War* (2 vols., London, 1925).
Charles Francis Adams, *With Lee at Appomattox* (New York, 1902).
H. C. Allen, *Great Britain and the United States* (London, 1954).
T. W. Balch, *The Alabama Arbitration* (Philadephia, 1900).
Frances Balfour, *Life of George, Fourth Earl of Aberdeen* (2 vols., London, 1905).
Frederick Bancroft, *The Life of W. H. Seward* (2 vols., London, 1900).
Samuel Flagg Bemis, ed., *The American Secretaries of State and Their Diplomacy* (10 vols., New York, 1927-9); *John Quincy Adams and the Foundations of American Foreign Policy* (New York, 1949).
T. H. Benton, *Thirty Years View* (New York, 1854).
C. A. Bodelsen, *Studies in Mid-Victorian Imperialism* (Copenhagen, 1924).
J. Boyd, *Sir George Etienne Cartier* (London, 1914).
John Bartlett Brebner, *North Atlantic Triangle* (London, 1945).
P. C. Brooks, *Diplomacy and the Border Lands* (New York, 1939).
G. Bryce, *Mackenzie, Selkirk and Simpson* (Toronto, 1926).
James Buchanan, *Works*, ed. J. B. Moore (12 vols., Philadelphia, 1908-11).
Viscount Bury, "Balance Sheet of the Treaty of Washington," Royal Colonial Institute *Proceedings, IV*, (1872-3), 7 ff.
J. M. Callahan, *American Foreign Policy in Canadian Relations* (New York, 1937).

Cambridge History of British Foreign Policy, ed. A. W. Ward and G. P. Gooch, II, III (London, 1923).
Cambridge History of the British Empire, VI (London, 1930).
Algernon Cecil, *British Foreign Secretaries of the 19th Century* (London, 1927).
W. F. Chamberlain, *Charles Sumner and the Treaty of Washington* (New York, 1901).
R. H. Coats and R. E. Gosnell, *Sir James Douglas* (London, 1926).
P. E. Corbett, *The Settlement of Canadian-American Disputes* (Toronto, 1937).
Donald G. Creighton, *John A. Macdonald* (2 vols., Toronto, 1952, 1955).
G. T. Curtis, *Life of James Buchanan* (2 vols., New York, 1883), I.
Caleb Cushing, *The Treaty of Washington* (New York, 1873).
A. G. Dallas, *San Juan, Alaska and the North-west Boundary* (London, 1873).
J. C. Bancroft Davis, *Mr. Fish and the Alabama Claims* (New York, 1893).
W. H. Dawson, *Richard Cobden and Foreign Policy* (London, 1926).
A. G. Dewey, *The Dominions and Diplomacy* (London, 1929).
Dictionary of National Biography (63 vols., 1885-1901).
W. A. Dunning, *The British Empire and the United States* (New York, 1912).
H. E. Egerton, *A Short History of British Colonial Policy* (London, 1932).
Mrs. M. A. P. Egerton, *Admiral Sir Geoffrey Phipps Hornby* (Edinburgh, 1896).
J. Ewart, *Canada and British Wars* (Ottawa, 1923).
—— *The Kingdom of Canada* (Ottawa, 1908).
—— *The Kingdom Papers* (Ottawa, 1911).
D. M. L. Farr, *The Colonial Office and Canada, 1867-87* (Toronto, 1955).
James E. Fitzgerald, *Examination of the Charter of the Hudson's Bay Company* (London, 1849).
E. S. M. Fitzmaurice, *Life of The Second Lord Granville* (2 vols., London, 1905).
J. W. Foster, *A Century of American Diplomacy* (New York, 1901).
H. R. Fox-Bourne, *English Newspapers* (2 vols., London, 1887).
P. R. Frotheringham, *Edward Everett* (New York, 1925).
W. Fuess, *Caleb Cushing* (2 vols., New York, 1923).
J. V. Fuller, *Hamilton Fish* in S. F. Bemis, ed., *American Secretaries of State and their Diplomacy*, vol. VII (New York, 1927).
John S. Galbraith, *The Hudson's Bay Company as an Imperial Factor, 1821-69* (Berkeley and London, 1957).
A. H. Gordon, *Life of Fourth Earl of Aberdeen* (London, 1905).
Great Britain, *Parliamentary Debates*, 3rd series, vols. LXXVIII, LXXXIII, LXXXIV, LXXXVII, CCXV.
Philip Guedalla, *Palmerston* (London, 1927).
R. Guyot, *La première entente cordiale* (Paris, 1926).
A. H. Hardinge *Fourth Earl of Carnarvon* (Oxford, 1925).
T. Hodgins, *British and American Diplomacy Affecting Canada* (Toronto, 1900).
F. W. Howay, *British Columbia, the Making of a Province* (Toronto, 1928).
F. W. Howay and E. O. S. Scholefield, *British Columbia from Earliest Times* (4 vols., Vancouver, 1914).
F. W. Howay, W. N. Sage, and H. F. Angus, *British Columbia and the United States* (Toronto, 1942).
M. A. de W. Howe, *Life and Letters of George Bancroft* (2 vols., New York and London, 1908).
L. H. Jenks, *The Migration of British Capital, to 1875* (London, 1927).
W. F. Johnson, *American Foreign Relations* (2 vols., New York, 1916).
H. L. Keenleyside, *Canada and the United States* (New York, 1929).
Paul Knaplund *Gladstone and Britain's Imperial Policy* (London, 1927).
Andrew Lang, *Life, Letters and Diaries of Stafford Northcote, Earl of Iddesleigh* (London, 1891).
Emil Ludwig, *Bismarck* (London, 1927).
E. J. McCormac, *James K. Polk* (Berkeley, 1922).
D. G. B. Macdonald, *British Columbia and Vancouver Island* (London, 1862).
Helen G. Macdonald, *Canadian Public Opinion and the American Civil War* (Columbia University Studies in History, CXXIV, New York, 1926).
R. M. McElroy, *The Winning of the Far West* (New York, 1914).
Matthew MacFie, *Vancouver Island and British Columbia* (London, 1865).
E. W. McInnes, *The Unguarded Frontier* (New York, 1942).
Douglas Mackay, *The Honourable Company* (London, 1937).
A. C. McLaughlin, *Lewis Cass* (New York, 1891).
Earl of Malmesbury, *Memoirs of an Ex-Minister* (2 vols., London, 1884).
W. R. Manning, *Diplomatic Correspondence of the United States: Canadian Relations, 1784-1860* (4 vols., Washington, 1940-45).

G. E. Marindin, *Letters of Lord Blachford* (London, 1896).

J. A. R. Marriott, *England Since Waterloo* (London, 1929).

R. M. Martin, *The Hudson's Bay Company Territories and Vancouver Island* (London, 1849).

H. E. Maxwell, *Life and Letters of the Fourth Lord Clarendon* (London, 1913).

E. S. Meany, *History of the State of Washington* (Seattle, 1924).

Frederick Merk, *Fur Trade and Empire* (Harvard University Studies, XXXI, London, 1931).

Hunter Miller, ed., *North West Water Boundary: Report of the Experts Summoned by the German Emperor as Arbitrator under Articles 34-42 of the Treaty of Washington of May 8, 1871, Preliminary to His Award Dated October 21, 1872* (University of Washington Publications, Social Sciences, XIII, no. 1, Seattle, January, 1942).

—— ed., *Treaties and Other International Acts of the United States of America* (8 vols., Washington, D.C., 1931-48).

J. Mildmay, *John Lothrop Motley* (London, 1913).

Viscount W. F. Milton, *A History of the San Juan Water Boundary Question, as Affecting the Division of Territory Between Great Britain and the United States* (London, 1869).

J. B. Moore, *History and Digest of the International Arbitrations to which the United States has been a Partner* (6 vols., Washington, D.C., 1898).

—— ed., *Works of James Buchanan* (12 vols., Philadelphia and London, 1908-11).

John Morley, *Life of Gladstone* (2 vols., London, 1905-06).

W. P. Morrell, *British Colonial Policy in the Age of Peel and Russell* (London, 1930).

R. B. Mowat, *Diplomatic Relations of Great Britain and the United States* (London, 1925).

Allan Nevins, *Hamilton Fish* (New York, 1937).

Thomas W. Legh, 2nd Baron Newton, *Lord Lyons: a Record of British Diplomacy* (2 vols., London, 1913).

Stafford Northcote (Earl of Iddesleigh), *Diaries of The First Earl of Iddesleigh* (London, 1907).

S. B. Okum, *The Russian American Company* (Boston, 1957).

Margaret Ormsby, *British Columbia: a History* (Toronto, 1958).

Roundell Palmer, (Earl of Selborne), *Memorials* (4 vols., London, 1896-8).

C. S. Parker, *Sir Robert Peel* (3 vols., London, 1899).

Christina Phelps, *The Anglo-American Peace Movement in Mid-Nineteenth Century* (New York, 1930).

L. S. C. Pickett, *Pickett and His Men* (Atlanta, 1900).

E. L. Pierce, *Memoir and Letters of Charles Sumner* (4 vols., Boston, 1877-93).

John K. Polk, *Diary*, ed. M. M. Quaife (4 vols., Chicago, 1910).

Joseph Pope, *Memoirs of Sir John A. Macdonald* (London, 1930).

Vernon J. Puryear, *England, Russia and the Straits Question (1844-56)* (Berkeley, 1931).

J. S. Reeves, *American Diplomacy Under Tyler and Polk* (New York, 1907).

E. E. Rich, ed., *The Letters of John McLoughlin from Fort Vancouver to the Governor and Committee, Second Series, 1839-44* (London and Toronto, 1943).

James D. Richardson, *A Compilation of the Messages and Papers of the Presidents* (10 vols., Washington, 1896-9).

Lord John Russell, *Recollections and Suggestions, 1813-73* (London, 1875).

Walter N. Sage, *Sir James Douglas and British Columbia* (University of Toronto Studies, History and Economics, VI, Toronto, 1930).

—— "The Annexation Movement in British Columbia," Royal Society of Canada *Transactions,* 3rd series, XXI (1927), sect. II.

Carl Schurz, *Reminiscences* (New York, 1909).

Winfield Scott, *Memoirs* (2 vols., New York, 1864).

W. O. Scroggs, *Filibusters and Financiers* (New York, 1916).

W. H. Seward, *Autobiography* (3 vols., New York, 1891).

Lester Burrell Shippee, *Canadian-American Relations (1849-74)* (New Haven and Toronto, 1939).

Adam Shortt and Arthur G. Doughty, eds., *Canada and Its Provinces,* (23 vols., Ottawa, 1914), VIII, 865-76.

George Simpson, *Narrative of a Voyage Round the World* (2 vols., London, 1847).

Goldwin Smith, *The Treaty of Washington, 1871* (New York, 1941).

Clinton A. Snowden, *History of the State of Washington* (4 vols., New York, 1909).

Henry Nash Smith, *Virgin Land: The American West as Symbol and Myth* (Cambridge, Mass., 1950).

C. P. Stacey, *Canada and the British Army* (London, 1936).

H. Stevens, *The Life of General Isaac I. Stevens* (2 vols., New York, 1900).

Moorfield Storey and Edward W. Emerson, *Ebenezer R. Hoar* (New York, 1911).

G. Sturgis, *The Oregon Question* (Boston, 1845).

Henry Taylor, *Autobiography* (2 vols., London, 1885).
J. Tilley and S. Gaselee, *The Foreign Office* (London, 1933).
Travers Twiss, *The Oregon Question Examined* (London, 1846).
Richard W. Van Alstyne, *American Diplomacy in Action* (London, 1944).
—— *The Rising American Empire* (London, 1960).
George Vancouver, *A Voyage of Discovery to the North Pacific Ocean and Round the World* (London, 1798).
H. R. Wagner, *The Cartography of the North West Coast of America* (2 vols., Berkeley, 1937).
Spencer Walpole, *Life of Lord John Russell* (London, 1891).
E. W. Watkin, *Canada and the United States* (London, 1887).
A. K. Weinberg, *Manifest Destiny* (New York, 1935).
Mrs. R. Wemyss, ed., *Memoirs and Letters of Sir Robert Morier* (2 vols., London, 1911).
Charles Wilkes, *Narrative of the United States Exploring Expedition, 1838-1842* (5 vols., Philadelphia, 1845).
M. W. Williams, *Anglo-American Isthmian Diplomacy* (London, 1916).
Beckles Willson, *The Great Company* (2 vols., London, 1900).
Lucien Wolf, *Life of the First Marquis of Ripon* (2 vols., London, 1921).
E. L. Woodward, *The Age of Reform (1815-70)* (London, 1938).
H. M. Wriston, *Executive Agents in American Foreign Relations* (London, 1929).
Hume Wrong, *The United States and Canada* (Toronto, 1927).

C. Periodicals

American Historical Review
John S. Galbraith, "Myths of the 'Little England' Era," LXVII (1961), 34-48.
Kathleen Judson, "Dr. McLoughlin's Last Letter to the Hudson's Bay Company," XXI (1916), 104.
Frederick Merk, "The Oregon Pioneers and the Boundary," XXLX (1924), 681-99.
Rising Lake Morrow, "The Negotiation of the Anglo-American Treaty of 1870," XXXIX (1933-4), 663-81.
Joseph Schafer, "Letters of Sir George Simpson 1841-43," XIV (1909), 70-94.
—— "The British Attitude toward the Oregon Question," XVI (1911), 273-99.
R. J. Turner, "The Colonization of the West," XI (1906), 302-27.

British Columbia Historical Quarterly
Donald C. Davidson, "The Relations of the Hudson's Bay Company with the Russian-American on the Northwest Coast, 1827-67," V (1941), 33-51.
W. E. Ireland, "The Annexation Petition of 1869," IV (1940), 267-87.
Paul Knaplund, "James Stephen and the Granting of Vancouver Island to the Hudson's Bay Company (1846-48)," IX (1945), 259-71.
F. W. Laing, "Hudson's Bay Company Lands on the Mainland of British Columbia, 1858-61," III, (1939), 75-100.
W. Kaye Lamb, "Some Notes on the Douglas Family," XVII (1953), 41 ff.
—— "The Founding of Fort Victoria," VII (1943), 71-92.
F. V. Longstaff and W. Kaye Lamb, "The Royal Navy on the Northwest Coast, 1813-50," IX (1945), 1-24; 113-28.
John T. Saywell, "Sir Joseph Trutch," XIX (1955), 71-92.
Reginald Saw, "Sir John H. Pelly, Bart.," XIII (1949), 23-32.

Canadian Historical Review
Alvin C. Gluek, Jr., "The Riel Rebellion and Canadian-American Relations," XXXVI, no. 3 (Sept., 1955), 199-221.
H. L. Keenleyside, "American Economic Penetration of Canada," VIII, no. 1 (March, 1927), 31-40.
Paul Knaplund, "Gladstone's Views on British Colonial Policy," IV, no. 4 (December, 1923), 304-15.
—— "Sir James Stephen and British North American Problems, 1840-1847," V, no. 1 (March, 1924), 22-41.
Dorothy E. T. Long, "The Elusive Mr. Ellice," XXIII, no. 1 (March, 1942), 42-57.
Morden H. Long, "Sir John Rose and the Informal Beginnings of the Canadian High Commissionership," XII, no. 1 (March, 1931), 23-43.
James O. McCabe, "Arbitration and the Oregon Question," XLI, no. 4 (Dec., 1960), 308-27.

Maureen M. Robson, "The *Alabama* Claims and the Anglo-American Reconciliation, 1865-71," XLII, no. 1 (March, 1961), 1-22.

F. E. Ross, "The Retreat of the Hudson's Bay Company in the Pacific North-west," XVIII, no. 3 (Sept., 1937), 262-80.

C. P. Stacey, "The Hudson's Bay Company and Anglo-American Military Rivalries during the Oregon Dispute," XVIII, no. 3 (Sept., 1937), 281-300.

—— "Fenianism and the Rise of National Feeling in Canada at the Time of Confederation," XII, no. 3 (Sept., 1931), 238-61.

—— "Britain's Withdrawal from North America, 1864-1871," XXXVI, no. 3 (Sept., 1955), 185-98.

R. G. Trotter, "Canada as a Factor in Anglo-American Relations of the 1860's," XVI, no. 1 (March, 1935), 19-26.

Oregon Historical Review

M. Bradley, "The Political Beginning of Oregon," IX (1908), 42-72.

Robert C. Clark, "How British and American Subjects United in a Common Government for Oregon Territory in 1844," XIII (1912), 140-59.

—— "The Last Stage in the Formation of a Provisional Government for Oregon," XVI (1915), 313-29.

Henry S. Commager, "England and the Oregon Treaty of 1846," XXVIII (1927), 18-38.

A. Fish, "The Last Phase of the Oregon Boundary Dispute," XXII (1921), 161-224.

Walter N. Sage, "James Douglas on the Columbia (1830-49)," XXVII (1926), 365-80.

Joseph Schafer, "The British Attitude towards the Oregon Question, 1845-46," XVI (1915), 273-99.

Richard W. Van Alstyne, "International Rivalries in the Pacific Northwest," XLVI (1945), 185-218.

M. L. Wardell, "Oregon Immigration Prior to 1846," XXVII (1926), 41-64.

Other Periodicals

Athenaeum, Review of books on Oregon Question, April 4, 1846, p. 288.

Blackwood's, "How They Manage Things in the Model Republic," LIX (1846), 439.

Bulletin of the Institute of Historical Research (London): Valerie Cromwell, "An Incident in the Development of the Permanent Under Secretaryship at the Foreign Office," XXXIII, no. 87 (May, 1960), 99-113.

Maureen M. Robson, "Liberals and Vital Interests: The Debate on International Arbitration, 1815-72," XXXII, no. 85 (May, 1959), 38-55.

Canadian Magazine for June, 1914 and March, 1926.

Canadian Monthly: C. Lindsey, "The Treaty of Washington," I, no. 1 (1872), 453.

Edinburgh Review: "The Oregon Question," LXXXIII (July, 1845), 238-65.

English Historical Review: Kenneth Bourne, "British Preparations for War with the North, 1861," LXXVI, no. 301 (October, 1961), 600-32.

E. Jones-Parry, "Under-Secretaries of State for Foreign Affairs, 1782-1855," XLIX, (1934), 308-20.

Fraser's Magazine: "England and Yankee-land," XXXIV (October, 1845), 485 ff.

Historical Journal (formerly *Cambridge Historical Journal*): W. E. Mosse, "Public Opinion and Foreign Policy: The British Public and the War-scare of November 1870," VI, no. 1 (1963), 38-58.

Zara Steiner, "The Last Years of the Old Foreign Office," VI, no. 1 (1963), 59-77.

Mississippi Valley Historical Review: Wilbur Devereux Jones, "Lord Ashburton and the Maine Boundary Negotiations," XL (Dec., 1953), 477-90.

North American Review: "The Oregon Question," Jan., 1846.

Overland Monthly: "The San Juan Difficulty," 77 (San Francisco, 1869).

Pacific Historical Review: W. D. Jones and J. C. Vinson, "British Preparedness and the Oregon Settlement," XXII (1953), 353-64.

Hollis R. Lynch, "Sir Joseph William Trutch, a British-American Pioneer on the Pacific Coast," XXX (August, 1961), 245-55.

Pacific North West Quarterly (formerly *Washington Historical Quarterly*): A. Tunem, "The Dispute over the San Juan Island Water Boundary," XXIII (Jan., April, July, 1932), 38-46, 133-36, 196-204.

Political Science Quarterly: R. L. Schuyler, "Polk and the Oregon Compromise of 1846," XXVI (1911), 443-61.

Quarterly Review: "The Oregon Question," LXXVII (March, 1846), 563-610.

Revue des Deux Mondes: Auguste Langel, "Le Traité de Washington," XCI-XCVI (1871), 795-810.

Spectator: "English Opinion of America," 1846, pp. 134ff.

Newspapers
Morning Chronicle, Morning Herald, Morning Post, Standard, The Times, Examiner, Daily News, Daily Telegraph, Pall Mall Gazette, Saturday Review. (All printed in London.)

NOTES

Abbreviations used in these notes are as follows: *A.H.R.—American Historical Review;* B.M.—British Museum; C.O.—Colonial Office; *C.H.R.—Canadian Historical Review;* D.S. Misc. Letters—Department of State, Miscellaneous Letters; F.O.—Foreign Office; G.D.—Granville Drafts H.B.C.—Hudson's Bay Company; P.R.O.—Public Record Office, London.

CHAPTER ONE

1. Copy of Pelly's letter giving the gist of the conversation with the foreign secretary is in F.O. 5/809.
2. *Ibid.*
3. Hunter Miller, ed., *Treaties and Other International Acts of the United States of America* (8 vols., Washington, 1931-48), VIII, 301.
4. F.O. 5/809, Memorandum by H. U. Addington, Feb. 27, 1854.
5. *Ibid.*, Memorandum by Addington, March 30, 1847.
6. *Ibid.*, Palmerston to Pakenham, no. 25, April 19, 1847.
7. Quoted in Lord Dalling, *Palmerston* (London, 1874), p. 143.
8. *Morning Chronicle,* Jan. 17, 1846, p. 4.
9. B.M., Aberdeen MSS., ff. 1-51, Aberdeen to Pakenham, June 30, 1846.
10. F.O. 5/809, Palmerston to Crampton, no. 21, Dec. 18, 1847.
11. *Ibid.*, Crampton to Palmerston, no. 2, Jan. 13, 1848.
12. F.O. 5/809.
13. Appendix to British statement, Treaty of Washington, 1872, copy in F.O. 5/1472.
14. F.O. 5/809, Crampton to Palmerston, no. 91, Oct. 29, 1849.
15. Miller, *Treaties*, VIII, 303.
16. *Ibid.*, VIII, 304.
17. F.O. 5/809, Douglas to Sir John Pakington, Dec. 9, 1852.
18. For accounts of his life and antecedents see Coats and Gosnell, *Sir James Douglas* (Toronto, 1926), and W. N. Sage, *Sir James Douglas and British Columbia* (Toronto, 1930), and W. Kaye Lamb, "Some Notes on the Douglas Family," *B. C. Hist. Q.*, XVII (1953) 41 ff.
19. C. F. Hickson, "Palmerston and the Clayton-Bulwer Treaty," *Cambridge Hist. J.*, III (1929-31), 295-303. Many fine points on the significance of the treaty throughout the fifties are made by R. W. Van Alstyne, "British Diplomacy and the Clayton-Bulwer Treaty," *J. Mod. Hist.*, XI (1938), 149-83.
20. F.O. 5/809, Douglas to C.O., Nov. 21, 1853.
21. *Ibid.*
22. *Ibid.*, Feb. 27, 1854. After discussion with Benjamin Hawes and James Stephen, permanent officials at the C.O., and Pelly of the H.B.C., Lord Grey, the colonial secretary, took the view that "looking to the encroaching spirit of the United States I think it is of importance to strengthen the British hold upon the territory now assigned to us." Quoted by P. Knaplund, "James Stephen and the Granting of Vancouver Island to the Hudson's Bay Company, (1846-48),"B. C. Hist. Q., IX (1945), 259-71.
23. Nov. 23, 1852. D.S. Misc. Letters, Jan.-Feb., 1853, enclosure in a letter from Senator John B. Weller to Secretary Everett, Feb. 10, 1853, quoted in Miller, *Treaties*, VIII, 307.
24. F.O. 5/809, Douglas to C. O., Feb. 27, 1854.
25. *Ibid.*, copy forwarded to F.O. May 20, 1854.
26. *Ibid.*, Sangster to Douglas, May 5, 1854, enclosure in Douglas to C.O., May 19.
27. Ebey to Secretary of the Treasury James Guthrie, May 15, 1854, in National Archives, Treasury Dept. Records, Secretary's Files, Series K, quoted in Miller, *Treaties*, VIII, 312-13.
28. P. Griffith, British Chargé *ad interim* at Washington to William Hunter, acting secretary of state, Sept. 3, 1854, in W. R. Manning, *Diplomatic Correspondence of the United States: Canadians Relations, 1784-1860* (4 vols., Washington, 1940-45), IV, 596-7.

29. Marcy to Griffith, Sept. 7, 1854, in Manning, *Diplomatic Correspondence*, IV, 101.
30. D.S. Misc. Letters, Sept.-Oct., 1854, Guthrie to Marcy, Sept. 11, 1854, quoted in Miller, *Treaties*, VIII, 313.
31. F.O. 5/809, Douglas to H.B.C., Oct. 20, 1854.
32. *Ibid.*, Douglas to C.O., Feb. 27, 1855, copy enclosed in C.O. to F.O., May 17, 1855.
33. H. R. Crosbie to Secretary Cass, April 3, 1860, printed in Serial 1056, House Ex. Doc. no. 77, 36th Cong., 1st Sess. Cf. F.O. 5/809, Douglas to H.B.C., Feb. 27, 1855, and Griffin to Douglas, April 2, 1855, encl. 11 in C.O. to F.O., Aug. 15, 1855.
34. F.O. 5/665, Douglas to Stevens, April 26, 1855.
35. *Ibid.*, copy of Steven to Douglas, May 12. Encl. in Douglas to C.O., Sept. 28, 1855; *also see* Serial 837, Report no. 251, 34th Cong., 1st Sess., p. 4.
36. James D. Richardson, *A Compilation of the Messages and Papers of the Presidents* (10 vols., Washington, 1896-99), V, 208.
37. F.O. 5/809, Douglas to C.O., Nov. 24, 1853.
38. *Ibid.*, Griffin to Douglas, April 2, 1855.
39. F.O. 5/810, H.B.C. to F.O., Feb. 29, 1856.
40. *Ibid.*, C.O. to H.B.C., March 22, 1856.
41. F.O. 5/664, Sept. 18, 1846.
42. F.O. 5/809, no. 156, Marcy to Stevens, July 14, 1855, copy enclosed in Crampton to F.O., July 30, 1855. *See also ibid.*, Marcy to Crampton, July 17, 1855. Copy in Manning, *Diplomatic Correspondence*, IV.
43. F.O. 5/809, copy of Marcy's letter to Stevens is encl. 1 to Gov.-Gen. Head of Canada from Crampton; Head's reply is encl. 5 in Crampton's no. 136.
44. Lord Lyons to Lord John Russell, Sept. 21, 1859, quoted in T. W. L., 2nd Baron Newton, *Lord Lyons: a Record of British Diplomacy* (2 vols., London, 1913), I, 20. Cf. Roundell Palmer, *Memorials* (4 vols., London, 1896-8), I, 203. *See also* Odo Russell's despatches from Berlin, *passim*.
45. R. L. Schuyler, "The Rise of Anti-Imperialism in England," *Political Science Q.*, XXXVII (1922), 467.
46. W. P. Morrell, *British Colonial Policy under Peel and Russell* (London, 1930), pp. 29-31.
47. *Ibid.*, p. 45.
48. G. E. Marindin, *Letters of Lord Blachford* (London, 1896), pp. 299-300. Cf. H. E. Egerton, *A Short History of British Colonial Policy* (London, 1932), p. 317, and Henry Taylor, *Autobiography* (2 vols., London, 1885), II, 234 ff.
49. Newton, *Lord Lyons, passim*.
50. S. Walrond, *Letters and Journals of the Eighth Earl of Elgin* (London, 1872), p. 60, quoted by H. L. Keenleyside, *Canada and the United States* (New York, 1929), p. 122.
51. *The Times*, leading article in issue of March 16, 1846.
52. *Ibid.*, Jan. 4, 1846.
53. Quoted by J. W. Pratt, "The Origin of Manifest Destiny," *A.H.R.*, XXXII, (1927), 795-8.
54. Quoted by E. D. Adams, *The Power of Ideals in American History* (London, 1913).

CHAPTER TWO

1. F.O. 5/812, Dallas to Clarendon, Aug. 28, 1856.
2. F.O. 5/810, no. 1, Clarendon to Prevost. Richards was to conduct a survey of the waters in the area.
3. Copies of the correspondence of the two commissioners are enclosed in Prevost's despatch no. 7, Dec. 7, 1857, in F.O. 5/810 and in Serial 1316, Sen. Ex. Doc. no. 29, 40th Cong., 2nd Sess., pp. 5-47.
4. F.O. 5/810, no. 2, Dec. 20, 1856; also in Serial 1316, p. 5.
5. *Ibid.*, Prevost to Campbell, no. 2, June 20, 1857.
6. Serial 1316, p. 96, Secretary of State W. Marcy to Campbell, Feb. 25, 1857.
7. A note on this in the F.O. archives (F.O. 5/813) by the permanent under-secretary is interesting: "After much hesitation and doubt I have come to the conclusion that we may safely give Mr. Dallas this extract of Captain Prevost's instructions. I understand privately from the Admiralty that a middle channel between Rosario and Arro Straits has been found."
8. F.O. 5/810, Prevost to F.O., no. 7, Dec. 7, 1857
9. *Papers Relating to the Treaty of Washington* (6 vols., Washington, 1872-4), V: *Berlin Arbitration*, p. 50.
10. Serial 1316, p. 73.
11. F.O. 5/810, Prevost to Campbell, no. 3, Nov. 24, 1857.

12. Copies of the correspondence between the two commissioners are enclosed in Prevost's despatch to Clarendon, no. 7, Dec. 7, 1857, in F.O. 5/810. The enclosures are: (1) Prevost to Campbell, no. 1, Oct. 28; (2) Campbell to Prevost, Nov. 2; (3) Prevost to Campbell, no. 2, Nov. 29; (4) Campbell to Prevost, Nov. 18; (5) Prevost to Campbell, No. 3, Nov. 24; (6) Arrowsmith to H.B.C., Sept. 29; (7) Campbell to Prevost, Nov. 28; (8) Crampton to Buchanan, Jan. 13, 1848; (9) Prevost to Campbell, No. 4, Dec. 1, 1857; (10) Campbell to Prevost, Dec. 2, 1857; (11) A map showing all claims. Copies of all the above are also printed in Serial 1316, pp. 5-47.
13. F.O. 5/810, Malmesbury to Prevost, May 14, 1858.
14. *Ibid.*, Prevost to Clarendon, no. 7, Dec. 7, 1857.
15. *Ibid.*, Prevost to Hammond, April 13, 1858.
16. Serial 1316, p. 90, Campbell to Cass, June 21, 1859.
17. F.O. 5/810, Prevost to F.O. "Private," Dec. 16, 1857.

CHAPTER THREE

1. F.O. 5/813, C.O. to F.O., March 6, 1858.
2. *Ibid.*, C.O. to F.O., Aug. 24, 1858.
3. *Ibid.*, Admiralty to F.O., April 8, 1858. This Admiralty attitude remained the same throughout the dispute. See their letter to the F.O. after Richards's survey report had arrived in London, April 9, 1859.
4. Aberdeen's reply was written by his son, Sir Arthur Gordon, who acted as his secretary *Ibid.*, Gordon to Russell, Aug. 21, 1858.
5. *Ibid.*, Pakenham to F.O., April 19, 1858.
6. Hammond's memorandum of April 20 is to be found in F.O. 5/813. Hammond also makes the remark that "we ought to come to an early decision and require an early decision on the part of the United States and not allow them to play their usual game of procrastination at which they always win."
7. F.O. 5/813, memorandum of Feb. 3, 1859.
8. Strictly speaking, the name "Douglas Strait" can be applied only to a passage which forms a part of the Middle Channel.
9. Richards's report is to be found in F.O. 5/813.
10. Quoted by Campbell in letter to Gen. Cass, Sept. 25, 1858, in Serial 1316, Sen. Ex Doc. no. 29, 40th Cong., 2nd Sess., p. 52.
11. *Ibid.*
12. *Ibid.*, p. 134.
13. Serial 1393, I, 2.
14. *Ibid.*, report of A. A. Humphreys, chief engineer, March 10, 1869.
15. Prevost to Hammond, April 13, 1858, in F.O. 5/810. Prevost in turn had been influenced by H.B.C. reports placed before him by the governor stressing the island's strategic value. See, for instance, enclosures with C.O. to F.O., Sept. 26, 1856, in F.O. 5/809. The famous Gen. Harney justified his seizure of the island (*infra*) in 1859 by telling his superiors that San Juan has "the most commanding position we possess on the sound ... one of the finest harbours on the coast is to be found, completely sheltered, offering the best location for a naval station on the Pacific coast." (Serial 1316, p. 148.)
16. F.O. 5/810, no. 7, Prevost to Malmesbury, no. 7, July 23, 1859.
17. F.O. 5/813, C.O. to F.O., March 6, 1858.
18. *Ibid.*, Russell to Lyons, Aug. 24, 1859.
19. Serial 1316, p. 75, Campbell to Cass, Jan. 20, 1859.
20. F.O. 5/813, Russell to Prevost, Aug. 24, 1859.

CHAPTER FOUR

1. Cass to Nugent, U.S. special agent, Aug. 2, 1858, quoted in W. R. Manning, *Diplomatic Correspondence of the United States: Canadian Relations, 1784-1860* (4 vols., Washington, 1940-45), IV, 169-72. Many despatches quoted by the present writer are printed in Manning.
2. *Ibid.*, IV, 754-79, Nugent to Cass, Jan. 8, 1859.
3. Serial 1056, House Ex. Doc., no. 77, 36th Cong., 1st Sess., p. 2 ff., H. R. Crosbie to Secretary of State Cass, April 3, 1860.
4. F.O. 5/813, no. 6, Douglas to colonial secretary, Feb. 19, 1859.
5. *Ibid.*, F.O. to C.O., April 27, 1859.
6. He later swore that he owned 160 acres, but Dallas, ridiculing such a statement, said

that Cutler's "farm" was a mere potato patch. This is the more likely view since he would hardly have established a farm in the short period of two months. See copy of Cutler's affidavit enclosed in Harney to Scott, Sept. 16, 1859, in F.O. 5/815 and Dallas to Harney, May 16, 1860. It is also printed as enclosure to no. 27, Lyons to Cass, in Serial 1027, pp. 49-50.

7. Serial 1316, pp. 146-8, Dallas to Harney, May 10, 1860.

8. Griffin to Douglas, June 15, 1859, copy in F.O. 5/815.

9. Serial 1316, p. 183.

10. Dallas to Harney, May 10, 1860. Copy in F.O. 5/815, enclosed in Lyons to Lord John Russell, no. 213, June 18, 1860. Also printed in Manning, *Diplomatic Correspondence*, IV, 855-6.

11. The letter in Serial 1316, p. 260, says "*an* unimpeachable witness," quoted in Hunter Miller, ed., *Treaties and Other International Acts of the United States of America* (8 vols., Washington, 1931-48), VIII, 337. Much of the official correspondence is quoted *in extenso* or in full by Miller on many aspects or the water boundary question.

12. Serial 1024, p. 107, Harney to Scott, July 19, 1859.

13. Serial 1027, p. 146, Harney to Pickett, July 18, 1859, letter no. 4. There were four military camps in the Pacific northwest: at Fort Vancouver, Fort Steilacoom, Fort Bellingham, and Fort Townsend.

14. H. Stevens, *The Life of General Isaac I. Stevens* (2 vols., New York, 1900), II, 292. Richard D. Gholson arrived to succeed Stevens on July 10, 1859.

15. Cutler's affidavit, Serial 1316, pp. 183 ff.

16. Serial 1056, p. 6. De Courcy's account appears in his letter to Douglas, July 29, 1859, copy enclosed in Douglas to C.O., Aug. 5, F.O. 5/730.

17. Prevost states that there were seven British settlers on the island, an estimate that is corroborated by Magistrate de Courcy. It is difficult correctly to determine the number of Americans. The petition to Harney had 22 signatures, though Harney claimed there were 25 *families* of Americans. H. R. Crosbie, a reliable authority who was appointed American magistrate on San Juan on July 29, 1859, found 29 actual settlers. Douglas claimed that up to 1859 there was only one American on the island, but in that year "a few more arrived." Magistrate Griffin on June 16, 1859, estimated that there were "upwards of sixteen" Americans on San Juan. Hunter Miller sums up the position thus: "By the summer of 1859 there were certainly twenty-five Americans on San Juan" though "it seems that from 1855 to some time in 1858, there were almost no Americans on the island." (Miller, *Treaties*, VIII, 331).

18. Serial 1056, p. 5, Crosbie to Cass, April 3, 1860.

19. Serial 1316, copy enclosed in Campbell to Cass, Aug. 18, 1859.

20. Hornby to his wife, July 31, 1859, in Mrs. M. A. P. Egerton, *Admiral Sir Geoffrey Phipps Hornby* (Edinburgh, 1896), p. 64. Cf. de Courcy to Baynes, Aug. 5, in F.O. 5/730, enclosed in Baynes to Admiralty of Oct. 3.

21. F.O. 5/730. De Courcy to Baynes, Aug. 5, encl. 2 in Baynes to Admiralty, Oct. 3.

22. *Ibid.*, Douglas to C.O., Aug. 1 (copy also in C.O. 305/11). Captain de Courcy left for San Francisco on Aug. 5 so that Capt. Hornby became senior naval officer in the region.

23. F.O. 5/810, Prevost to Douglas, Aug. 1, 1859, encl. 3 in Prevost to F.O., Aug. 3.

24. F.O. 5/730, Minute of Council of Principal Officers of Vancouver Island and British Columbia, enclosure in Douglas to C.O., Aug. 1.

25. *Ibid.*, Douglas to Hornby, Aug. 2, encl. 1 in Douglas to C.O., no. 31, Aug. 8.

26. Copies of the correspondence dealing with this interview are to be found as enclosures in Douglas to the C.O., Aug. 8, 1859, F.O. 5/815: Encl. 1, Douglas to Hornby, Aug. 2. Encl. 2, Hornby to Douglas, Aug. 4. Encl. 4, Hornby to Pickett, Aug. 3. Encl. 5, Pickett to Hornby, Aug. 3. The two last mentioned are printed in Serial 1027, pp. 155-6.

27. Baynes to Admiralty, no. 107, copy in F.O. 5/730. See also Serial 1316, p. 166. Steps were taken at once to increase this force, a first-class frigate and a vessel of the *Clio* class being sent to the troubled waters. See F.O. 5/730, F.O. to Admiralty, Oct. 2, 1859.

28. Serial 1316, p. 176.

29. John S. Galbraith, *The Hudson's Bay Company as an Imperial Factor, 1821-69* (London, 1957), p. 305.

30. F.O. 5/730, Douglas to C.O., no. 3, Executive, Aug. 5, 1859.

31. F.O. 5/813, Douglas to C.O., Feb. 19, 1859.

32. F.O. 5/809, Crampton to F.O., no. 156, July 30, 1855. Crampton had also written to the governor-general of British North America urging "the same spirit of forbearance which is inculcated upon the authorities and Citizens of the United States."

33. Marcy to Stevens, July 17, 1855.

34. F.O. 5/813, F.O. to C.O. F.O. to Lyons, April 25, 1859.

35. F.O. 5/814, Douglas to Lyons, Aug. 8.

36. F.O. 5/730, Douglas to colonial secretary, no. 30, Aug. 5.
37. Douglas Mackay, *The Honourable Company* (London, 1937), p. 219.
38. F.O. 5/634, Douglas to C.O., Jan. 30, 1855, enclosure in C.O. to F.O., May 3, 1855.
39. Douglas to H.B.C., Nov. 21, 1853.
40. F.O. 5/815, Douglas to Newcastle, "Confidential," Dec. 15, 1859.
41. *Ibid.*
42. Serial 1027, p. 153, Pickett to Pleasanton, Aug. 3, 1859.
43. Serial 1316, p. 158.
44. F.O. 5/815 Baynes to Admiralty, Aug. 19, 1859.
45. Douglas to Harney, Aug. 13, 1859, enclosure in C.O. to F.O., Oct. 22, in F.O. 5/814. Copy also in Serial 1316, pp. 170 ff. Hunter Miller, *Treaties*, VIII, convicts Douglas of deception on several counts: (1) He cannot accept Douglas's assertion that the Company and the government of Vancouver Island were "entirely distinct," for "it was notorious that influence of Hudson's Bay Company with the administration of Vancouver Island was great and relations necessarily very close" (p. 371). (2) Douglas told the government on Nov. 24, 1853, that there was not a settlement of whites on San Juan when in fact it had been decided some months previously to establish Griffin and assistants there (p. 306). (3) The governor represented to his own government that Griffin's establishment was in the personal name of Griffin and not of the company, though the company's explanation of this seems reasonable. Thus the deputy-governor, J. Shepherd, told the British government that they were "of opinion that the claims of an independent British subject would be more likely to be respected by the Authorities of the United States . . ." (*See* Shepherd to C.O., Feb. 29, 1856, in F.O. 5/812). (4) "In his letter of complaint to Governor Stevens of Washington Territory, dated April 26, 1855, Governor Douglas presents the episode as a wrong done to "Charles Griffin, a British Subject" and does not mention the company.
46. C.O. 305/11. It is apparent from the Foreign Office records that there was considerable doubt about the wisdom of repudiating Douglas's policy, and a memorandum by the C.O.'s permanent under-secretary speaks of this: "From the tenour of the Governor's remarks it is evident that he considers that passing events strongly support the original view that it would have been better to effect a landing of a British Force immediately that the Americans had landed theirs . . . it is difficult to receive the daily arriving accounts of the manner in which the Americans are strengthening themselves without having some uncomfortable misgivings whether after all Governor Douglas was not right and whether it would not have been better to land some of our people likewise and announce that we should maintain a joint occupation until the Americans withdrew. We have preserved the peace, but I greatly doubt we may have lost San Juan." This was evoked by the nature of the colonial secretary's despatch of Oct. 29 to Douglas (*infra*). Newcastle's reply to the memorandum is his of the same date quoted below.

CHAPTER FIVE

1. F.O. 5/730. Harney to Douglas, Aug. 6, encl. 5 in Baynes to Admiralty, no. 110. Printed in Serial 1316, Sen. Ex. Doc. no. 29, 40th Cong., 2nd Sess., p. 157.
2. F.O. 5/730, Prevost to Campbell, encl. 1 in Admiralty to F.O., Oct. 1, 1859.
3. F.O. 5/815, Harney to adjutant-general, Aug. 7, copy enclosed in Lyons to F.O., no. 74, Feb. 28, 1860, printed in Serial 1027, Sen. Ex. Doc. no. 10, 36th Cong., 1st Sess., p. 159.
4. F.O. 5/730, Baynes to Admiralty, Aug. 12, no. 110. A copy of Casey's letter to Baynes and the reply are enclosed. Printed as Enclosure 11b in Serial 1027. Casey to Pleasanton, Aug. 12: "I had gone 25 miles and he would not come 100 yards."
5. F.O. 5/730, Hornby to Baynes, Aug. 15. Cf. Chapter IV (*supra*), n. 46.
6. F.O. 5/814, Baynes to Hornby, Aug. 16, 1859.
7. Copy of letter printed in Serial 1027, p. 143.
8. F.O. 5/814, Douglas to Harney, Aug. 13, copy as enclosure in C.O. to F.O. Oct. 22.
9. F.O. 5/815, Douglas to C.O. Aug. 22.
10. British subjects had been warned that if they settled on San Juan they did so at their own risk. The company had been given, by their charter in 1849, the exclusive right to sell land "at a reasonable figure" on Vancouver Island and the adjacent islands. No British subjects other than company servants ever settled in this area; a despatch to Douglas by the then colonial secretary, Sir William Molesworth, dated Aug. 13, 1855, distinctly disavowed on the part of the British government any intention to sanction the colonization of the area.
11. Lyons to Lord John Russell, no. 189, Sept. 13, 1859. See also his despatch to the F.O. of Oct. 3 in F.O. 5/814.
12. Lord John Russell to Lyons, Sept. 21, T.W.L., 2nd Baron Newton, *Lord Lyons: a Record of British Diplomacy* (2 vols., London, 1913), I, 20.

13. F.O. 5/730, Lord John Russell to Douglas, Sept. 29.

14. Secretary of war to Harney, Sept. 3, printed as Letter 15 in Serial 1027. A copy was shown by Gen. Cass to the British minister before its despatch. Cf. F.O. 5/715, Lyons to Russell, Sept. 12.

15. Acting secretary of war to Scott, Sept. 16, Serial 1027, pp. 161-2. The basis of the instructions to Scott, so Cass assured Lyons, was Marcy's letter of July 14, 1855. See Lyons's cipher despatch of Sept. 15 in F.O. 5/813.

16. F.O. 5/815, Baynes to Admiralty, Nov. 9, enclosed in C.O. to F.O. Jan. 2, 1860.

17. Copies of the Douglas-Scott correspondence appear as enclosures to Letter 23, Serial 1027, pp. 189ff. See also enclosures in Douglas's despatch to the C.O. of Nov. 19, F.O. 5/815. They are: Scott to Douglas, Oct. 25 and Nov. 2, and Douglas to Scott, Oct. 29 and Nov. 3. Scott's letter of November encloses a project for a temporary settlement.

18. Nov. 16, 1859, copy enclosed in C.O. to F.O., Nov. 24.

19. Printed as encl. 0 to Letter 23 in Serial 1027.

20. F.O. 5/815, Baynes to Admiralty, March 28, 1860. Approval by the foreign secretary of these instructions was intimated on May 17.

21. A copy of the instructions was transmitted by Pickett, thence to Bazelgette and thence to Douglas and Lyons.

22. F.O. 5/815, copy enclosed in Lyons to Russell, no. 204, June 7.

23. *Ibid.*

24. *Ibid.*, Douglas to Newcastle, no. 24, May 7, 1860.

25. *Ibid.*, Russell to Lyons, July 20, 1860, "Seen by Lord Palmerston and the Queen."

26. C.O. 305/15, F.O. to C.O., Jan. 30, 1860. The colonial secretary, the Duke of Newcastle, would have withdrawn civil magistrates "who were more likely to clash than military officers."

27. Harney to Scott, July 19, 1859, copy in Serial 1024, p. 107ff. Cf. Harney to adjutant-general, Aug. 29, in Serial 1027, p. 179. ". . . the power that possesses it [San Juan] will command a supremacy on this coast." "A one-time Indian fighter in Florida, Harney pictured himself as the Andrew Jackson of the Northwest, appointed to invade that country as Jackson had in 1818 invaded East Florida." (R. W. Van Alstyne, *The Rising American Empire* (London, 1960), p. 118.)

28. Serial 1027.

29. L. C. Pickett, *Pickett and His Men* (Atlanta, 1899), pp. 123-4.

30. C. A. Snowden, *History of the State of Washington* (4 vols., New York, 1909), IV, 60. Snowden asserts that both the war in Italy and the secessional sympathies of Harney and Secretary of War Floyd had their influence.

CHAPTER SIX

1. Lyons communicated the proposal of Aug. 24 to Cass on Sept. 12 (*supra*).

2. F.O. 5/814; also printed in Serial 1027, Sen. Ex. Doc. no. 10, 36th Cong., 1st Sess., pp. 231-40.

3. F.O. 5/814, F.O. to Lyons, Nov. 29, 1859.

4. *Ibid.*, "Confidential."

5. F.O. 5/815; also printed as Letter no. 20 in Serial 1027.

6. F.O. 5/815, Russell to Lyons, no. 62, "Seen by Lord Palmerston," March 9, 1860; printed as Letter no. 21, in Serial 1027. The name "Douglas" properly applies only to part of the Middle Channel.

7. F.O. 5/815, Lyons to foreign secretary, no. 126, April 2, 1860.

8. Cass to Dallas, no. 252, April 23, 1860, "Communicated to Lord John Russell by Mr. Dallas," May 10, in Serial 1027, letter 22.

9. For an account of the Central-American dispute see S. F. Bemis ed., *The American Secretaries of State and Their Diplomacy* (10 vols., New York, 1927), VI. Cf. *The Cambridge History of British Foreign Policy*, ed. A. W. Ward and G. P. Gooch (London, 1923), 282ff. Also see R. W. Van Alstyne, "British Diplomacy and the Clayton-Bulwer Treaty," *J. Mod. Hist.*, XI (1939) pp. 149-83. The most illustrious of the peace-makers, President Buchanan, was able, in his message of December, 1860, proudly to announce: "Our relations with Great Britain are of the most friendly character . . . The discordant construction of the Clayton and Bulwer treaty between the two governments, which at different periods of the discussion bore a threatening aspect, have resulted in a final settlement entirely satisfactory to this government."

10. F.O. 5/815, Russell to Lyons, Nov. 22, 1860. There is little subtlety about the phraseology; the hint that a middle channel will satisfy Britain is unmistakeable.

11.   F.O. 5/816A, Russell to Lyons, no. 18, Jan. 25, 1861. In Art. 3 of the Oregon treaty of 1846 the United States pledged herself to respect the possessory rights of the company in Oregon. If they were to be sold, it was to be "at a proper valuation to be agreed upon between the parties." For the history of the negotiations over the claims see R. R. Martig, "Hudson's Bay Company Claims," *Oregon Hist. Q.*, XXXVI (1935), 60-9.

12.   F.O. 5/816A, Lyons to Russell, no. 88, March 3.

13.   Lyons to Russell, "Private," Jan. 7, 1861, in T.W.L., 2nd Baron Newton, *Lord Lyons: a Record of British Diplomacy* (2 vols., London, 1913), I, 30. During the Central-American dispute Seward had spoken threateningly of "war and favoured making positive demands upon Great Britain" (Frederick Bancroft, *The Life of W. H. Seward* (2 vols., London, 1900), I, 485). Seward had more than once advocated the acquisition of Canada (T. H. Lothrop, *William H. Seward* (New York, 1896), 297). He was the "central figure of nineteenth century imperialism" in the United States. "He understood the nature and the direction which American expansion historically strove to follow . . . the effort to absorb British North America . . . ." His purchase of Alaska in 1867 was a "master stroke comparable to Jefferson's deal with Napoleon over Louisiana," for "Alaska is the north star of the American empire, shedding its light on two continents," though he "overlooked the potentialities of the new Canadian Federation [in 1867] . . ." (R. W. Van Alstyne, *The Rising American Empire* (London, 1960), 170).

14.   F.O. 5/816A, Lyons to Russell, "Private," March 4, 1861.

15.   *Ibid.*, Lyons to Russell, no. 124, April 1, 1861.

16.   Newton, *Lord Lyons*, I, 43.

17.   Pickett to Bazelgette, June 25, enclosed in Admiral Maitland's despatch to the Admiralty, July 9, 1861, F.O. 5/816A.

18.   Lyons to Russell, "Private," Dec. 23, 1861, Newton, *Lord Lyons*, I, 69.

19.   *Ibid.*, I, 72.

20.   S. E. Morrison, *History of the United States* (2 vols., London, 1927), II, 203. Cf. Lord John Russell, *Recollections and Suggestions, 1813-73* (London, 1875), 276. See also Kenneth Bourne, "British Preparations for War with the North, 1861," *English Hist. Rev.*, LXXVI (Oct. 1961), 600-32. He notes that Lyons was constantly reminding his government in May and June, 1861, that Seward might try to avert civil war by precipitating a foreign one and that war seemed inevitable until the *Trent* affair. Lyons was not exactly an admirer of Seward, for he wrote privately to Russell about "the difficulty of keeping Mr. Seward within the bounds of decency even in ordinary social intercourse."

CHAPTER SEVEN

1.   F.O. 5/1471, C.O. memorandum, Nov., 1872.

2.   F.O. 5/816A, Russell to Lyons, no. 191, April 9, 1863, "Seen by Lord Palmerston and the Queen."

3.   *Ibid.*, Russell to Lyons, no. 637, Dec. 24.

4.   *Ibid.*, Russell to Lyons, no. 49, Feb. 4, 1864. The commission did not meet until Jan., 1865, and the Company's case was not concluded until Aug., 1868. The final award was promulgated in Sept., 1869.

5.   *Ibid.*

6.   *Ibid.*, Lyons to Russell, no. 184, March 11, 1864.

7.   Thomas W. L., 2nd Baron Newton, *Lord Lyons: a Record of British Diplomacy* (2 vols., London, 1913), II, 127.

8.   There was, for example, the Hughes incident of 1867. Details are given in the relative correspondence: Seymour to Oldfield, Jan. 3, 1867, encl. 3 in Seymour to Carnarvon, Jan. 4, in F.O. 5/816B. See also *ibid.*, Halleck to Oldfield, Jan. 21, 1867.

9.   *Papers relating to the Foreign Relations of the United States*, 1867-8, pt. 1, vol. I, 329, Seward to Johnson, no. 2, July 20. Cf. H. L. Keenleyside, *Canada and the United States* (New York, 1929), pp. 137ff. "It is equally manifest that the sympathy of the whole American people goes with such movements [sedition in Ireland] for the reason that there is a habitual jealousy of British proximity across our northern border, and especially for the reason that this nation indulges a profound sense that it sustained great injury from the sympathy extended in Great Britain to the rebels during the civil war." Seward to Adams, "Confidential," no. 1952, March 28, 1867, printed in *Foreign Relations*, 1866-67, pt. 1, p. 75.

10.   J. B. Brebner, *North Atlantic Triangle* (New York, 1946), p. 169.

11.   Seward to Adams, *Foreign Relations*, 1868, pt. 1, p. 355.

12.   F.O. 5/1129, Thornton to F.O., March 14, 1868.

13.   Seward to Adams, Jan. 13, 1868, *Foreign Relations*, 1867-8, pt. 1, vol. I, p. 141.

14. D.S. Misc. Letters, March, 1866, pt. 2, quoted in Hunter Miller, ed., *Treaties and Other International Acts of the United States of America* (8 vols., Washington, 1931-48), VIII, 436.

15. *Foreign Relations*, 1867-8, pt. 1, vol. I, p. 183, Seward to Adams, March 23, 1868. Copy also in F.O. 5/816B.

16. D.S. Misc. Letters, Jan., 1868, p. 2, Stanton to Seward, Jan. 24, quoted in Miller, *Treaties*, VIII, 439-42.

17. *Ibid.*, 443.

18. It is agreed today by international authorities that the declaration of neutrality was quite within British rights.

19. Caleb Cushing, *The Treaty of Washington* (New York, 1873), p. 15.

20. F.O. 83/2225, quoted by R. L. Morrow, "The Negotiations of the Anglo-American Treaty of 1870," *A.H.R.*, XXXIX (1933-4), 669.

21. A supplementary protocol was arranged appointing the president of the Federal Council of the Swiss Confederation as arbiter. Copy, dated Nov. 10, 1868, in F.O. 5/816B. See also Seward to Johnson, telegram, Nov. 7, in *Foreign Relations*, 1867-68, pt. 1, vol. I, p. 361.

22. Copy of protocol, F.O. 5/816B. Art. 5 was omitted from the subsequent convention.

23. Hunter Miller who has examined the Senate file of the treaty in the National Archives says that the Senate contemplated changes. One of these added to Art. 1: "but the referee shall have no authority to establish any other line than that intended in the Treaty," and Art. 2 is deleted. It was obvious that the Senate were not going to be easily converted to Britain's view of the subject matter to come within the purview of the arbiter. See Miller, *Treaties*, VIII, 446.

24. Fish to Motley, no. 151, Feb. 15, 1870, copy in F.O. 5/1469.

25. On March 1, 1869, Gladstone outlined to the House of Commons the terms of his bill for the disestablishment of the Irish Church; the third reading was successfully negotiated on May 31. The subject therefore did take up a great deal of time.

26. F.O. 5/1469, Clarendon to Thornton, March 11, 1870.

27. *Ibid.*, Clarendon to Thornton, cipher, Jan. 10, 1870.

28. Charles Francis Adams, *With Lee at Appomattox* (New York, 1902), pp. 103-4.

29. J. C. Bancroft Davis, *Mr. Fish and the Alabama Claims* (New York, 1893), p. 45.

30. Allan Nevins, *Hamilton Fish*, (New York, 1936), p. 165.

CHAPTER EIGHT

1. A. K. Weinberg, *Manifest Destiny* (New York, 1935). On May 22, 1861, Lord Lyons wrote from Washington to Sir Edmund Head: "Canada is, as you know, looked upon here as our weak point. There are in the Cabinet men who are no doubt as ignorant af the state of feeling in Canada as they were of that in the Southern States and who believed that there is a strong American feeling in Canada. You will not have forgotten that Mr. Seward, during the Presidential canvass, publicly advocated the annexation of Canada as a compensation for any loss which might be occasioned by the disaffection of the South." T.W.L., 2nd Baron Newton, *Lord Lyons: a Record of British Diplomacy* (2 vols., London, 1913), II, 39-40.

2. In debate Gladstone declared that the Government had vowed "that nothing should induce it to add to the territory, or the territorial responsibilities" of Britain. Quoted by Paul Knaplund, *Gladstone and Britain's Imperial Policy* (London, 1927), p. 133. Cf. Newton, *Lord Lyons*, I, 292. Clarendon wrote shortly before his death in June, 1870: "We cannot throw them off, and it is very desirable we should part as friends." Cf. also John Morley, *Life of Gladstone* (2 vols., London, 1903), I, 363.

3. J. A. R. Marriott, *England Since Waterloo* (London, 1929), p. 411.

4. "If reared in freedom, Gladstone believed the new communities would overcome the difficulties of the early critical years, and later remain faithful to the mother country." (Paul Knaplund, "Gladstone's Views on British Colonial Policy." *C.H.R.*, IV, no. 4 (Dec., 1923), 304.) He wanted a "union of hearts, a union of many happy Englands, a Commonwealth such as the one which is now fairly definitely taking shape." Knaplund, *Gladstone and Britain's Imperial Policy*, p. 16. Cf. John S. Galbraith, "Myths of the 'Little England' Era," *A.H.R.*, LXVII (1961-2), 34-48.

5. Great Britain, *Parliamentary Debates*, CXCVIII, 783.

6. J. M. Callahan, *American Foreign Policy in Canadian Relations* (New York, 1937), 304. American politicians, particularly in the states bordering Canada, could always whip up support for annexation by appealing to anti-English elements.

7. "As such a policy [Summer's on Canadian annexation] found much support in the country, in government circles, and with the President, Fish felt obliged to adopt it though he did

so with serious misgivings as to the difficulties and dangers in carrying it through." J. V. Fuller, "Hamilton Fish," in Samuel F. Bemis, ed., *The American Secretaries of State and Their Diplomacy* (10 vols., New York, 1927-9), VII, 135.

8. Allan Nevins, *Hamilton Fish* (New York, 1937), p. 223.

9. C. P. Stacey, "Fenianism and the Rise of National Feeling in Canada at the Time of Confederation," *C.H.R.*, XII, no. 3 (Sept., 1931), 259. Cf. Joe Patterson Smith, "A United States of North America — Shadow or Substance, 1815-1915," *C.H.R.*, XXVI, no. 2 (June, 1945), 109-18, who develops the thesis that "since the movement [for annexation] lacked a leader around whom all would rally, it gradually ran its course and was forgotten," (p. 117), and "an organised political group in the United States with sufficient strength to bring about the absorption of Canada never existed" (p. 118).

10. J. B. Brebner, *North Atlantic Triangle* (New York, 1945), pp. 174-5.

11. Stacey, "Fenianism," p. 258. "The hatred aroused in the United States by Britain's attitude during the war was vented on her colonies, finding expression in talk of annexation." The Fenians planned to call Canada "New Ireland," and, as Gen. T. W. Sweeny had it: "By the offer of a surrender of Canada to the United States, Mr. Seward, it is hoped, will wink at connivance between American citizens and the Fenian conquerors..." J. A. Macdonald, *The Fenian Raids* (Toronto, 1910), p. 15. President Andrew Johnson and Secretary Seward had held back for five days, in June, 1866, the issue of a proclamation forbidding Americans to break the Neutrality Act by joining the Fenians. In 1870, however, Grant and Fish were careful to act very properly. United States General Foster attempted to dissuade the Fenians from taking combative action, and President Grant issued his proclamation on the very day of the invasion.

12. "The Treaty of Washington," *Canadian Monthly*, I, no. 1 (1872), p. 453.

13. Fish to J. C. Hamilton, quoted by Nevins, *Hamilton Fish*, p. 222.

14. Nevins, *Hamilton Fish*, p. 397.

15. J. C. Bancroft Davis to Sir Curtis Lampson, March 12, 1870, Davis Papers, MS Division, Library of Congress, quoted by Alvin C. Gluek, Jr., in "The Riel Rebellion and Canadian-American Relations," *C.H.R.*, XXXVI, no. 3 (Sept., 1955), 199-221.

16. Nevins, *Hamilton Fish*, p. 219 n.

17. H. M. Wriston, *Executive Agents in American Foreign Relations* (London, 1929), p. 742. The reports of secret-service agents are always open to suspicion because such agents usually mingle only with the people who share their views.

18. Nevins, *Hamilton Fish*, p. 219.

19. *Ibid.*, p. 200.

20. A. H. de Trémaudan, "Louis Riel and the Fenian Raid of 1871," *C.H.R.*, IV, no. 2 (June, 1923), 137. Red River Valley "is the meeting place of three historic routes into the interior; the Hudson Bay from York Factory, whence had come the first settlers in 1812; the old canoe route from Canada and Lake Superior... and the route from Minnesota in the upper Mississippi Valley," (R. W. Van Alstyne, *The Rising American Empire* (London, 1960), p. 119).

21. Malmros to Davis, quoted by Gluek, "The Riel Rebellion," p. 202.

22. Washington *Morning Chronicle*, Jan. 30, 1871. An account of the O'Donoghue incident is given in John P. Pritchett, "The Origin of the So-called Fenian Raid on Manitoba in 1871," *C.H.R.*, X, no. 1 (March, 1929), 23-42. Pritchett describes O'Donoghue as "a Fenian with annexationist tendencies."

23. *Congressional Globe*, 40th Congress, 2nd Sess., (1868), 79. "The Banks scheme... really originated with one of the general agents whom the United States maintained in Canada," (Smith, "A United States of North America," p. 112).

24. Englishmen held all the official positions in the colony, which was ruled by a "Crown Colony clique which had consolidated its position through marriage and friendship..." (Margaret A. Ormsby, *British Columbia: a History* (Toronto, 1958), p. 230). In 1869 eight British Columbia colonists became members of the Royal Colonial Institute, a British organization dedicated to the task of nullifying the efforts of anti-colonialists. The British Columbia annexation movement is dealt with by F. W. Howay, W. N. Sage, and H. F. Angus in their *British Columbia and the United States* (London, 1942), chap. VIII. See also W. N. Sage, "The Annexation Movement in British Columbia," Royal Society of Canada *Transactions*, 3rd ser., XXI (1927) sect. II, 97.

25. W. E. Ireland, "The Annexation Petition of 1869," *B. C. Hist. Q.*, IV, (1940), 270.

26. Ormsby, *British Columbia*, p. 244. "The frequent notices of this matter in the American Press have become fruitful source of pleasantry in the Colony," Musgrave told Thornton C.O. 60/38, Musgrave to Thornton, Feb. 23, 1870, enclosed in Musgrave to C.O., March 7, 1870, "Confidential".

27. Ireland, "Annexation Petition," p. 270.
28. Howay, *et al., B.C. and the U.S.*, p. 191.
29. Granville to Musgrave, Aug. 14, 1870, Sessional Papers of Canada, 33 Vict., 1870, no. 33, quoted in Howay, *et al., B.C. and the U.S.*, p. 195. Cf. Ormsby, *British Columbia* pp. 242-4.
30. Fish, Diary, Sept. 19, in Nevins, *Hamilton Fish*, p. 412.
31. P.R.O. 30 G.D. 29/80, Thornton to Granville, Sept. 27, 1870.
32. *Ibid.*, Thornton to Granville, Oct. 4, 1870.
33. Toronto *Globe*, May 27, 1865, quoted by F. H. Underhill, "Canada's Relations with the Empire as seen by the Toronto Globe, 1857-1867," *C.H.R.*, X, no. 2 (June, 1929), 125.
34. P.R.O., 30 G.D., 29/80, Thornton to Granville.
35. Nevins, *Hamilton Fish*, p. 427.
36. Diary for Sept. 26, 1870, in *ibid.*, p. 425.
37. *Ibid.*, p. 426. The secretary of state, "little by little had brought Grant to realise that Canada had chosen to remain with the motherland, and could not be bullied or lured away."
38. Maureen M. Robson, "The *Alabama* Claims and the Anglo-American Reconciliation, 1865-71," *C.H.R.*, XLII, no. 1 (March, 1961), 19.

CHAPTER NINE

1. E. S. M. Fitzmaurice, *Life of the Second Lord Granville* (2 vols., London, 1905), II, 73. The force of public opinion almost drove the British government into war, for the press was almost unanimous for firmness. The *Standard*, the *Morning Post*, even the pacific *Daily News*, endorsed the view expressed in *The Times* on Nov. 16 that "retraction of the Russian circular should be demanded under penalty of immediate war." John Bright, about to leave the government on grounds of ill-health, wrote to the prime minister reminding him that any interference on behalf of Turkey would fail "and General Grant would come down on him for payment of Alabama claims and for an apology." The situation is fully discussed by Dr. W. E. Mosse of Glasgow University in his article, "Public Opinion and Foreign Policy: The British Public and the War-scare of November 1870," (Cambridge) *Hist. J.*, VI, no. I (1963), 38-58.
2. Granville to John Bright, Nov. 21, 1870, quoted by Fitzmaurice, *Life of Granville*, II, 28. Granville was reputed to be pro-French and anti-German. See Mrs. R. Wemyss, ed., *Memoirs and Letters of Sir Robert Morier*, (2 vols., London, 1911), II, 161. Granville told Thornton that "it has long been Bismarck's favourite idea to establish such intimate relations with the United States as to neutralise our influence in Europe. That he meant to trade upon the 'Alabama' wrongs in order to effect this object . . ." (F.O. 362/11, "Private").
3. J. D. Richardson, *A Compilation of the Messages and Papers of the Presidents* (10 vols., Washington, 1896-9), 102.
4. John Morley, *Life of Gladstone* (2 vols., London, 1905-06), II, 8. How this accords with Fish's views is more than clear from Nevins, *Hamilton Fish*, p. 384: "Fish always had an instinctive comprehension that, in the swift-changing, treacherous modern world, a cordial understanding between the United States and Great Britain would protect not only both peoples, but all mankind, from many possible calamities."
5. Richardson, *Messages and Papers*, VII, 104.
6. Joseph Pope, *Memoirs of Sir John Macdonald* (London, 1930), p. 491. "Lord de Grey has told me several times that the chief cause of England's apparent want of firmness in action with respect to European and Russian complications was the dread of being attacked in the rear by the United States, and that Russia in case of war with England, would be sure to draw the United States into the conflict." Cf. Auguste Langel, "Le Traité de Washington," *Revue des Deux Mondes*, 1871, pp. 795-810.
7. Fitzmaurice, *Life of Granville*, II, 29.
8. Morden H. Long, "Sir John Rose and the Informal Beginnings of the Canadian High Commissionership," *C.H.R.*, XII, no. 1 (March, 1931), 23-43.
9. *Ibid.*, 32.
10. F.O. 5/1298, Granville to Rose, no. 1, Dec. 19, 1870.
11. *Ibid.*, Rose to Granville, "Strictly Confidential," Jan. 10, 1871.
12. *Ibid.*, Jan. 16.
13. *Ibid.*, Jan. 19.
14. *Ibid.*, Memorandum of Jan. 22.
15. F.O. 5/1296, Granville to Thornton, Jan. 24.
16. P.R.O. 30 G.D. 29/106, Tenterden to Meade, March 21.

CHAPTER TEN

1. F.O. 5/1299, Feb. 9, 1871.

2. Stafford Northcote, *Diaries of the First Earl of Iddesleigh*, (London, 1907), p. 213.

3. J. C. Bancroft Davis, *Mr. Fish and the Alabama Claims* (New York, 1893), p. 70.

4. P.R.O. 30 G.D. 29/63, de Grey to Granville, Feb. 28.

5. *Ibid.*, de Grey to Granville, March 12.

6. Musgrave to Kimberley, Feb. 22, copy in F.O. 5/1298. In April, while the commission still sat, the British members were visited by Mr. (later Sir) J. W. Trutch (destined to become in the succeeding July the first lieutenant-governor of British Columbia) who strongly exhorted them not to give way on San Juan. H. R. Lynch, "Sir Joseph William Trutch, a British-American Pioneer on the Pacific Coast," *Pacific Hist. Rev.*, XXX (August, 1961), p. 254.

7. P.R.O. 30 G. D. 29/59, Granville to Gladstone, Jan. 27. Tenterden had been sent to Lord Derby to show him all the papers for the Joint High Commission. Derby demanded "firmness" in treating with the Americans.

8. Northcote, *Diaries*, p. 193. Cf. Andrew Lang, *Life, Letters and Diaries of Stafford Northcote, Earl of Iddesleigh*, (London, 1891), p. 239. Cf. also P.R.O. 30 G.D. 29/63, de Grey to Granville, March 21.

9. Northcote, *Diaries*, 195.

10. F.O. 5/1301, de Grey to Granville, "Secret," March 20.

11. P.R.O. 30 G.D. 29/80, Thornton to Granville, March 21. Cf. Fish, Diary for March 16 and 18, quoted by Allan Nevins, *Hamilton Fish*, (New York, 1937), p. 480. De Grey divined the secretary's intention and wrote home secretly that the Americans wanted to negotiate an opportunity to buy British Columbia in whole or part. Had Fish pursued this line he might have had unexpected success, for the great man himself, W. E. Gladstone, would have agreed to sell San Juan. In a private letter to Granville of Jan. 23, 1871, P.R.O. 30 G.D. 29/59 he asked: "Would it be possible for the U.S. to buy San Juan from the Colonists?"

12. P.R.O. 30 G.D. 29/63, de Grey to Granville, March 21. See also chap. x, *supra*.

13. *Ibid.*, March 17. Cf. F.O. 5/1301, telegram, March 19, de Grey to Granville. Cf. also P.R.O. 30 G.D. 29/80, Thornton to Granville, March 21.

14. P.R.O. 30 G.D. 29/80, Thornton to Granville, March 21.

15. F.O. 5/1301, F.O. to de Grey, nos. 43 and 49, April 1, "Seen by the Queen."

16. P.R.O. 30 G.D. 29/63, de Grey to Granville, April 14.

17. *Ibid.*, April 7. In conversation with de Grey, Fish had hinted that Britain might give up all Vancouver Island either for a money payment or for other territory. See also P.R.O. 30 G.D. 29/63 de Grey to Granville, March 17.

18. *Ibid.*

19. P.R.O. 30 G.D. 29/106, Tenterden to Granville, April 7.

20. F.O. 5/1302, de Grey to F.O., no. 102, April 15.

21. Nevins, *Hamilton Fish*, p. 474. Fish found Sumner "malicious." "He had, I am told, declared that no settlement with Great Britain shall be made by Grant's Administration" (*ibid.*, p. 460). But Sumner after March 10 ceased to be chairman of the Foreign Relations Committee.

22. Fish, Diary, April 13, quoted by Nevins, *Hamilton Fish*, pp. 477-8.

23. *Ibid.*, April 12.

24. Joseph Pope, *Memoirs of Sir John A. Macdonald* (London, 1930), p. 450.

25. P.R.O. 30 G.D. 29/63, Granville to de Grey, March 25.

26. Pope, *Memoirs*, p. 473.

27. Macdonald to Tupper, April 29, Macdonald Papers, Treaty of Washington Correspondence, I, 296, quoted by Goldwin Smith, *The Treaty of Washington*, (New York, 1941), p. 80. Smith gives an excellent account of the Washington negotiations, mainly from the Canadian angle.

28. P.R.O. 30 G.D. 29/63, de Grey to Granville, Feb. 28.

29. *Ibid.*, de Grey to Macdonald, May 6.

30. Macdonald Papers, Letter Book XV, Macdonald to Tupper, quoted by L. B. Shippee, *Canadian-American Relations (1849-74)* (New Haven and Toronto, 1939), p. 361 n.

31. Macdonald Papers, Letter Book XV, quoted by Smith, *Treaty of Washington*, p. 76 n.

32. P.R.O. 30 G.D. 29/63, Granville to de Grey, April 6.

33. F.O. 5/1302, de Grey to Granville, no. 102, April 15.

34. Pope, *Memoirs*, p. 457.

35. F.O. 5/1302, de Grey to Granville, "Private and Personal," April 15.

36. P.R.O. 30 G.D. 29/63, de Grey to Granville, April 15. De Grey mentioned that Northcote, Bernard, Thornton, and Tenterden "are entirely of the some opinion." Actually Bernard and Northcote had at first been with Macdonald against any permanent surrender of the fisheries.

37. *Ibid.*

38. P.R.O. 30 G.D. 29/63, de Grey to Granville, March 12.

39. F.O. 5/1302, de Grey to Granville, "Private and Personal" telegram.
40. Northcote, *Diaries*, p. 300.
41. Macdonald Papers, Treaty of Washington Correspondence, II, 248, Macdonald to Cartier, April 16, quoted by Smith, *Treaty of Washington*, p. 77.
42. P.R.O. 30 G.D. 29/59, Gladstone to Granville, April 12.
43. Macdonald to Cartier, May 6, in Pope, *Memoirs*, p. 494.
44. Fish, Diary, April 19, quoted by Nevins, *Hamilton Fish*, p. 478.
45. F.O. 5/1303, de Grey to Granville, "Secret," April 19.
46. *Ibid.*
47. F.O. 5/1301, de Grey to F.O., telegram in cipher, April 19.
48. *Ibid.*
49. F.O. 5/1303, de Grey to F.O., telegram in cipher, April 20.
50. *Ibid.*, de Grey to Granville, April 22.
51. F.O. 5/1302, de Grey to F.O., "Secret," April 21.
52. P.R.O. 30 G.D. 29/59, Gladstone to Granville, Feb. 21.
53. *Ibid.*, 29/63, Granville to de Grey, March 25.
54. F.O. 5/1299, F.O. to de Grey, May 1.
55. Macdonald to de Grey, April 26, 1871, in Macdonald Papers, Letter Book XV, quoted by Smith, *Treaty of Washington*, p. 85.
56. *Papers Relating to the Foreign Relations of the United States*, 1870-71, pp. 508-15.

CHAPTER ELEVEN

1. F.O. 5/1470, Prevost to Hammond, May 26, 1871, and Hammond to Prevost, June 22, 1871.
2. *Ibid.*, Memorandum by "T(enterden)" of Nov. 25, 1871.
3. F.O. 5/1472, Trutch to Kimberley, March 20, 1872, enclosed in C.O. to F.O., April 30.
4. *Ibid.*, Granville to the Treasury, April 8, 1872.
5. See article by W. M. Sloane, Bancroft's assistant at Berlin, in *Century*, January, 1887, pp. 473-87. A copy of Bancroft's letter to President Grant appears in M. A. de W. Howe, *Life and Letters of George Bancroft* (2 vols., New York, 1908), II, 225.
6. A copy of the British case is to be found in F.O. 5/1472. It has also been printed in *Papers Relating to the Treaty of Washington* (6 vols., Washington, 1872-4), V: *Berlin Arbitration*, pp. 58-129.
7. *Berlin Arbitration*, pp. 1-17; copies of the maps of Vancouver, Wilkes, and de Mofras are appended to the statement together with letters from Everett to Aberdeen of 1843-44, copies of speeches in the Senate and of Peel's speech in Parliament of June 29, 1846.
8. Hunter Miller, trans. and ed., *North West Water Boundary: Report of the Experts Summoned by the German Emperor as Arbitrator under Articles 34-42 of the Treaty of Washington of May 8, 1871, Preliminary to His Award Dated October 21, 1872* (University of Washington Pubs., Social Sciences, XIII, no. 1, Seattle, January, 1942).
9. *Ibid.*, p. 12.
10. *Ibid.*, p. 13.
11. *Ibid.*, p. 15.
12. *Ibid.*, p. 37.
13. *Ibid.*, p. 39.
14. *Ibid.*, p. 57.
15. *Ibid.*, p. 57.
16. Priority of discovery counts little, particularly since the results of early Spanish discoveries in the region of Juan de Fuca strait were published only after the publication of Vancouver's work in 1798. An excellent account of the earlier discoveries is to be found in H. R. Wagner, *The Cartography of the North West Coast of America to 1800* (2 vols., Berkeley, 1937). Here it is shown that Manuel Quimper was in charge of an expedition to examine the strait in 1791, and he sent Lt. Carrasco to examine Rosario Strait which he called "Boca de Fidalgo." No examination was made of Haro, but he named it "Lopez de Haro" after the pilot of the *San Carlos*, which had sailed to Nootka in 1788. Vancouver, who seldom changed the Spanish nomenclature, called the strait "Arro." His maps were copied by the famous geographer, Aaron Arrowsmith, and that explains the general adoption of Vancouver's nomenclature. Wagner, II, 253).
17. *Berlin Arbitration*, V, 139.
18. *Ibid.*, p. 141.
19. Miller, *North West Water Boundary*, 23.

20. American Case, in *Berlin Arbitration*, p. 46.
21. *Ibid.,* p. 50.
22. *Ibid.,* p. 53.
23. Miller, *North West Water Boundary,* p. 27.
24. *Ibid.,* p. 47.
25. *Ibid.,* p. 49.
26. *Ibid.,* p. 59.
27. *Ibid.,* p. 57.
28. *Ibid.,* p. 59.
29. *Ibid.,* p. 45.
30. Wilkes definitely shows Haro as the chief channel, and he has Rosario, called "Ringgold's" on his map, in a very minor position.
31. F.O. 5/809, Pelly to Aberdeen, May 22, 1846.
32. H.B.C. Archives, D-5/17, Pelly to Simpson, June 3, 1846, quoted by John S. Galbraith, *The Hudson's Bay Company as an Imperial Factor, 1821-69* (Berkeley and London, 1957), p. 247.
33. F.O. 5/809, Pelly to Aberdeen, May 22, 1846.
34. He talks of "King George's Sound" (a name never before or afterwards used) when clearly he means the Gulf of Georgia.
35. *Supra.*
36. F.O. 5/809, p. 2.
37. *Ibid.,* Addington's memorandum of Feb. 27, 1854. When Viscount Palmerston succeeded Aberdeen at the F.O. in 1846, he was reminded almost at once of the disputed islands. Pelly saw him on July 29, 1846, and to him the fact that "there are numerous islands and I believe passages between them ... but I believe the largest to be the one Vancouver sailed through and coloured red in the tracing, and I think this is the one which should be the boundary." Another illuminating fact in this connection may be noted. When in Dec., 1859, Lord John Russell was drawing up instructions on the water boundary controversy for Lord Lyons at Washington, he spoke of Aberdeen's failure in 1846 to draw the line through the islands of the San Juan Archipelago as being owing to "the absence of precise information as to the water and lands in question," and he also spoke of the "imperfect information" in their hands in 1846. But a significant marginal note by the permanent official explains that the two phrases just quoted were omitted from the final draft "because Sir J. Pelly's letter shows that Lord Aberdeen *had* accurate information." (F.O. 5/814.)
38. Buchanan to McLane, private letter, June 6, 1846, quoted in J. B. Moore, ed., *Works of James Buchanan* (12 vols., Philadelphia and London, 1908-11), VII, 3-4. Buchanan notes that McLane's outline of the proposition "most probably" to be offered mentioned the "Canal de Arro," but he took no steps to have the projected treaty emended appropriately.
39. F.O. 5/449.

CHAPTER TWELVE

1. *Supra,* chap. x. Also F.O. 5/1303, *passim.*
2. F.O. 5/813, Memorandum of April 20, 1858.
3. Richard Croker, Tory gossip and organizer, so steeped in Tory trends and policy, wrote to Aberdeen on May 13, 1846: "If you get 49° and the Columbia you will have done a miracle, but I have no hope of miracles now-a-days, and I shall gladly assent to 49° and *half* the Straits of Fuca but for God's sake end it." (Croker to Aberdeen, quoted by Robert C. Clark, *History of the Willamette Valley, Oregon* (2 vols., Chicago, 1927), I, 856.
4. For a discussion of both countries' attitude to arbitration see James O. McCabe, "Arbitration and the Oregon Question," *C.H.R.* XLI, no. 4 (Dec., 1960), 308-27.
5. Hunter Miller, trans. and ed., *North West Water Boundary: Report of the Experts Summoned by the German Emperor as Arbitrator under Articles 34-42 of the Treaty of Washington of May 8, 1871, Preliminary to His Award Dated October 21, 1872* (University of Washington Pubs., Social Sciences, XIII, no. 1, Seattle, January, 1942), p. 9.
6. *Ibid.,* p. 59.
7. *Ibid.,* p. 37.
8. *Ibid.,* p. 51.
9. *Ibid.,* p. 63.
10. *Ibid.,* p. 65.
11. *Ibid.*
12. *Ibid.,* p. 73.
13. Copy, F.O. 5/810.

14. Great Britain, *Parliamentary Debates*, CCXV, 1441.

15. F.O. 5/1470.

16. Chester Martin, "The United States and Canadian Nationality," *C.H.R.*, XVIII, no. 1 (March, 1937), 1-11.

17. F.O. 5/1474, Memorandum of July 4, 1873, in Thornton's draft to Granville, no. 26. Cf. F.O. 244/258, Odo Russell to F.O., "Most Confidential," Sept. 2, 1872. "... the gentlemen of the Press and other Germans to whom Mr. Bancroft has communicated his case and countercase in gorgeous gilt bindings expect the Imperial decision will be in favour of America ..."

18. *Daily Telegraph*, Oct. 29, 1872.

19. They had been at school together; indeed, Bismarck is the "Otto von Rabenmark" of Motley's novel. "To Motley he has given the real love of his life ... he loves the American without reason or purpose." Emil Ludwig, *Bismarck*, (London, 1927), p. 338.

20. M. A. de W. Howe, *Life and Letters of George Bancroft* (2 vols., New York and London, 1908), II, 247. Of Bancroft the chancellor said: "It is known that he is our friend, he has never concealed it:..." (G. W. Curtis, *Life and Correspondence of J. L. Motley* (London, 1889), 313). When in the autumn of 1869 there had been talk of Bancroft's recall, Bismarck had used his influence to have him remain. Bismarck had assured Fish on April 15 that "the Emperor treats me with the kindness which has never varied ... So you need have no anxiety about the Emperor's fidelity in our San Juan reference." Allan Nevins, *Hamilton Fish* (New York, 1937), p. 536.

21. F.O. 244/258, Odo Russell (British ambassador in Berlin) to the F.O., "Most Confidential," Oct. 30, 1872, Cf. F.O. 362/1, Granville to Thornton, Oct. 13, 1870.

22. *The Times*, Oct. 26, 1872.

23. *Daily Telegraph*, Oct. 25, 1872.

24. *Standard*, Oct. 28.

25. *Morning Post*, Oct. 25.

26. *Pall Mall Gazette*, Oct. 25.

27. *Daily News*, Oct. 28.

28. Quoted in H. E. Egerton, *Short History of British Colonial Policy* (London, 1932), p. 311.

29. F.O. 5/809, memorandum by H. U. Addington, Feb. 27, 1854.

30. *Cambridge History of British Foreign Policy*, ed. A. W. Ward and G. P. Gooch, III (1923), 585.

31. Frederick Merk, "The Oregon Question in the Webster-Ashburton Negotiations," *Mississippi Valley Hist. Rev.*, XLIII (1956-7), p. 388.

32. F.O. 5/809.

33. J. Tilley and S. Gaselee, *The Foreign Office* (London, 1933), p. 234.

34. Zara Steiner, "The Last Years of the Old Foreign Office," *Hist. J.*, VI, no. 1 (April, 1963), 63. Another authority states: "... from the time of Canning ... the Permanent Under-Secretary shared with his chief in decisions on most great matters of foreign policy. The real extent of his influence, too subtle, perhaps, to be readily apprehended and, consequently, not willingly admitted by some foreign ministers, is, from the very nature of it, almost incalculable." (E. Jones-Parry, "Under-Secretaries of State for Foreign Affairs, 1782-1885," *English Hist. Rev.*, XLIV (1934), 320.) See also Valerie Cromwell, "Incident in the Development of Permanent Under-Secretaryship," Institute of Historical Research *Bulletin*, LXXIX (May, 1960).

35. The project of the treaty was shown to Louis McLane, the United States minister, before it was sent to Washington, and six weeks later, on July 1, the foreign secretary refreshed his memory on this point: "I have conversed with Mr. McLane since writing the above [letter of June 29 to Pakenham in Washington] and he has confirmed all I say." (F.O. 5/809.)

36. To Sir Robert Morier (chargé in Munich) Oct. 21, 1873, quoted in Mrs. R. Wemyss. *Memoirs of Sir Robert Morier* (2 vols., London, 1911), II, 275.

INDEX